Political Society

A Macrosociology of Politics

Political Society

A Macrosociology of Politics

Edward W. Lehman

1977
Columbia University Press
New York

Library of Congress Cataloging in Publication Data

Lehman, Edward W
  Political society.

  Bibliography: p.
  Includes index.
  1. Political sociology.   I. Title.
JA76.L43   301.5'92   77-23887
ISBN 0-231-04003-2

Columbia University Press
New York—Guildford, Surrey

For Robbie

Contents

Preface

TRACES of autobiography, however subliminal (but rarely sublime), permeate all writings in social science. This book is no exception. Usually authors acknowledge these strands in a section such as this, by citing their intellectual and moral debts to teachers, colleagues, friends, and rivals. I intend to do so as well. But for a book such as mine, whose focus is explicitly macrosociological and political, the world in which it was written is perhaps as important as its author's own professional roots.

The purpose of this book is to develop a macrosociological way of talking about political life. As I indicate in the opening chapter, the categories of macrosociology are particularly well suited both for explaining variance in the polity and locating those forces capable of constraining, promoting, and redirecting social change. Frankly, I am still surprised at (and slightly uneasy about) admitting a sociologist's responsibility in the second of these areas—for *praxis,* as Marxists call it. Little in my formative professional days prepared me for such a position. Indeed, a decade ago I would have willingly gone to the barricades for Value-Free Sociology in its struggle with Normative Theory. I think this book will show I have become something of an agnostic in the matter.

I began my first regular academic appointment in the fall of 1967, and I would never trade that time with anyone. For a few

short years, we in the universities were at the hub of American political upheaval. The events of the 1960s (the war, race relations,
drugs and the counterculture) were given dramatic expression on
many campuses. Mouthing the old shibboleths about objectivity
and the ways of pure science to student activists (and even to those
outside the university who were forever asking: *"What* do the
students *really* want?"*) seemed more and more fatuous. Had sociology nothing to say to a society in disarray or to academia seemingly forever on the brink of turmoil?

I never occupied a building, roughed up a dean, or even
burned a draft card—as some of my more radical colleagues probably will gladly attest. Yet, I think the events in the university,
and the forces outside that triggered them, changed me permanently; I hope for the better, at least as a sociologist. I learned a
deceptively simple lesson: Eschewing the role of social engineer is
no excuse for glorifying the status of sociological mandarin. The
founders of modern sociology knew that, but many of us educated
in the 1950s and early 1960s had acquired a trained incapacity to
assimilate the lesson.

Still, there is substance to academic sociology. Over the decades we have managed to compile innumerable and ingenious
skills, many useful categories, and even some bits of wisdom.
Ironically, what my sociological training told me would happen to
"the Movement" has in fact come about. In the pale pessimism of
the 1970s it would be soothing simply to retreat to the comforting
categories of a bygone era. But we cannot. The questions raised in
the 1960s have not been answered. They deserve to be, even if
fewer are asking them at the moment.

The central question, I think, is whether the categories of
contemporary sociology can be applied to the dilemmas of political
life and societal misery without lapsing into pure ideology or intellectual rabble-rousing. I think they can. Thus, I have not abandoned "establishment sociology" as many of my more radical
contemporaries have. "Establishment sociology" did not ask the
wrong questions; it just did not ask *enough* questions.

This brings me to the more personal part of my autobiographical acknowledgments. My intellectual debt to Amitai Etzioni is immeasurable. This book could not have been written without the stimulus of *The Active Society* and Amitai's telling comments on earlier drafts of most of my chapters. The idea for writing this book first came from Dennis Wrong, who continued to be a source of enlightenment and moral support throughout the enterprise. Herbert Gans read and commented in detail on the first draft of this manuscript. I hope the final version reflects his insights and common sense. Marvin Olsen provided a meticulous reading and detailed critique of the second draft, for which I am grateful. Without Ethna Lehman's suggestions, encouragement, and affection, this book would never have been finished. I hope I have more than occasionally met her excruciatingly high standards.

Those writing sociological theory must also acknowledge the teachers who made a lasting impression. My theoretical interests and foci have been influenced especially by Bernard Barber, Robert Merton, Thomas O'Dea, and Hans Zetterberg. Moreover, I would like to acknowledge the comments and useful suggestions of Eliot Freidson, David Greenberg, Michael Hechter, Wolf Heydebrand, Mark Levy, Caroline Hodges Persell, Richard Sennett, and Ezra Zask. Finally, I want to express my appreciation to the administrative and clerical staff of the Center for Policy Research for their aid in the preparation of the manuscript, especially to Andrew Finnel, Toni Goldsmith and most particularly Evelyn Ledyard, who did the bulk of the typing with skill, patience, and good cheer.

Chapter 2 is a revised and expanded version of a paper on political culture which first appeared in *Social Forces* (1972a). It has been rewritten completely for this book. The most important substantive addition is an analysis of the role of less passive political ideas, particularly of ideology and knowledge. Chapters 3 and 4 on power incorporate elements from an earlier paper in the *American Sociological Review* (1969). These two chapters represent a considerable expansion of my views on the topic. The principal substantive additions are an effort to justify the status of collective goals and an examination of the part played by information in the exercise of power.

Part One

Prologue

chapter one

Why Macrosociology?

The men of action and conviction have failed enough of late to warrant reversing a famous apothegm of Marx: philosophers have tried to change the world; now it is time to understand it.

—Barrington Moore, Jr.,
Reflections on the Causes of Human Misery

CAN we ask for a more fitting turn-of-phrase by a more pivotal author to reflect the mood of the 1970s? Barrington Moore is asking those who seek substantial change in our society to engage in a stocktaking, in an effort to discern what went wrong and why. He is calling for a reexamination of theoretical preconceptions and prevailing methodologies in order to rethink what a "decent society" is and whether it is really obtainable.

My book is intended to contribute to such a stocktaking. Yet, by doing so, I am not implying that the pessimism of the 1970s is a more accurate assessment of the prospects for societal transformation than was the naïve euphoria of the 1960s. Specifically, I want to examine political life in the modern world, relying on categories drawn from contemporary sociology. I believe that these categories, although at times ponderous and labored, are surer guides to understanding and to action than is the rhetoric of the professional polemicist and the impassioned ideologue. In the final analysis, statements by the social scientist must face the scrutiny of logic and of empirical investigation. This self-imposed discipline is scorned by the ideologue.

I agree with Moore that a reasoned and empirical study of political life must "let the political chips fall where they will. There is no innate guarantee that valid social analysis will always yield conclusions favorable to the humanitarian impulse . . ." (pp. 8–9). Thus, while a social-science approach may seem dry and academic, it is also an adventure. We are never sure where our facts and categories will lead us, nor are we ever certain about how our conclusions will fit in with our cherished policies, beliefs, and ideals.

This book is unabashedly theoretical. A commonsense style might seem refreshing in the face of the arid theorizing and puffed-up Hegelianism pervading so much of sociological and political discourse. But abandoning formal theory leads to the avoidance of *praxis* and hence reinforces the pessimistic aura of the 1970s. Much of what passes for sociological theory probably deserves the ridicule that has been heaped upon it. However, sociologists of diverse ideological and academic styles now recognize that theory, implicitly or explicitly, has a built-in *praxis*. That is, theories rise and fall on how closely they meet the canons of scientific adequacy, but, in addition, they must be judged by how they tell men and women to lead their lives. This is as true for the theories of Talcott Parsons as it is for those of Karl Marx. Abhorrence of technical language may promote a picturesque understanding of the present, but it prevents us from generalizing in a rigorous manner and from searching out those aspects of past and present societies that are levers for transformation in the future.

Nevertheless, some tension between the understanding and the *praxis* aspects of sociological theory is inevitable. On the personal level most of us find it difficult, if not impossible, to maximize our scientific and social-activist commitments simultaneously. The same is true in the realm of ideas. An adequate theory should point to where and how history can be made. Still, theory cannot be totally absorbed or justified by *praxis*. To do so promotes circular reasoning and tautology which make falsifiability, the keystone of authentic science, an impossibility. If theory is legitimated by *praxis* or if existing *praxis* is rationalized in terms of an unsubstantiated theory, then science as we know it cannot exist.[1]

Thus, if there is a "tilt" in my book, it is toward theory building before we again joust with the windmills of wholesale change. What I am offering is a generalized language for the fuller appreciation of political phenomena. I see this as a prerequisite for successful political action. The language is that of macrosociology. Its focus is not on the study of particular events or societies, such as the sources of political upheaval in today's America. Nor is it a language of one class of events or societies: that is, it is not a theory of "advanced capitalist" society, or "state socialist" society, or "postindustrial" society. Rather, its aim is to analyze several classes of events and societies; to understand the bases of stability and instability in all modern political systems. Most of my illustrations are from the United States and other capitalist democracies, but the utility of my formulations depends on their applicability to other political systems as well.

I believe macrosociology provides the surest ground for connecting theory and *praxis* while retaining a scientific perspective. The major focus here is in the elaboration of this language. This task must precede the adoption of broad, new social policies, and it must be begun before we claim to possess a theory that explains political phenomena. It is illusory to declare a theory is being built simply because we have gone on a fishing expedition with particular and often contradictory bits of abstraction to explain isolated pockets of data. It seems far more productive to outline a coherent approach and then to investigate how far it takes us.

By characterizing my stance as "macrosociological," I do not mean to juxtapose it to political science. In the past, political scientists were often concerned with the development of political philosophy or with the formal structures and proceedings of official organizations. (It is no accident that university departments that may now call themselves "Political Science" or "Politics" in the past had names like "Political Philosophy" and "Public Law and Government.") But if we examine the current work of political scientists, we see that much of what they do is impossible to distinguish from what is done by political sociologists. Nor, as Giovanni Sartori reminds us, is the convergence one-way. While political science is less absorbed with formal political structures and legal proceedings, political sociology now recognizes that the political superstructure (the state, political parties, and so on) does not merely reflect "real" factors in the substructure of society. What goes on in society's more "natural" groupings is also shaped by conscious political interventions (1969a, pp. 65–100).

Macrosociology

Given the flux sociology is in, a claim to discern trends is probably foolhardy. In the growth of phenomenological concerns, we see a tendency to move into ever more microscopic and subinstitutional directions and even to submerge sociology entirely in the morass of epistemological controversy. Yet the last two decades have also witnessed a resurgence of macrosociological concerns. More sociologists are talking about the state versus society, class conflict, political power, bureaucratization, postindustrialism, and societal change than in the late 1950s, when many were invoking status-sets, role-sets, reference groups, and so on. In part, the transition is a result of methodological and theoretical progress made on the microsociological level. S. M. Lipset's *Political Man* (1959) is the best example of trying to build on the postwar breakthroughs of the Lazarsfelds and Mertons and to give their work a macroscopic and "relevant" turn. It is ironic that a subsequent generation of sociologists, clamoring for a macroscopic focus and for greater "relevance," should turn not *to* Lipset but *on* him. One of the great banalities of radical sociology is to invoke—often out of context—Lipset's 1959 declaration that ". . . the fundamental politi-

cal problems of the industrial revolution have been solved . . ."
(1959, p. 406).

But the radical assault on "establishment sociology" during
the 1960s is important because it provides the second major impetus for a renewed macrosociology. The radicals asked, "What
has sociology done to alleviate societal miseries and international
injustice?" Their most benign answer was "nothing"; their most
scathing one was that "establishment sociology" has been a willing tool of the forces of "oppression." (See, for example, Nicolaus 1969a, pp. 375–89; 1969b, pp. 103–6.) The ensuing debate
between establishmentarians and radicals produced considerable
obscurantism. But controversy also brought progress. Important
books like Amitai Etzioni's *The Active Society* (1968), William
Gamson's *Power and Discontent* (1968), Alvin Gouldner's *The
Coming Crisis in Western Sociology* (1970), Gerhard Lenski's
Power and Privilege (1966), and Barrington Moore, Jr.'s *The
Social Origins of Dictatorship and Democracy* (1967), as well as
Moore's *Reflections on the Causes of Human Misery* (1972), prove
that the polemics of the 1960s bore rich macrosociological fruit
and did not just generate hot air.

The Perspective

What, then, is macrosociology? Although it represents a distinctive way of looking at society and politics, a precise definition of
where microsociology ends and macrosociology begins is difficult
to formulate. Formally, we talk about a group in macroscopic
terms if we see its parts (its "members") as other collectivities
and not as individual actors. We can analyze American society in
either microsociological or macrosociological languages. To view
America microsociologically is to describe it as the sum of all the
status-sets and role-sets in the population. To treat America macrosociologically is to see it as a system composed of such units as
ethnic and religious groups, classes, interest groups, business corporations, labor unions, political parties, local, state, and federal

governments, and so forth. However, further clarity is provided when we examine what macrosociologists do, as opposed to merely striving for a formalistic definition. Macrosociology is the study of total societies, their major subunits, and the relations among societies. (For a more detailed treatment of methodological and substantive assumptions underlying macrosociological analysis, see Etzioni 1968, pp. 41–93.)

Embedded in both the formal and substantive definitions is the assumption that societies and their subunits have *emergent properties*. Macrosociologists presume that these entities have characteristics that are not reducible to the attributes of the individual members or their microscopic ("face-to-face") bonds. For instance, when Marxians assert that capitalists exploit and oppress workers, they are not hypothesizing about the personality or social character of capitalists as individuals (or as statistical aggregations); nor are they hypothesizing about the personalities or social character of workers; nor, for that matter, are they making statements about personal bonds between particular capitalists and particular workers. Marxism, as one type of macrosociology, theorizes that the relation between the two great macroscopic groups created by the Industrial Revolution is one of conflict, deriving from their relationship as classes, vis à vis the means of production. These groups and their interaction have a "reality" that is, to some degree, independent of the desires, motives, and affections of individual capitalists and particular workers. While I quarrel with Marxians over the empirical adequacy of their hypotheses, I accept the macrosociological premises upon which these hypotheses rest. My own perspective on the major factors in a macrosociology of politics is outlined in the subsequent chapters of this book.

I, therefore, disagree with one of the most able of the younger generation of social theorists, who calls macrosociological categories "metaphors" and who says, speaking of social inequality:

Our prominent images of stratification share the propensity to cloud our eyes with reifications. Stratification is seen as a ladder of success, as a hierarchy of geological layers, as a pyramid. . . ; but this is not what human society *looks like*. What it looks like, as anyone can verify by opening his eyes as he goes about his daily business, is nothing more than people in houses, buildings, automobiles, streets—some of whom give orders, get deference, hold material property, talk about particular subjects, and so on. No one has ever seen anything human that looks like a ladder or a pyramid, except perhaps in a high school variety show. . . . (Collins 1975, p. 51)

In fact, macrosocial forces, such as political parties, multinational corporations, classes, ethnic groups, and governments, are as "real" as individual human beings, their face-to-face encounters, or, for that matter, their cars and houses. Individuals are, of course, more directly experienced in everyday life. Moreover, macrosocial factors are not real in the same way human beings are; but then, human beings have a different reality from their houses and cars, not to mention the molecules, cells, and organs that make up their bodies. The greatest pitfall for macrosociological analysis would be to treat these realities as strictly comparable, and, for example, to speak of society as if it were a biological organism.

To cede causal or existential priority to immediately apprehended reality encourages a radical empiricism that makes authentic science impossible. The macrosocial is as real as the microsocial or the individual. Sociology has overcome the antinomy of individualism and collectivism by recognizing it as the social-science version of the chicken or the egg controversy. It is a false dichotomy: the individual is born into a collectivity, and he or she is not an individual until socialization occurs; at the same time, a group cannot exist without people. *I* and *We* are contemporaneous phenomena. The micro- and macrosocial are also contemporaneous. For every instance of microbonds sustaining macrobonds—for example, Rist's (1970) research on how interactions in a ghetto classroom help perpetuate existing societal inequities—there is a case of how macrostructures make microbonds possible—for example, how relations in the Bank Wiring Observation

Room represent an adaptation to the constraints set by the management of the Western Electric Company.

In short, the individual, the microsocial, and the macrosocial levels together make up social reality. None has necessary existential or explanatory priority. Each is capable of accounting for significant portions of the variance in human social life (as are, under certain circumstances, variables drawn from biology, chemistry, and physics). Which of them accounts for the most variance cannot be predicted on a priori grounds. Empirical research is required in every case.

The Benefits

What are the benefits of talking macrosociologically about political life? The principal theoretical gain is that a reductionist analysis of society and politics is avoided. Macrosociology alerts us to larger forces that shape our lives and cautions us about trying to explain national and international events in terms of the personalities or microscopic bonds of the participants.

For example, those who explain the student revolts of the 1960s solely in terms of "unresolved Oedipal conflicts" or other psychologistic categories lapse into reductionism. To be sure, some of what went on at Berkeley, Columbia, and Kent State can be explained in terms of a psychology of late adolescence. But such a psychological state is a constant and not a variable. Any study of these events that ignores the larger societal and political factors operative at the time (the civil rights movement, the Vietnam war, the expansion of technology, the politicization of the universities) overlooks probably the most important variables. These variables are the subject-matter of macrosociology. Psychology and microsociology cannot adequately formulate them, since neither is concerned with emergent properties of complex human groupings.

When we talk about major changes or abiding patterns in a society—or in one of its key components like the political or educational sectors—we are pointing to the operation of macrosocial forces. The effects of individual or small-group behaviors are more commonly short-lived and idiosyncratic. Consider, for example, the inability of four successive administrations to extricate the United States from the quagmire of Vietnam which dignity and dispatch. This failure is more fully explained by the contradictions in America's position on the international scene and by the character of the federal executive than by the personalities of Kennedy, Johnson, Nixon, and Ford or the nature of the social circles around them. (See Maitland 1976 for a cogent treatment of this issue.)

To speak macrosociologically about political life means that some topics are emphasized more than others. For example, this book deals with elections and voting behavior. But I do not dwell on the social-psychological questions of who votes and who does not, nor on the social determinants of voting preferences. Rather, I see voting as one strategic process in the political system (or polity, as it is sometimes called). In addition, skillful use of voting data can tell us much about the relations among society's key macroscopic groups, irrespective of the electoral process, and how these relations affect political viability.

Macrosociology also has a practical benefit. Anyone concerned with changing society—via direct action or policy analysis—is advised to look for levers in the macrosocial domain. I have just alluded to one reason for this: the longevity of macrosocial factors. The ability to persist and have long-range effects makes this realm a better bet for investing energy, time, and resources in the pursuit of change. Moreover, the strategic assets necessary for transformation are found mainly on the macro level.[2] Units like states, political parties, business corporations, and interest groups control the principal instruments of change. These resources "belong" to them. They are not usually controlled by microunits. More types of resources and larger amounts occur on the macro level than elsewhere in social life. The micro level cannot match the macro's nuclear weapons, police powers, fuel and energy, technological know-how, educational opportunities, mass media, dams, and factories. The profusion of resources is staggering.

Finally, macrosocial factors are often more malleable than individual or micro-level properties and thus are more readily changed. For example, the redistribution of income through tax reform, negative income tax, or income-maintenance programs is an easier way to overcome the impoverishing effects of racism than efforts to change the "hearts and minds" of individual white Americans. If we wait for the latter to occur, we condemn unborn generations of American blacks to second-class citizenship.

The Hobbesian Problem:
A Macrosociological Perspective

Talcott Parsons, at once the most eminent and controversial American theorist, sees one beginning of modern sociology in the works of Thomas Hobbes (1588–1679), particularly in *The Leviathan* (Parsons 1937, pp. 89–94).[3] Hobbes discerned an innate trend toward chaos in social life. The end product of this drift he called "the war of all against all." While Hobbes spoke of these tendencies as occurring in an allegorical presocial "state of nature," he recognized that the slide toward the "war of all against all" always remains a possibility; beneath every tranquil societal surface there lurks the chance for life to become "nasty, brutish and short."

The specter of chaos exists, Hobbes felt, because human desires and needs are potentially unlimited; men and women, never permanently satisfied, always strive for new goals and gratifications. "And the cause of this," Hobbes went on to say, "is not always that a man hopes for a more intensive delight than he has already attained to . . . but because he cannot assure the power and the means to live well, which he has at present, without the acquisition of more" (1956, p. 92). Other humans are often the most expedient instruments for one's own ends; hence, force and fraud become the best ways to satisfy wants. The inclinations to expand gratifications, to protect gains, to use others as means not ends, and to rely on force and fraud are, for Hobbes, the main facilitators of the "war of all against all."

Chaos is averted, he said, by a political solution. Mutually antagonistic individuals, motivated by a desire for security, come together and make a social contract. They agree to create the state, the Leviathan, by surrendering to it some freedom and coercive powers in exchange for a guaranteed limitation on force and fraud. In a word, Hobbes argued that the "war of all against all" was checked by utilitarian and coercive factors. Order flows from utilitarian sources insofar as people, beneath competing goals, are united by a common interest in security. Order has a coercive component because of the state's monopoly on the means of violence (voluntarily ceded to it by the social contractors). Hobbes saw state power as the ultimate safeguard against the "war of all against all."

My concern here is not the history of political philosophy or sociological theory but with a contemporary macrosociology of politics. Consequently I am not interested in an exegesis of Hobbes's work for its own sake. I focus on Hobbes for three reasons. First, the Hobbesian formulation of the problem of order is an intellectual landmark. Hobbes may or may not have been the first thinker to focus on this dilemma in descriptive and scientific terms rather than ethical and theological categories. But he has come to symbolize this shift in Western social thought at the end of the Middle Ages. Modern sociology and political science continue his quest insofar as they struggle to understand what constitutes and causes social order and social chaos (as opposed to speculating about the nature of utopia, the ideal social order).

Second, Hobbes is important because of how he viewed social disorder. Hobbes's formulation contains an assumption of what Etzioni calls *social entropy*. Such a perspective regards order as problematic and chaos as the "natural" order of events—unless there is deliberate human intervention. Etzioni says, "This assumption of social entropy highlights our premise that activation of the social potential and, in this sense, the establishment of social order are 'unnatural' in that their introduction and maintenance require continual effort'' (1968, p. 95).

My third reason for focusing on Hobbes is the most important one. *The Leviathan* points to society's two main political problems. For Hobbes, the primary struggle in society occurs among members for things that are highly valued. The inability to control this struggle generates both human misery and social conflict. Yet, there is a second theme: political intervention is necessary to check the ''war of all against all.'' Hobbes, at times, sounded like an apologist for the absolutist state. But he was also aware that the state's attempts to regulate members and impose common goals was a source of additional friction.

Deciding ''who gets what, when, how'' and making binding decisions are as much the central problems of political order now as they were in Hobbes's time.[4] Only their concrete manifestations have changed. We still focus on inequality and conflict, on the one hand, as well as the needs for and dangers of societal guidance, on the other. Both are potential sources of chaos and not just the struggle over resources. William Gamson (1968) calls these dilemmas the problems of influence and social control, and I have called them the intermember and systemic aspects of power (1969). How these strains are played out is at the heart of political life and is the core topic of political sociology.

Hobbes provides a useful vehicle for introducing the problem of order and its two axes. Nevertheless, a macrosociology of politics departs from his approach in three respects. Specifically, it rejects what Parsons calls his analytical individualism; it is concerned over his slighting of the normative component of social order; and it does not accept his tendency to reduce macrosocial issues to microsociological terms. First, regarding individualism, Hobbes postulated a presocial ''state of nature'' in which humanity once existed. Modern sociology, as noted above, tends to see the antinomy of individualism and collectivism as a false dichotomy. To search for presocial human beings is no more valuable than is trying to locate a society without people (or, for that matter, a world populated by naked apes—see Alland 1972).

Hobbes's analytic individualism is linked to his disregard of the normative component of social order. While he recognized that utilitarian self-interest and the coercive power of the state help contain social chaos, Hobbes overlooked the significance of shared beliefs, values, and sentiments. This book assumes that order rests, to some degree, on all three elements—normative, utilitarian, and coercive—and that empirical research must determine which accounts for how much in a given situation. The normative element may be especially important for microcohesion, for the binding of individuals into groups. Small, face-to-face bonds seem to be more dependent on normative factors for their sustenance than are macrobonds. But normative factors are also present on the macro level. (This point is developed in more detail in chapter 4.)

Hence, problems of microcohesion and macrocohesion are not identical. Unfortunately, because Hobbes spoke of the appetites and conflicts of individuals, this point is obscured in his work. Clearly, he sometimes addressed issues of macrocohesion. For example, he noted that the relation among "kings and persons of sovereign authority" approaches a situation in the state of nature. In effect, he implied that the threat of chaos is strong in international relations. But the most strategic actors here are societies and their governments, not individual rulers. A macrosociology of international relations assumes that, over time, more of the variance is explained by emergent "historical" factors and less by personal bonds among particular heads of state.

Microcohesion aims to explain how and why individuals fit into groups. The answers do not illuminate the relations between groups, the relation between society and its subgroups, or the relations among societies. The study of macrocohesion asks different questions and gets different answers. Karl Marx saw this when he hypothesized a growing cohesion *within* classes concurrent with increased conflict *between* classes. The macrosociology of politics brackets the question of the relation of individuals to the group; it focuses instead on the macrosociological problems of order: the inevitability of competition over valued resources and the strains created by trying to impose collective goals.

An
Organizing Concept

Macrosociological perspectives exist in both political sociology and political science. But the two specialties emphasize different organizing concepts. Sociologists generally begin their analyses with the concept of social power, whereas many political scientists anchor their work in the notion of political culture. This cleavage in academia is mirrored in popular interpretations of America's current malaise. One interpretation sees our "current crisis" largely in terms of disruptions of social structure and power. Proponents of this view search for remedies in the reorganization of economic and political life. The second disposition is to see our crisis as lodged in culture and ideology. Here the diagnoses include "moral decline," "crises of legitimacy," and "failure of nerve."[5] Of course, academics who build their professional work on the concept of power sometimes diagnose the United States in terms of "moral crisis."

How does one select an organizing concept for the macrosociology of politics? Two criteria loom large. First, a concept or set of concepts should hold out promise of explaining significant portions of the variance in political life. That is, it should have the potential for generating powerful explanatory variables. Second, a successful organizing concept should serve as a guide for *praxis*. It should help us to identify the malleable factors in social life and hence to locate the forces that promote and constrain deliberate change.

As I have indicated, there are two possible organizing concepts—political culture and social power. One is a language of symbols, the other is a language of social structure. As I detail in

Part 2 of this book, I prefer power as the organizing concept, because I think power can explain and change the world better. Moreover, I view America's malaise as primarily an organizational problem, not a moral crisis. Of course, there is a moral component involved; but the moral crisis can be solved only when power is made more responsive to the members' needs and is used to enforce what we all presumably cherish.

Plan of the Book

The remainder of the book is divided into three parts. Part 2 weighs the benefits of political culture and social power as organizing concepts. In chapter 2 I examine the components of political culture and argue they have only modified explanatory potential and low malleability. Yet, political symbols are more than the reflection of material interests in social structures. Political structures do not exist as objectified entities in the manner of physical or biological phenomena. They are always lodged in a cultural context. Chapters 3 and 4 explore why I prefer social power as the organizing concept. Power is at the core of allocating and reallocating valued resources, as well as the ability to set collective goals and make them stick. Chapter 3 contains an analysis of power as a universal phenomenon. Chapter 4 elaborates five attributes of macropower and examines how these heighten its prospects for explanation and *praxis*.

Part 3 is concerned with mapping societal power. Two distinct systems of power develop in the modern world, the intermember network and the political system. The first is concerned with the struggle over resources; the second with the struggle to impose collective goals. Chapters 5 and 6 analyze the organization of these two systems of power. In chapter 5 I treat the structure of intermember power. To those who know the literature on social stratification, much of what is said will seem familiar. Yet, I have tried to give this analysis a new twist by deliberately focusing on the macrosociology of societal inequality and not all inequality in

society. Chapter 5 is intended to make clear that any political sociology that ignores the issue of macroinequality is hopelessly trun-
cated. Chapter 6 examines the organization of systems of political
power (or political systems or polities as I sometimes call them for
brevity). Such an analysis is at the heart of a macrosociology of
politics. Special attention is paid to the factors that promote or impede political viability.

Part 4 contains a concluding chapter. The main barriers to
transformation in our society are considered, using the categories
developed in the preceding chapters. A focus on the limits to successful action is an appropriate way to end this book, in light of
the current somber view of history making. But while acknowledging that real change is never easy, I try to make plain why significant improvement remains possible.

Part Two

Organizing Concepts

chapter two

Political Culture

DO ideas make history? Those who rely on political culture as an organizing concept implicitly assume that they do. Karl Marx, for one, would have disagreed. "Ideas cannot carry out anything at all," he and Engels wrote. For ideas to become real, "men are needed who [apply] a certain practical force" (Marx and Engels, 1956, p. 160). This statement provides a starting-point, but elaboration is essential before it helps us build a macrosociology of politics. The Marxian formulation implies that political culture has weak explanatory potential and low malleability. Yet ideas are more than dim reflections of what goes on within social systems. Although ideas do not make history, neither are they merely the refuse of history. Anyone wishing to understand and redirect political processes cannot ignore political culture.

This chapter attempts to stake out a middle ground for political culture between cultural determinism, on the one hand, and a view of culture as epiphenomonal, on the other. Specifically considered are the parameters of political culture; some pitfalls in current usages of the term; the "causal status" of political-culture variables for explaining and effecting change; the interaction of political-culture variables; and the special cases of ideology and knowledge.

Parameters
of Political Culture

The notion of political culture has been popular among researchers
interested in cross-national political comparisons for more than
two decades. Gabriel Almond, his colleagues, and his students
have been the prime movers in this area. They have grafted
categories from Parsonian sociological theory onto the empirical
concerns of political science.[1] Popularity, however, has had a
price: the term "political culture" has been used too broadly, raising doubts as to its scientific precision. Even Lucian Pye, a prominent figure in the Almond School, expresses reservations. "The
very ease with which the term can be used," he says, "means that
there is considerable danger that it will be employed as a 'missing
link' to fill in anything which cannot be explained in political analysis" (1968, p. 224).

   If the term "political culture" is to be used with greater accu-
racy, we need to understand clearly (1) what culture is; (2) the
place of the political culture within culture generally; and (3) the
elements of political culture.

What Is Culture?

Parsonian theory maintains strict logical frontiers among social,
cultural, and personality systems. (See Parsons 1951, pp. 3–23.)
Each describes a different analytic aspect of group life (analogous
to the way that mass, velocity, and density portray separate analytic properties of the physical world). A social system is the
network of interactions produced by actors who make up a
group. These actors may be individuals or subgroups. The culture
of a group is the set of abstract meanings (beliefs, values, and
expressive symbols) that provides the basis for mutual orientation
among these actors. The meanings are internalized by the individuals (to varying degrees) via socialization. The concept of personality system refers to the motivational integration of the individual

actors who have been socialized. Culture and social system have a place in macrosociology; personality usually does not. The notion of personality is most productively employed in psychology, social psychology, and microsociology.

Culture, in Parsonian sociology, is always nonmaterial because it is a system of meanings, not an element of physical objects. The meanings lodged in cathedrals, flags, and books are cultural, not the artifacts themselves. Further, the essence of culture is not reducible to the properties of systems of interaction nor to the interior state of individuals. If the boundaries of the three systems become blurred or overlap, difficulties arise. Many of the vital questions of social science could not be handled without lapsing into tautology. Two perennial ones are: how social meanings and human character are articulated; and how the structure of a group is connected with its beliefs, values, and sentiments. Neither issue can be studied scientifically unless social, cultural, and personality systems are kept separate.

All human groups have a culture, including informal groups, mental hospitals, churches, factories, prisons, communities, and political parties. Yet the concept applies most unequivocally to society. There, culture is presumed to be more comprehensive than in any of the other units. The cultures of these "lesser" entities are treated as parts (or determined by) societal culture. Those who use the concept of culture regard societies as set off from one another by distinctive systems of symbols. Indeed, intersocietal comparisons are often called "cross-cultural research," even though noncultural factors are also contrasted.

Political Culture
and General Culture

Political culture is not all of a society's culture. Donald J. Devine suggests: "Political culture is, simply, the political aspect of the culture of a society" (1972, p. 14).

Within this definition, the general culture seems to be of little interest to students of political behavior. However, the general culture occasionally takes on political relevance. Some analysts have invoked it to explain political events. Parsons, for instance, says that the interplay of universalistic and ascriptive values in German culture helps account for the success of National Socialism (1951, pp. 191–95; 1954, pp. 104–23). He is not talking about a segment of Germany's culture but about its overall cultural system. Parsons here treats the general culture as political since it orients political conduct. He argues that the contradictions between the two value patterns (one emphasizing impersonal rules, the other stressing the special position of elites) led to excessive stress on hierarchy, authority, and submissiveness. This outlook made the Nazis more socially acceptable.

In short, both the general and the political culture can have political implications. What is the relationship between the two? They are not on the same theoretical level, since the former is broader than the latter; rather, the relationship is that of the whole to a part. Symbols that orient conduct in the polity (the political culture) and in the other subsectors of society (the economic culture, the religious culture, the educational culture, and so on) are parts of a suprasystem of symbols (the general culture). The central themes of the overall culture place limits on the content of particular subcultures.

The character of a political culture is better understood when examined as part of the general culture that constrains it and limits how it can evolve. For instance, the overarching culture of medieval Europe encouraged feudal values within the political culture. In the modern world, a general culture glorifying equality and achievement makes a democratic political culture more likely. Conversely, it makes a political culture resting on the doctrine of divine right of kings improbable.

Elements
of Political Culture

Political culture itself is not of a single cloth. In an earlier work, I found it helpful to see its main parts as *political institutions* and *political legitimations.*[2] Political institutions are the rules embedded in recurrent patterns of political conduct. Writers who speak of the "rules of the game" in political life are analyzing political institutions. But orderly political life needs more than institutions: institutions do not contain a moral imperative capable of promoting compliance. Institutions must be associated with a set of ideas that integrate and explain them and render them plausible. Legitimations are second-order symbols that endow institutions with moral worth.

Political institutions Political institutions include rules that cover two kinds of conduct. Some rules spell out how a society's members should participate in influencing political authorities. (These members may be either groups or individuals.) Other rules indicate how political authorities should use their power.

According to Almond and Verba, rules for participation in modern polities can take two directions: toward subject or participatory orientations. (Almond and Verba relegate their third type, the parochial, to premodern systems.) With subject orientations, an actor "is aware of specialized governmental authority; he is affectively oriented to it, perhaps taking pride in it, perhaps disliking it . . . but the relationship is toward the system on the general level, and toward the output, administrative or 'downward flow' side of the political system: it is essentially a passive relationship." Under participatory orientations, "members of the society tend to be explicitly oriented to the system as a whole and to both the political and administrative structures and processes . . . they tend to be oriented toward an 'activist' role of the self in the polity, though their feeling and evaluations of such a role may vary . . ." (1963, pp. 17–18).

Rules that define the responsibility of political authorities tend to be either guiding or regulating. Guiding rules call for strong control by authorities in order to introduce significant changes but regulating rules do not. Both dictatorships and democracies may be oriented by guiding cultural patterns (for example, the Soviet Union and Nazi Germany on the one hand, and Israel and Sweden on the other). However, earlier capitalist democracies rarely were, partly because of the laissez-faire values in capitalist ideology.

Figure 1. A Typology of Political Institutions Based on Participational Institutions and Political-Power Institutions

Political-Power
Institutions

Guiding   *Regulating*

	Participatory	Responsive	Liberal
Participational *Institutions*			
	Subject	Totalitarian	Dormant

Four analytical types of political institutions emerge by combining participational rules with rules for political authorities. They are: responsive, dormant, totalitarian, and liberal[3] (see Figure 1). Responsive and dormant institutions are the most "congruent" combinations of political themes. *Responsive* political institutions are congruent because they encourage members to make demands on rulers and permit authorities to respond with major efforts. The closest approximations to such orientations today are found in Scandinavia and Israel. *Dormant* political institutions are congruent since the populace is not expected to take an active interest in political life, and authorities are asked to shoulder only "housekeeping" responsibilities. Old-style Latin-American dictatorships are illustrations of polities whose outlooks were shaped by dormant institutions.

Totalitarian political institutions contain rules that call for authorities to transform the society but that dictate that rank-and-file participation remain minimal. Such patterns are incongruent because a state must mobilize citizen support to guide effectively, but the subject orientations of totalitarian institutions define autonomous political activity (which mobilization tends to unleash) as a threat. States with totalitarian institutions generally value co-

ercion too highly in the hopes of developing support while restrict-
ing demands. Possibly the best example of totalitarian institutions
is the Soviet Union during the Stalinist era. The intermittent efforts
at de-Stalinization since 1953 may be interpreted as attempts to
create more congruent political institutions. On the cultural level at
least, the Soviet Union is probably less totalitarian and more responsive than two decades ago.

Liberal political institutions contain values that call for a government to be more regulating than guiding but that tell society's
members to press political demands. Institutions mix incongruent
political themes when they elicit such demands but do not require
the state to process them systematically. The United States until
the New Deal is close to an ideal type of a polity with this orientation.

Legitimations Despite acknowledged flaws,[4] Weber's classification of legitimacy still provides the best perspective in the
field. Political rules of the game are routinely legitimated by either
(1) a body of "sacred" symbols viewed as the product of immemorial tradition—that is, traditional legitimation; or (2) a set of abstract rules perceived as rational, from which lower-level directives are felt to be logically derived—that is, rational-legal
legitimation. Weber's third type, charismatic legitimation, is the
antithesis of the other two because it arises when routine doctrines
lose their moral appeal. (See Weber 1947, pp. 324–406.)

The two facets of political institutions (rules orienting
member participation and the power of political authorities) are legitimated in similar ways. The same doctrines give moral significance to both. This symmetry is essential. If it did not exist, reciprocal ties between rulers and ruled (of even the most elementary
form) would be difficult, especially over long periods. For example, a polity is likely to be unstable if participation is given
moral worth in rational-legal terms, while state power is sanctioned by traditional doctrines.

Political institutions in premodern societies tend to be legitimated by traditional themes. However, the doctrines of most ad-

vanced societies are mixtures of both kinds. This is not to say that
legitimacy in the modern world cannot be ranged on a continuum
from more traditional to more rational-legal. Societies whose ultimate moral appeals are to written constitutions are likely to be
marked by legitimacy near the rational-legal end of the continuum.
The United States is an example, although the Constitution is not
without sacred strands. When doctrines give ultimate authority to a
revolutionary ideology (as in the Soviet Union) or to a social unit
that is "above the fray" (such as the British monarchy), we have a
good indication that the mode of legitimation retains more traditional elements. However, both these cases include more rational-
legal components than in most premodern political cultures.

Some Deficiencies

Those laboring in the vineyards of political culture usually focus
on one or two of their elements but rarely on all of them. Thus,
work in the area is beset by lack of both conceptual clarity and
comprehensiveness. Sociologists since Weber's time have had a
special interest in legitimacy. The Almond School gives most of
its attention to political institutions. Their study of political culture
is concerned mainly with rules for citizen participation. Yet, failure to cover all the dimensions of the concept is only one of the
problems arising from the use of political culture and related
terms. Two other problems plaguing current usages are: (1) a tendency to reduce cultural factors to social-system or personality
ones; and (2) an uncritical acceptance of certain Normative assumptions about the role of ideas in history. Reductionism raises
doubts about the need for a separate cultural domain. Normative
bias exaggerates the importance of culture in shaping the future.

Reductionism

The social-personality-cultural distinction is not devised to portray
empirical reality more accurately. The concrete social world is not

made up of separately packaged personalities, social systems, and cultures. The classification is presumed to be more fruitful for theorizing and for ordering data. The main benefit of the concept of culture is not its ability to label separate entities but its capacity to promote productive ways of talking about and explaining social reality.

Since the tripartite distinction is an analytical one, empirical referents of "living" cultural systems are, needless to say, hard to find. Even among those who draw upon the Parsonian approach, there is a tendency to reduce cultural factors either to social-system characteristics or to the sum of psychological orientations.

Statements claiming to be about political symbols often contain global descriptions of social structures. Take, for instance, the following statement from Lipset's *The First New Nation:* "Diffuse elitism of the variety which exists in most of the democratic monarchies of Europe tends to place a buffer between the elites and the population. The generalized deference which the latter give to the former means that even if the bulk of the electorate do not understand or support the 'rules,' they accept the leadership of those who do . . ." (1963, p. 269).

This excerpt does not make clear what the linkages are between cultural concepts (such as diffuse elitism) and structural ones (such as the existence of buffers between elites and the population). Does the statement represent loosely phrased propositions? Is the passage an explication of the elements in the definition of diffuse elitism, or what? Social structure never reflects cultural values perfectly, and joining them in a discursive way diverts attention from how they interact. Moreover, sliding back and forth between cultural and structural terms makes us wonder whether we need two sets of categories (one cultural, the other structural).

Other writers treat political culture as the sum of individual attitudes and opinions. This approach is clear in Almond and Verba's definition of culture as a "psychological orientation toward social objects," and the political culture of a nation as "the particular distribution of patterns of orientation toward political objects among the members of the nation" (1963, pp. 12–13). This definition is convenient for those comparing different political cultures via the survey method; but it suffers from allowing one's methodological preferences to define one's theoretical perspective. Indeed, it exposes the concept of political culture to the charge of being "too democratic" that has been leveled at the survey method in general. Johan Galtung says:

> . . . The democratic principle is one person-one vote; the principle of statistical analysis is usually the same: one card-one count, where one individual has one punch card. Thus a democratic bias is introduced. This may be valid in systems where individuals count about equally much and equally little, but not in systems with tremendous differences in the degree to which the properties of people count. . . . (1967, p. 152)

It may be advantageous to measure properties of culture by studying individuals. But cultural items are supramembership in nature so that their analytical status does not flow directly from the properties of individuals.[5] The typical survey employing multivariate analysis can make us aware that cultural patterns are not distributed uniformly throughout society. However, reliance on survey data may lead the unwary to assume that all the members have the same leverage in shaping cultural patterns or that all members subscribe to them equally. Michael Mann has suggested this is not the case—at least for liberal democracies (1970, pp. 423–39). He feels that political values are supported mainly by an elite minority.

Normative Bias

Normative bias has its roots in the history of sociological theory. The Normative (or Consensus) School is the principal source of the notion of culture and related concepts. All members of this school believe that a society can be portrayed by a distinctive set of orientations. Many members go on to assume that the sharing of symbols always rests on moral commitment, since culture itself is "moral." They are then just a short step away from arguing that consensus must be the major safeguard blocking the "war of all against all." This step has been taken too often without reflection. It has led others to assume that the concept of culture is a Trojan horse for sneaking an unsubstantiated conservative view of social order into sociological analysis. Thus, those who emphasize coercion or self-interest are often leery of culture and similar concepts.

We do not have to drag along the entire baggage of Normative assumptions because we see some benefit in the concept of political culture. There is no reason why societies cannot be described and compared by their collective symbols. Yet to do so does not tell us how symbols are distributed within a society or on what grounds—moral obligation, self-interest, or fear—various members accept the symbols. Only when these two questions have been dealt with can the role of consensus in any society be clarified.[6]

A second aspect of Normative bias is the inclination to treat the causal status of ideas as nonproblematic. Given the centrality of culture in portraying a society, some in the Normative tradition uncritically accept the dictum that "ideas make history," that symbols can be indiscriminately used as independent variables in accounting for change. Critics of this approach argue that it violates the canons of scientific inquiry to say that disembodied ideas are able to affect social structures in a social vacuum. (See, for example, Stinchcombe 1968, pp. 108–18, 181–88.) In their strongest form, these criticisms follow the Marxian assertion that ideas are epiphenomenal, that is to say, only the shadows cast by material interest in social structures.

Causal Status
of Political Culture

I cannot predict who will win the World Series by reading baseball's rule book (its institutions) or by studying its place in American folklore (its legitimation). But it is helpful to learn about both if I want to understand what goes on during the games. Rules and folklore won't help me pick the winner, but they are more than tools that winners use to put down the losers.

Much the same logic applies to general culture and political culture. Social scientists who want to describe and explain who wins and who loses in life are advised *not* to use cultural variables as isolated, independent variables. To follow this advice does not require that we adopt a vulgar Marxism which sees symbols as epiphenomenal or as a source of spurious variables.

Generally, new symbol systems emerge, diffuse, and gain acceptance quite slowly. Of all the items on the societal landscape, culture changes so little in the short run that Parsons and Smelser have compared it to a computer program: culture provides the basic channels for social-system processes and changes without itself changing (Parsons and Smelser 1956, pp. 69–70). Naturally, there is some "give" in culture. Lipset (1963, pp. 99–204) suggests that American culture alternates between putting greater emphasis on egalitarian and achievement values. Each is a permanent feature of our culture, but at different times one is more highly regarded than the other. However, these alternations are not sufficient to explain the historic changes in U.S. society (although Lipset believes they tend to coincide with shifts from liberal to conservative governments or vice versa).

The lack of short-term variation diminishes the explanatory potential of cultural variables. Constants cannot account for change. Thus, political culture and culture in general are better treated as specifying variables for understanding political events.[7] A specifying variable has only a modified explanatory impact: it specifies the conditions under which more strategic correlations will exist in greater or lesser intensity. In this light, culture is one condition in the broader context that encourages or inhibits interaction among social-system properties. For example, Weber's hypothesis about religious beliefs and economic modernization suggests that Calvinism provided the broad frame within which political and economic forces in Europe were able to affect the emergence of capitalism. Confucianism, on the other hand, failed to provide such an orientation, even though the more favorable political and economic circumstances in Imperial China by themselves might have been decisive.

Similarly, political culture in isolation does not account for what is going on within political systems. For instance, there is limited value in explaining the presence of a more stable polity in the United States compared to Argentina in terms of the latter's failure to develop a favorable political ethos. True, differences in political culture are translated into differences in political structure; thus the United States is less likely to generate a Peron, but more likely to generate a Nixon. But we cannot assume a one-to-one relationship between political symbols and the behavior of individuals and groups engaged in the political process.

In short, political culture affects political processes indirectly, the way the culture of baseball determines the outcome of the World Series. One might say that symbols "nudge" rather than "impact" on structures. Those who want to explain what is going on in a political system (or in a baseball game) are advised to give more attention to structural factors than to cultural ones. When the game is politics (not baseball), power becomes decisive.

Culture is also a poor vehicle for planned social change because of its low short-run variability. Culture cannot be molded for the sake of societal transformation. For instance, how seriously should a regime struggling to modernize take a recommendation to wait for the evolution of a new political culture or for the rise of a work ethic? New values might be helpful, but emerging states can hardly stand by for several generations hoping for cultural improvements to take place.

Yet, in two respects, facets of political culture depart from the quietistic portrait just sketched. First, cultural variables have more of a direct impact on one another than on social-system properties. In theory, one set of symbols can explain at least as much of the variation in another set as structural variables. Weber, for example, argued that there is an "elective affinity" between the values of Calvinism and the values of capitalism which exists regardless of political and economic factors. Therefore, I suggest below how the elements of political culture directly impinge on each other. Since symbols do "nudge" political structures, these relationships are worth spelling out.

A second departure from a quietistic portrait is the fact that some ideas are weapons in political competition. Groups wield symbols in their struggles with other groups. These symbols are relatively active compared to the passive nature of much of culture. They can be spawned and reshaped in a way political institutions and political legitimations cannot be. Ideology and knowledge are often used for these purposes.

The next section offers some hypotheses about the relationship of the elements making up political culture. Then the special statuses of ideology and knowledge are discussed. There I indicate why these two cannot serve as organizing concepts, despite their greater malleability.

Some Propositions

Earlier, I said that political culture is encased in the more general culture and is itself composed mainly of institutions and legitimations. The propositions presented here are intended to trace the relationship of these elements. First, the articulation of the general culture and the political culture is discussed; then some propositions about the association between political institutions and political legitimations are put forward.

General Culture
and Political Culture

The general culture's impact on political behavior is usually even less direct than the political culture's. Its influence is ordinarily felt through the political culture: it constrains the forms political culture may take.[8] I have previously noted the nature of this whole-part relationship (see pp. 23–24 above). However, the general culture occasionally has more direct political relevance. Sometimes the general culture defines what is and is not political. This occurs, for instance, when the general culture contains a motif emphasizing authority and power. The stress in pre-Nazi German culture on hierarchy, authority, and submissiveness (previously discussed) is probably such a case. General culture has a similar impact when it defines key power relations as nonpolitical. For example, American individualistic, laissez-faire values for a long time viewed industrial and race relations as off limits to governmental intervention. The struggles of industrial workers and blacks were made more difficult because the stress on achievement defined their disadvantaged positions as inappropriate loci for political reform.

The general culture of a society forms a higher-order symbolic system; it is more than the sum of its subcultures (i.e., the political, economic, religious, kinship, and so on). Nevertheless, the relationship between an overarching culture and its subcultures (including the political) is never one-way but always reciprocal. Under certain circumstances, a change in the political culture may encourage change in the general culture and not just vice versa.

However, whether the political culture has a lasting impact on the general culture or is "washed out" by it, how completely the political culture transforms the general culture, as well as the pacing of its impact, do not depend entirely on the affinity between symbols. The existing structure of society and polity intervene between the political culture and the general culture. For example, a revolutionary movement's success in making its values pervasive depends on the new regime's power and effectiveness, the power of opposing forces, the magnitude of intrasocietal cleavages, and so on, and not just on the "congruence" of ideas. Structural factors exercise a similar effect on the interaction of political institutions and political legitimations.

Political Institutions
and Political Legitimations

Neither political institutions nor political legitimations totally pre-
determine the other. New political institutions may lead to new
doctrines of legitimacy (for example, the French Revolution's appeal to Natural Law instead of the divine right of kings); but legitimacy also affects institutions. For instance, the stress on citizenship rights for all Americans—especially regarding the
franchise—reflects the gradual modification of political institutions
to bring them into conformity with patterns of legitimacy (found in
the Constitution and the "American creed").

Although there is no necessary causal sequence, certain af-
finities between political institutions and political legitimations are
evident. These, of course, may be altered by structural factors—
the amount of conflict in the society, the effectiveness of the
regime, and so on. First, responsive political institutions tend to
coincide with rational-legal political legitimations. Since responsive values call for societal guidance and high participation, they
are best realized in a society with preferences for rationality, flexibility, and pragmatism. Traditional legitimations are rarely adapt-
able enough to render plausible all possible directions of the pragmatic impulse. The long-term prospect for democratic political
institutions in the Third World depends partly on the ability of the
political system to break the grip of traditional orientations and to
invoke acceptable rational-legal appeals.

Second, dormant political institutions are most often associated with traditional political legitimations. The values of dormant institutions entail obligations that are not relegated to a narrow political sector. They are defined as open-ended and
communal. These obligations depend in part on the particular position of the subject. Weber held that the patriarchal relationship is
the "pure type" of such cases (1960 pp. 4–13). He also argued
that such a relationship rests most firmly on "the belief in the
sacredness of the social order and its prerogative as existing of

yore. . . . People obey the lord personally since his dignity is hallowed by tradition; obedience rests on piety'' (p. 7).

The incongruence in totalitarian and liberal political institutions makes it difficult to predict their link with doctrines of legitimacy. Structural factors may be crucial here. However, how a society resolves the incongruence also is determined by prevailing legitimations. If legitimation is relatively traditional, it may push totalitarian institutions in a more traditionalist direction (e.g., Salazarism in Portugal) and hence toward more dormant institutional values. If the doctrine is more rational-legal, the regime may have to act as if its institutions were genuinely responsive (e.g., Gaullism).

Liberal institutions with rational-legal legitimations may experience a movement toward responsiveness with an increased activist orientation by the state. The United States' political culture since the Depression is moving along this path. Liberal institutions legitimated by relatively traditional doctrines may adapt in a variety of ways. In advanced societies, the presence of some rational-legal patterns may lead to a downgrading of remaining traditional themes (e.g., the decline in the devotion to constitutional monarchs in Sweden, Belgium, and Holland). The future is more in doubt in emerging nations whose traditional legitimations are more pervasive. Whether liberal institutions (inherited from colonial rulers) overcome traditional doctrines or are dissolved will be seen in the next few decades. New nations subscribing to guiding orientations (associated with responsive and totalitarian institutions) have a better chance to break the bonds of traditional legitimations. Those with liberal values are, by definition, less committed to mobilization.

Traditional-dormant and rational-legal-responsive are, then, the most congruent combinations of legitimations and institutions. Yet, these two patterns do not necessarily yield smoother-functioning political systems. Congruence of political ideals is no guarantee of viability within political structures. Both conbinations can serve as an indirect source of strain in a polity. Traditional legitimations and dormant institutions may encourage a *wel-tanschauung* that blocks the visibility of emerging threats, fails to recognize rational remedies, or fosters a lackadaisical (*mañana*) approach.

Modern political systems are more susceptible to the snares of the rational-legal-responsive combination. A positive evaluation of rationality, governmental activism, and expanded public involvement encourages a view that social problems have easy political remedies. Such an orientation inspires a heightened demand for "payoff" from the polity. Modern democratic states often find it difficult to keep pace with these demands. Their relative ineffectiveness is a factor. However, their difficulties are also due to the open-ended character of the political agenda which the political culture may indirectly stimulate. In the short run, the dissatisfaction that develops leads only to the withdrawal of support from particular leaders or regimes. If the process goes unchecked for longer periods, however, it may foster doubt about the moral worth of the political order. Thus, in advanced societies, political payoff becomes more directly bound up with legitimacy. The system's failure to deliver is more likely to lead to a crisis of legitimacy than in premodern settings. (The relationship between payoffs and legitimacy and how it shapes the viability of a polity is discussed in chapter 6.)

Ideas as Weapons: Ideology and Knowledge

Political struggle frequently entails the mobilization of ideas. When ideas become weapons, they no longer conform to the passive image I have been sketching. Marxian theory considers all active ideas as *ideology*.[9] I believe *knowledge* plays a distinctive enough role in modern life to deserve separate treatment. Yet, there is more overlap between the two than some think.

Parsons sees ideology as a combining of descriptive and eval-

uative statements about empirical reality—ordinarily an aspect of
the social world (1951, pp. 348–59). When compared to Marxian
or other conflict perspectives, Parsons' usage relegates ideology to
a passive sector of culture. The treatment of the ideology of the
professions provides a clear example of the differences in emphasis. For Parsons, a collectivity or service orientation is the distinguishing characteristic of such professions as medicine and law.
Physicians, for instance, are said to differ from businesspeople
because their profession demands greater commitment to client
welfare (Parsons 1954, pp. 34–49). Here service orientation is
viewed as a given and unchanging element in the professional
ethos. Compare this view of service orientation to Eliot Freidson's:

As a property of occupational institutions, it can be deliberately
created . . . to persuade politically important figures of the virtues
of the occupation . . . it can be created out of whole cloth, to
improve the public image of the occupation . . . all that may be
distinct to professions about a service orientation is *general acceptance of their claim,* acceptance that is fruit of their earlier success
at persuasion. . . . *The profession's service orientation is a public
imputation it has successfully won in a process by which its leaders
have persuaded society to grant and support its autonomy.* Such
imputation does not mean its members more commonly or more in-
tensely subscribe to a service orientation than members of other occupations. (1970, pp. 81–82)

For Freidson, a service orientation is a weapon that a powerful occupation uses to advance its political claims. It is not a passive condition of the broader situation. Ideology here is closer to
being a normative resource. (See chapter 3, pp. 48–52.) But
while ideology can be more easily molded than most of culture,
resources are even more malleable. They can be created, de-
stroyed, invested, or redeployed in a way ideology cannot be. Further, the general and political cultures limit the forms ideology
may take. China's Marxism-Leninism is different from Russia's in
part because the two general cultures differ.

Ideology does not play as direct a role in political struggles as
do resources. Ideology is a set of deliberately activated ideas in-

tended to reflect themes in the broader culture. In a sense, it mobilizes the larger culture by rationalizing incompatible elements, emphasizing dormant themes, or reinterpreting unpopular components. Culture, as a result, becomes a surer ground for a common orientation toward collective action.

While ideology is more malleable than most of culture, as a variable it has less explanatory potential than political culture or culture in general. Ideology is deliberately created. It is the product of group processes and interests, modified by the symbolic constraints of the larger culture. Thus ideology is more commonly a dependent variable than an explanatory one. Ideology may lend itself more easily to *praxis* than the rest of political culture, but it has less explanatory potential.

Knowledge resembles ideology in three ways. First, like ideology, some kinds of knowledge are more malleable than most of culture. Empirical knowledge especially tends to be the deliberate outcome of group processes. In the modern world, science is defined by a distinctive set of (cultural) belief systems as well as by an organizational and professional division of labor. The latter (the social organization of science) is in the business of creating the former (scientific ideas). Moreover, today's macrounits increasingly try to use knowledge to shape their relations with others and to direct their own transformations.

A second similarity between ideology and knowledge is that they both contain cognitive and evaluative components. This view is a departure from the conventional one which sees empirical knowledge as purely cognitive. Yet, "pure" knowledge cannot be used for political purposes. For knowledge to be successfully employed, it must be converted into information. This conversion entails condensation plus the adding of value by those conducting the processing. (See especially chapter 4, pp. 75–80.) The insertion of an evaluative component is not a dysfunction to be overcome. It is indispensable for turning pure knowledge into effective information.

Finally, ideology and knowledge are similar because as the outcomes of group processes both are usually dependent variables. They generally have less explanatory potential than most cultural categories. This lower potential makes ideology and knowledge unlikely prospects for organizing concepts in the macrosociology of politics—even though they have greater implications for *praxis* than much of culture.

Of course, knowledge and ideology are not the same thing. Information is more malleable than ideology. It may sometimes be considered a resource whereas ideology cannot. (The possible theoretical groundings of knowledge and information are discussed in chapter 3.) Moreover, knowledge is less evaluative than ideology. In the process of becoming usable information, knowledge does have value added; but if information is to be *practical*, the cognitive elements must dominate. The hallmark of ideology, on the other hand, is the primacy of the evaluative, which promotes an orthodox and simplistic view of issues in place of one that is skeptical and appreciative of the complexities of political life. Ideological statements are difficult, if not impossible, to falsify. The acid test that processed knowledge has not tipped irrevocably in the ideological direction is whether or not its key ingredients are based on scientifically verified data or are capable of being tested by such procedures.

Nevertheless, through most of human history, decision makers have relied on "knowledge" which was, in fact, a mixture of science, "practical" facts, common sense, ideology, religion, and folklore—with the scientific by no means predominating. Heavy reliance on ideology is not confined to state socialist or fascist systems. In our own country, conflicting strategies for combatting inflation and recession are offered by economists linked to the Republican and Democratic parties. These strategies are as much ideological as scientific products.

Summary
and Conclusions

Four points raised in this chapter are requirements for using the concept of political culture in the macrosociology of politics.

First, the concept of culture is multitiered. The general culture encompasses and is on a higher level than the political culture. But it is relevant for the study of poltical culture, since it sets limits within which the political culture can vary and defines what social activities are political.

Second, political culture is multidimensional. It contains both symbols that typify behavior in the political sector (political institutions) as well as the doctrines for integrating and rendering them plausible (political legitimations). It is multidimensional also because both institutions and legitimations are focused on two types of conduct: member participation and the role of political authorities.

Third, the effective use of the concept requires that its referents not be treated as intrapsychic orientations toward political objects, their statistical aggregation, or as synonyms for social structure. Political culture, if it is to retain its theoretical power, must refer to something other than subjective states or global portraits of political systems. Else, why not dispense with the term?

Fourth, regardless of how parsimoniously political culture allows us to make cross-national political comparisons, it is not suitable as an organizing concept. Political-culture variables do not possess the explanatory potential of structural variables. They are better treated as specifying variables in accounting for political events. Nor do they have the malleability to make them guides to *praxis*. Ideology and knowledge are partial exceptions because they serve as weapons in political conflicts; but they also lack explanatory potential.

In sum, political ideas can "nudge" political structures, albeit indirectly. Consequently, a macrosociology of politics cannot ignore the realm of meanings. Still, knowledge is advanced further when we grasp what it is that political culture modifies. These factors are in the domains of intermember and political power. I now turn to their consideration.

chapter three

Fundamentals of Social Power

Power is a good way to get things done; it offers you the best prospect for changing the world or of holding on to what you've got. Power's ability to provide a difference makes it the more promising organizing concept. Its strengths for explaining events and for guiding political action are most evident on the macrosocial level. The present chapter explores the universal properties of power. Reflection on what is common to power on all system-levels is necessary even though this book's thrust is macrosociological. I cannot convey what is special about macropower without a backdrop that tells us about power in general. The next chapter examines five features of power as a macrosociological force and explains why these give macropower unique advantages as an organizing concept.

Four Fundamentals

My starting-point is Max Weber's classic definition of power. He saw it as "the chance of a man or a number of men to realize their own will in a communal action even against the resistance of others who are participating in the action'' (Gerth and Mills 1946, p. 180).[1] Weber's definition says that power as a universal phenomenon has four components: it is relational, intentional, impositional, and potential.

Power is always *relational* and thus relative. It is never the property of a single individual or group. Rather, the term refers to a social bond between or among actors. The concept of power considers how powerful one actor (*ego*) is vis-à-vis other actors (*alters*). Power did not exist in the Garden of Eden until Eve joined Adam. Robinson Crusoe had no power until Friday appeared on the island. If "to be human is to be social," then to be social is to be immersed in power relations. When power is an aspect of recurrent, patterned interactions, it is a structural attribute.[2]

Social interaction is a process of mutual modification. But power refers to a narrower set of events than ego's chances of modifying alter's behavior. If both intended and unintended efforts at modification are included in the definition, "social interaction" and "social power" become synonyms (rather the latter being an aspect of the former). With this formulation, social structure and power structure are the same thing. Yet, common sense suggests that the total patterning of behavior in a group (its social structure) is more than its network of power. Otherwise, studies of the relationship between who dominates and a group's overall organization lapse into tautology. For example, the operation of a hospital is affected by the physicians' power over patients and the rest of the staff. But the social system of any hospital consists of more than the dominance by one profession over other participants. To ensure that the two provinces are not confused, power is restricted to ego's chances of obtaining *desired* outcomes. The notion of power is thus confined to *intentional* conduct. This does not preclude the examination of its unintended consequences. After all, each exercise of power does not meet with the same success, nor are all of its ramifications foreseen by ego (for example, the generation of alienation).

Power entails getting others to do what they would not do left to their own devices. A power wielder comes to expect resistance because not all ends are shared. School desegregation, for example, did not occur overnight simply because the Supreme Court commanded it in 1954. Power is thus *impositional,* since ego cannot count on alters' automatic compliance. Ego must have the ability to apply sanctions—to make threats and promises. The impositional nature of power (making others do what they would otherwise not do) reveals its *alienative* character. Alienation is the potential for resistance to commands implicit in all power relations. Resistance may be active (revolutions, strikes, demonstrations) or passive (apathy, "passive-aggressive behavior," minimal job performances). Resistance arises in several ways: because of a conflict over basic values and goals (as in the "right-to-life" movement's opposition to legal abortions); because of a conflict over goal priorities or the allocation of resources among goals (for example, undergraduates' resentment over professors' "excessive" interest in research); or because of disagreement over how to implement a particular goal (for example, the debate over how much to invest in national defense).

The successful use of power results in the domination of people or groups. The impositional and intentional nature of power demands domination. The link between the impositional component and the mandate to dominate is perhaps more clear-cut. Domination is intrinsic to overcoming resistance. For example, the management of General Motors must dominate workers to gain their cooperation for producing automobiles at a profit. Doctors dominate patients when they get their consent to painful medical procedures. The federal government must dominate local opposition to implement court-ordered school busing.

However, goal attainment also entails domination when the processing of people is at the core of ego's goals. For instance, a teacher seeking improved reading skills modifies behavior to obtain this end. If the teacher succeeds, domination has occurred, albeit in a narrow sector of the students' lives. Of course, dominations for the impositional aspect of power and for its intentional component are often fused empirically. It is also true that domination that has overcome resistance does not necessarily yield domination for successful goal attainment—or vice versa. For example, teachers who rely on a heavy-handed use of negative sanctions sometimes find their educational effectiveness weakened by too much order.

Domination is rarely total. It occurs in sectors. Parents can more easily wield power over children at home than at school. But sectors of domination exist not only among groups, but within them. Teachers dominate students more in academic matters than in their peer groups or in extracurricular activities. Further, domination is usually not total within a given sector because power relations are not "zero-sum games." Successful power depends on resources, knowledge, and symbolic attributions. None of these necessarily exists in fixed quantities. The amounts of each may increase or decrease during power struggles. Thus, simply because one actor gains more of them at one time does not mean that other actors have less: the United States and the USSR are both more powerful now than at the end of World War II. The language of ego and alter is a heuristic device. In the real world, all actors are sometimes ego and sometimes alter. Although, if Orwellians will pardon the pun, some are more ego than others.

Finally, those subscribing to Weber's definition find themselves using such terms as "chance," "capacity," and "potential." Unless social scientists view power as a prospect for future action, they have to be satisfied with ex post facto analyses, that is, with the study of power as past dominations. Ego's power potential rests on the likelihood of being able to attain a goal in the future even if alter has to be brought into line. This potential is said to have two sources. These have been called potential for power versus power as a potential (Rose 1967, p. 47), the objective versus symbolic bases of power (Etzioni 1968, pp. 338–42), and possible power versus latent power (Wrong 1968, p. 680). All three distinctions tell us the power comes from its wielder (ego) as well as from the subjects of commands (alters). Ego's own source of power is based on the control of resources. Ego's potential from alter is the symbolic basis for power. Alter is a source of power when ego is attributed the right or the ability to issue commands.

People who think of themselves as "hardheaded" or as "realistic" stress the role of tangible resources. Mao's aphorism, "Political power springs from the barrel of a gun," supports this view. Others are inclined to see power as something mercurial—based on moods or on shared definitions—which can arise unexpectedly and evaporate suddenly. In fact, power, like most social behavior, depends on both objective factors (resources at hand) and subjective definitions (symbolic attributions). The place of knowledge makes matters more complicated. Knowledge is vital for domination; but at some points it looks more like a resource, and at other times, more like a cultural item defining the situation.

Resources, Knowledge and the Symbolic Bases for Power

Resource Bases

The type of resource used is linked with how ego seeks acquiescence. Following Etzioni and others,[3] I suggest that resources fall into three categories—utilitarian, coercive, and normative—and that this classification is exhaustive. Each application of power uses either one of these types or some combination of them.

Utilitarian resources are material rewards such as goods, services, property, and income. On a macro level, they include such assets as manpower, technical and administrative procedures, and industrial capabilities. This type of resource lends itself to domination through inducement. Ego gets alters to acquiesce in exchange for material rewards. Alters hope these will lead to a positive change in their external situations.

Coercive resources are objects capable of doing violence to alter's body or psyche. Examples from the microsociological level are guns, whips, and knives. On the macro level, coercive resources include weapon stockpiles, military installations, military and paramilitary manpower, and the police. Coercive resources are used most effectively when constraint is the desired mode of domination. Constraint, as opposed to inducement, means adding disadvantages to alter's situation. The aim is to limit—and perhaps to eliminate—alter's options in an encounter with ego.

Normative resources are symbols that invoke shared values, beliefs, and sentiments, rather than material rewards or physical threats. The most universal normative resources are prestige, esteem, love, and acceptance. The threat of excommunication by the pope, a government's control of information, and the president's special access to the mass media are illustrations of normative resources in macrosystems. Normative resources are especially effective for domination via persuasion. They work best in getting acquiescence by changing alter's intentions rather than the external situation. They are used to change interior dispositions and not to promote "going along." William Gamson (1968) notes that complimentary as well as pejorative words have been employed in described persuasion, depending on the speaker's attitude. He says, "The approving words include education, persuasion, therapy, rehabilitation, and perhaps more neutrally, socialization. The disapproving words include indoctrination, manipulation, propaganda and 'brainwashing' " (p. 125).

Knowledge and Information

In the last chapter I said that knowledge can be more than a cultural item. Generally, the more knowledge ego has on hand, the more successfully goals are pursued and resistance eliminated. Knowledge looks like a resource in these situations. This role for knowledge appears to be a stumbling-block for our classification of resources. Is knowledge a resource? If so, what kind?

Knowledge is anchored on three theoretical levels: (1) as a cultural item; (2) as a resource, and (3) as information, that is, a mechanism for mobilizing resources. There is no one best way to classify knowledge for all times and in all situations. But in the study of power, knowledge is best treated as an informational capacity that ego uses to make the application of resources more rational.

Knowledge consists of beliefs about reality. In this light, it is a part of a group's culture. Under these circumstances, knowledge is a symbolic basis for power because culture provides group members with an orientation to the world. For example, our knowledge of the police's rights, obligations, and capabilities in American society gives them a modicum of power over us.

There are two reasons for not stopping here. First, as I detailed in chapter 2, some knowledge has greater malleability than most of culture (political or general). Second, ego sometimes manipulates knowledge to dominate alter. Consequently, knowledge is more than a passive definition of the situation.

If knowledge has implications beyond a symbolic basis for power, should I call it a resource? Why not add knowledge to the classification as a fourth type? On the whole, this solution is the least satisfactory one, for it converts an analytical classification into an ad hoc listing devoid of underlying logic. What stops us from adding fifth, sixth, or more types? The theoretical power of the three-way classification rests on logical completeness, which the piecemeal addition of elements destroys.

Another tactic is to subsume knowledge under one of the three resource types. Knowledge looks most like a normative asset, since it is neither a material nor a physical object. The problem here is that knowledge, like that in theological discourses on ritual practices, in administrative know-how, or in military strategies, is better labeled normative, utilitarian or coercive, respectively. Certainly, each promotes a different type of domination.

Thus, knowledge as a resource can be categorized as normative, utilitarian, or coercive, depending on circumstances. For example, data about sacred texts are normative; about the stock market, utilitarian; and about the effects of torture, coercive. Yet, knowledge's main contribution to power is not as a resource, but as a mechanism for mobilizing resources. When knowledge is made practical it becomes information. The more information a resource has attached, the more successfully it is employed. Ideally, information should tell ego how to produce or to acquire a resource, when and how to use it, and something about its side-effects. The better such information is, the more able ego is to dominate alter.

The use of resources in the exercise of power requires more than brute application because the resource basis of power, alone, is blind. Etzioni (1968, pp. 334–38) offers another metaphor; he suggests that power (based on resources) provides the "muscle" for pursuing goals but that muscle is not enough. It cannot identify problems, formulate objectives, or evaluate how well resources are handled. Domination needs "nerves" as well as muscle (Deutsch 1963). Without an informational capacity, ego cannot make decisions, use resources, and evaluate policy; without resources, decisions remain empty gestures because there is no system of sanctions to back them up.

Knowledge is vital for converting resources to power and power to domination, but other factors also affect mobilization. Among these are the types and quantities of resources available, their distribution, the cost (in units of resources) of a given goal, the "liquidity" of resources (how readily they can be mobilized), and the "slack" in resources (the ratio being held in reserve). (See Gamson 1968, pp. 93–110.) Yet, ego's informational capacity is more general than these others. The more ego knows about the types, availability, distribution, cost, liquidity, and slack of the resources at hand, the more skillfully they will be used.

In sum, knowledge contributes to domination in three ways. As an item of culture, it provides a basis for subjective attributions of power. As a resource, it can have normative, utilitarian, or coercive significance. But its most important role is as a capability attached to resources. The most critical impact of knowledge on power is as an informational capacity to mobilize resources.

Symbolic Bases

What distinguishes the symbolic bases for power from resources? Dennis Wrong, echoing Hobbes, sheds considerable light when he states: *"If* an actor is believed to be powerful, *if* he knows that others hold such a belief, and *if* he encourages it . . . *then* he truly has power and his power has indeed been conferred upon him by the attributions, perhaps initially without foundation, of others" (1968, p. 679). Wrong alerts us that power also exists when people suspend judgment. Ego gains a symbolic basis for power because of a reputation attributed by alter. Because of this reputation, alter may comply without resistance. Reputation sometimes exists because ego's gestures of power seem credible. Thus students listen to teachers because they hope that teachers know something. A hold-up man, hand in pocket, is credible because he *may* have a gun. The coercive powers of the Soviet Union and the United States are credible because each possesses nuclear weapons and *might* be willing to use them. Ego's reputation may also derive from the attribution of a right to issue commands. Here, alters suspend judgment because they feel it is the moral thing to do. Doctrines of political legitimacy (discussed in chapter 2) often provide this moral right on the macro level. When power is seen as legitimate, sociologists call it *authority*.

The symbolic basis of power lies behind "power plays" or "bluffing."[4] At times, ego obtains acquiescence solely because of a reputation. Thus, ego is able to obtain an end without depleting resource stockpiles. For example, most people who obey traffic laws have never been arrested or convicted for traffic violations. When power wielders deliberately seek dominance via reputations alone, they are engaging in power plays. Even parents sometimes get away with bluffing behavior. On rare occasions, they can get children to finish dinner, to turn off the T.V., and even to go to bed because their offspring feel that mother and father really "know best." As we shall see in chapter 4, power plays become routine on the macro level.

The symbolic basis of power bears a resemblance to normative resources. Both are associated with shared meanings, not the allocation of material or physical objects. In a sense, ego can use each to wield power. However, the symbolic basis of power highlights the less malleable aspects of shared meanings, that is, those over which ego exercises few controls. Normative resources are symbols that ego possesses, manipulates, and is able to ''spend.'' Hence, the symbolic basis is a given—a condition of the situation—while normative resources generally represent means at ego's disposal. For example, the president of the United States can play on the fundamental constitutional prerogatives of his office to obtain consensus, but he cannot ''spend'' or ''exchange'' these definitions. On the other hand, the president is quite able to manage the news to obtain acceptance of his policies.

Intermember versus Systemic Power

There are other aspects of power that cannot be culled directly from Weber's definition. Power means more than an actor's chances for dominating others. The capacity takes two directions: as *intermember power* or as *systemic power*.

Power's intermember form focuses on the competition over a group's valued resources. This struggle is endemic to social life, for no resource exists in infinite supply. Generally, the value of a resource is defined in terms of its cost and its scarcity. The struggle for resources is found on all system-levels. It is evident in the rivalry for love in families and for a ''rep'' in teen-age gangs; Marx saw the intermember struggles of modern societies as combat between classes for the means of industrial production; and the arms race is an intermember contest by nation-states for control of coercive resources.

Unequal possession of resources is called *privilege*. Over time, differential privilege magnifies inequality in intermember power—which, in turn, provides the grounds for even greater privilege. (See Lenski 1966.) This cycle is self-sustaining because possession of resources is critical for both privilege and power. An initial edge in assets promotes progressively greater slanting in allocative processes: all else being equal, the rich get richer, the loved more beloved, and the strong stronger.

Yet, competition for resources does not exhaust the topic of power. At times, power is exercised for collective purposes (and only secondarily, if at all, to increase the privileges of particular members). This capacity is not mindless; change is not only the unintended backwash of intermember conflict. Some potential to set, pursue, and implement collective goals exists in all groups. This manifestation is power's *systemic* dimension. The more a group develops systemic power, the greater are its hopes for mastering problems and opportunities. Systemic power is also a check on the cycle of privilege and intermember power. The cycle can only be arrested if checking it is a collective purpose. In chapter 4, I argue that specialization in systemic power is more frequent in macrosystems: Agents acting for the group as a whole are more common in such entities as bureaucracies and societies than they are, let us say, in small, face-to-face groups.

The distinction between intermember and systemic powers has theoretical application to all system-levels. Microunits also have some systemic power capacity (for example, "Doc's" direction of the Norton Street Gang in Whyte's *Street Corner Society*). Similarly, intermember power is present both on the micro level (as when children compete for esteem and prestige in play groups) and on the macro level (as when management and labor struggle over profits and wages). But the empirical expression of the two elements varies by level. Intermember and systemic powers on the macro level have attributes not found elsewhere. The study of macropower, thus, should not rely on analogies to microbonds (for example, international relations as a "game"). Unwarranted use of analogies deflects attention from what is unique about systemic and intermember powers in macrosystems.

The value of distinguishing between intermember and systemic powers does not depend on their empirical separation. Sociological analysis benefits even when the two types are fused in the real world. The distinction permits observers to ask questions they could not otherwise raise. For example, they are able to classify discrete acts by whether or not they foster intermember rivalry or promote collective goals. This may be done even in settings where participants do not acknowledge these categories. Observers also are able to consider how well a group shapes its destiny with or without a visible agent of systemic power. The distinction is useful where states seem to be the tool of a few elite members. There, it alerts us to the possibility that a modern state does more than mirror intermember power—that it usually has some power focus of its own. The modern state is never just a tool. Often, it molds its apparent masters.

Systemic Power
and Collective Goals

Where there are only particular goals, there is no systemic power. The value of distinguishing between systemic and intermember powers depends on the reality of collective goals. *If* goals are always private purposes, *if* there are never goals for the overarching system, then the notion of systemic power has no scientific merit. At best, invoking systemic power would be a lapse from scientific to metaphorical language; at worst, it would represent the infiltration of prejudices about social solidarity or the beneficence of political authorities.

However, there are sound reasons for the reality of collective goals. The discussion that follows defines collective goals, weighs the major objections to them, and presents four criteria for deciding on the collective character of goals.

Definition
of Collective Goals

A collective goal is a desired future state for a group that the membership is mobilized (to some degree) to pursue. Collective goals, unlike the goals of individuals, are supramembership properties. They are group attributes and do not depend directly on the purposes of individual members. The goals of the New York Mets,

General Motors, or the United States Army are not the same as those of their personnel singly or in aggregate. A collective goal is at the interface of a group's culture and social structure. It is in the realm of culture because it involves symbols, especially orientations to preferred future situations. It is in the realm of social structure because members are activated for its implementation. Mobilization entails the organizing of group life and is essential for converting values into collective goals. Collective goals are thus "energized symbols" (Etzioni 1968, pp. 34–36). When symbols are energized, that is, backed by social effort, we speak of them as operative collective goals and merely stated collective goals.

Collective goals are often confused with the "common good." The latter concept has been with us for several millenia, in one guise or another. Basically, it asks whether or not a given practice is good for an entire group. Simplified forms of cost-benefit analysis frequently have been employed to identify a common good: an item is said to promote the common good if its benefits outweigh its costs.[5]

In contemporary sociology, the Structural-Functional School has been most associated with efforts to give scientific respectability to this idea. Functionalists focus on how a group's structure and processes mesh with the problems it faces. Items that promote adaptation are called *functions;* those that undermine it are called *dysfunctions.* Sociologists who perform these analyses hold that a scientific observer can gauge functions and dysfunctions. Thus, the approach includes more than the description of outcomes. It also has an evaluational dimension; it assumes that we are able to judge how well the needs of the social system are being met.[6]

But the language of collective goals is different from that of common good, function, or even outcome. The difference rests on the distinction between social action and its consequences. Individuals and groups have the potential for purposive, goal-oriented behavior. However, the results of such conduct are not the same as the conduct itself. The recognition that purposive behavior has unforeseen side-effects is central to the perspective of most contemporary social scientists. (See Merton 1936.) For instance, the apparent impact of the Protestant ethic on the spirit of capitalism was not intended by the early Calvinists. They would have been horrified if they knew how their asceticism was to form modern life.

To speak of collective goals is to use the language of purposive action on the level of groups. Collective goals, like power, are intentional. To perceive the difference between a group's intentions and their consequences is essential for the study of goals. The goals of a complex organization, for example, are not the same as its functions or dysfunctions for society. Even when the evaluational component of Structural-Functionalism is stripped away, we are not left with collective goals; we are reduced to the description of outcomes. "Goals" and "outcomes" are not synonyms: not all goal pursuit is equally successful; some ends in failure, and virtually all has unanticipated effects. Certainly the antiwar movement was not a goal of American intervention in Southeast Asia.

Two Objections

Collective goals are easier to identify on the macro level. Ironically, objections to the idea of collective goals occur mainly in macrosociological analysis—among those engaged in political and societal studies. Objections are on theoretical or empirical grounds. That is, critics argue either that collective goals are an a priori impossibility or that they fail to appear in our type of system.

Those partial to a conflict perspective are inclined to reject the theoretical possibility of collective goals for society. After all, if society is held together by conflict, not consensus, how can we speak of mobilization for the pursuit of common values? The simplest answer is that values need not be uniformly shared to provide a common orientation. (This issue has been explored in the preceding chapter, pp. 29–30.)

An a priori rejection of collective goals for society has troubling theoretical implications. It triggers an infinitely regressing reductionism. Opponents of collective goals usually also exhort the "oppressed" to mobilize to pursue their rights. Yet, once we dismiss the theoretical possibility of societal goals, the prospect of collective goals for other groups disappears too. If, on a priori grounds, American society does not have goals, how can the corporate establishment, workers, blacks, or the poor have them? If there is no theoretical basis for a society's collective goals, it is difficult to argue that other macroscopic actors pursue them. Such an approach ultimately leads to a rejection of collective goals for all groups—both on the micro and macro levels. Only individuals then have goals. The next step is to dismiss the possibility of group ("emergent") properties in general. If there is no reality arising from human interaction, then a distinctive sociological perspective no longer exists.

Objections to collective goals on empirical grounds have less dire consequences. Here there is no a priori rejection; the nature of modern society is rather the obstacle. The contemporary world, the argument runs, is too heterogeneous for an entire society to have goals in common. Those who reject collective goals on these grounds usually do so in the context of attacking the Structural-Functional image of society. They adhere to a view of society offered by Herbert Gans:

In a modern heterogeneous society, few phenomena are functional or dysfunctional for the society as a whole, and most result in benefits to some groups and costs to others. Given the level of differentiation in modern society, I am even skeptical whether one can empirically identify a social system called "society." Society exists, of course, but is closer to being a very large aggregate, and when sociologists talk about society as a system, they often really mean the nation, a system which, among other things, sets up boundaries and other distinguishing characteristics between societal aggregates. (1972, p. 277)

Yet, Gans's argument is not an attack on collective goals. At most, he rejects the likelihood that collective goals can promote the common good in our kind of system. While Gans disparages the capacity to apply the language of function and dysfunction to a total society, he does not question the power of political authorities to make policies binding on all. Indeed, Gans's general view of governmental policy is that it has a profound impact (albeit a differential one).

Critiques of the empirical possibility of collective goals tend to blur goals with their consequences. Evidence is usually offered that society's most privileged members are the prime beneficiaries of public policy. Critiques go on to suggest that what passes for a collective goal is actually the private interest of a "power elite."

But the consequences of goal-oriented behavior are not the same as the goals themselves. It follows that we cannot eliminate collective goals from society merely because powerful interests benefit the most. The argument does warn us that the setting of collective goals is often controlled by the most privileged. Demonstrations of when, how, and why political influence is skewed in favor of elites are important contributions. However, their impact is diminished when they are stretched into attacks on collective goals.

Criteria
for Collective Goals

But what gives a goal its collective character, if all members do not have to benefit from it? Four criteria are important for judging whether a given goal is collective. The first criterion deals with ego, the actor who issues commands. The remaining three focus on the alters in the situation. According to Cyert and March (1963) and Simon (1964), these alters limit or put constraints on ego's goal-making ability.

First, ego must have the resources or the reputation to impose his or her will on a group; otherwise there can be no collective goals. The more resources ego can muster, the more likely commands are linked to collective goals. The same is true of reputation: as ego's credibility increases, the probability grows that commands are part of collective goals. If ego has both resources and

responsibility, the prospect for collective goals is enhanced further. Ego here becomes an agent with the formal charge of acting
for the group.

Yet, ego's resources and reputation are not sufficient to make
a goal collective. Those who form the context of commands also
shape a goal's character. The second criterion focuses on the audience of commands. The issue here is who is considered before
decisions are made. A goal is more likely to be collective when
ego's deliberations take many members into account. Sheer
numbers of individuals are not always the best indicator: the array
of classes or levels of members provides a more precise measure
of an audience's scope. Sometimes scope is so broad that the audience extends beyond group boundaries. For example, U.S. economic policy takes foreign nations into consideration. A program
is usually a collective goal (or part of one) if authorities touch base
with many interest groups. This second criterion should not be
confused with democratic politics; totalitarian polities also form
goals while keeping an eye on the potential constraints created by
the membership.

The audience of commands is not the only constraint on ego's
decisions. Intended targets of commands provide more visible constraints. Intended targets are included in the third and fourth criteria. The audience and the intended targets are sometimes the
same actors—but not always, especially in large, complex groups
marked by extensive political wheeling-and-dealing. Simply because many actors are considered before a goal is set does not
mean all or most are its intended targets. Programs for the men-
tally ill, for prisoners, and for orphans probably are instances
where there is no overlap between audience and targets.

The third criterion asks whether commands are aimed at a
broad or narrow segment of actors. The narrower the band of intended targets, the less likely a goal is to be collective. As with the
second criterion, classes and levels of actors are a better indicator
of the collective character of a goal than are numbers of individuals.

The value of the second and third criteria depends on how we view collective goals. If we define them too concretely, not many meet the standards. Suppose each command were called a goal. Then, probably only a narrow range of actors would be the audience and intended targets. For instance, a small number of constituencies form the context for most single pieces of legislation before the U.S. Congress. With a concrete perspective, few goals would pass muster as collective.

It is more helpful to see the projects of decision makers as falling on one of three levels of generality: (1) particular decisions or directives; (2) policies; and (3) grand designs. In some situations, all three may be treated as a collective goal. In most cases, only the last two carry this label with minimum confusion. A grand design is a comprehensive plan whose elements are logically related. Much of the planning in the Soviet Union is of this character. A policy is less comprehensive and integrated than a grand design but entails a commitment to a set of related programs and not just to one. The decisions and directives flowing from policies are not always logically consistent. The New Deal and the War on Poverty are good examples of policies. The possibility that a broad array of the actors are the audience and targets of commands exists *only* when goals are seen as policies or grand designs—not as isolated decisions or directives.

The fourth criterion also deals with ego's relationship with the targets of command. The third criterion focused on the extensiveness of the relationship; the fourth focuses on its intensity. This criterion asks how deeply ego seeks to penetrate the lives of the targets. Deep penetration means high performance obligations. In general, the modern state penetrates societal groups more deeply than earlier political forms and requires higher role performances from "citizens." This capacity to exact higher levels of performance is indicative of collective goal activity. In earlier times, a central authority had a weaker chance to modify behavior significantly. Hence, the collective character of goals was more diluted, and perhaps nonexistent.

In sum, a goal is collective if it meets four criteria: (1) it is produced by a commander who has the resources and reputation to make decisions in the name of the group as a whole; (2) a broad array of actors provides the audience of commands; (3) the intended targets also represent a broad array of actors; and (4) ego's commands contain high performance requirements for the intended targets. Obviously, these criteria are phrased in general terms. In part, this is deliberate, for it points to the fact that they are better thought of as ordinal or interval dimensions (in terms of varying degrees, of more or less than) not as categorical ones (yes versus no; either/or). This view of the criteria is appropriate because the collective nature of goals is itself a matter of degree. Our understanding is advanced further when we talk about the extent to which, and along which dimensions, a goal is collective, rather than trying to label it as either totally collective or particular.

Thus, the classification of goals is relative. Multiple criteria make it so. But the classification of goals as more or less collective—and power as systemic or intermember—is relative for two other reasons. First, actors who are formally charged with generating collective goals are not immune to the intermember power struggles. Research on complex organizations demonstrates that they frequently neglect their original goals to satisfy the special needs of administrators. It is probable that the state (as a kind of supraorganization charged with societal goals) is from time to time just another competitor for society's resources. As I indicated earlier, the two foci are even more difficult to disentangle on the micro level.

The second source of relativity stems from the fact that social systems are "Chinese nesting boxes" in which smaller units are encased in larger ones. (See chapter 4, pp. 80–83.) What is systemic power and a collective goal on one level—the intragroup, intraorganizational, or intrasocietal ᐟlevel—becomes intermember power and a particular goal on the next higher level—the intergroup, interorganizational, or intersocietal. For example, increased military spending is an exercise in systemic power and is a collective goal for the American system. But from the vantage point of the international system, which also includes the Soviet Union, China, France, Great Britain, and other nations, it is more appropriately treated in terms of intermember power and particular goals. It makes no sense to talk about systemic power and collective goals unless the system of reference is circumscribed clearly.

Conclusions

This chapter serves as a prologue to the analysis of power in the realm of the macrosocial which begins in chapter 4. The nature of macropower cannot be grasped unless there is an understanding of the fundamentals of power as a universal phenomenon.

I have argued that power is always a property of a social relationship (it is relational); it is geared toward the pursuit of goals (it is intentional); it contains the prospect of compelling others to do what they would otherwise not do (it is impositional); and it speaks of a capacity for future domination (it is potential). This last aspect of power derives both from the resources at ego's disposal as well as from symbolic attributions by alter. Knowledge can be thought of as either a resource or as a symbolic basis. But in the study of power, it is most productively seen as an informational capacity for mobilizing resources. The fact that the supply of resources, symbolic attributions, and knowledge is rarely fixed means that power relations are not usually "zero-sum games."

All these elements are critical for an understanding of power on any system level. Yet, the distinction between its intermember and systemic dimensions is the most important one for the analysis of macropower. Every group contains some struggle over resources and incipient attempts to impose collective goals. The next chapter argues that the difference between the two factors is likely to be just analytical in microsystems but tends to become "real" in macrosystems. Systemic power is macropower *par excellence*. It is in the domain of the macrosocial that the prospects for comprehensive change become possible. Only there is systemic power sufficiently liberated to advance those collective goals that make history.

chapter four

Macropower

MACROPOWER requires separate treatment because it is never simply micropower "blown-up." The two domains differ in many respects. But five features of macropower illuminate its potential as an organizing concept. Specifically, this chapter explores why macropower is more likely: (1) to be a generalized capacity; (2) to foster "power plays"; (3) to possess a multiresource base; (4) to develop an informational capacity; and (5) to be marked by the separation of systemic power from intermember power. These characteristics clarify macropower's strengths for explaining what has happened and for directing what will happen.

Generalized Capacity

Power abides in relationships. On the microsocial plane, these relationships are commonly informal and noninstitutionalized. The macrosocial, for instance, has no counterpart of friendship cliques. Moreover, power bonds in microsettings tend to be specific: ego's dominance is often limited to particular events and to concrete commands. Macropower, in contrast, is frequently a generalized capacity: ego is able to exercise designated types of power within prescribed sectors at specified and recurrent intervals. The government's ability to levy taxes, raise an army, and make economic policy reflects a generalized capacity. The same is true of General Motors' power within its plants and throughout the automobile industry. The United States' position on the world scene is a generalized capacity. But my friend's prospects for getting a loan from me is not.

Of course, there are institutionalized power statuses in microunits—such as "father" and "mother" in the nuclear family. But macropower has a greater chance of being institutionalized. The nuclear family is probably the exception which proves the rule about the informality of microsocial life. I also do not deny that some micropower wielders dominate repeatedly in more than one sector of behavior—as witnessed by "Doc's" role in the Norton Street Gang. Nevertheless, on the micro level, more of conduct is the result of personality and unique situational factors. Structural factors account for more of the variance in macropower. Thus, micropower is less often institutionalized and more open to a wide expression of personal styles. For example, there is greater latitude in how American fathers are expected to behave than in how the federal judiciary is allowed to perform.

Reputation is decisive in forming a generalized capacity. In many microunits, alter's attributions to ego rest on personal qualities. Alter submits because ego is seen as holier, smarter, or kinder. George's power over Lenny in Steinbeck's *Of Mice and Men* flows from this kind of reputation. The personal grounding of their bond also explains why George's domination was often tenuous. Ego's reputation tends to have firmer roots on the macro level. Here, to a large. extent, it stems from shared or imposed definitions. When enough of the "right" members subscribe to cultural orientations, ego is defined as having the resources and the responsibility to issue certain types of commands.

Culture can provide macro actors with stable, intersubjective contexts of power, As we saw in chapter 2, most of culture changes very little in the short run. Thus, macro reputation is not will-o'-the-wisp. It is a label that may stick for many generations. The tenacity of the papacy is a vivid example of this. The Iron Age of the Papacy, the Great Schism, the Reformation and Counterreformation, and the Enlightenment all tarnished its image in the past. Yet it survived. In our own time, its reputation was battered by the controversy over *Humanae Vitae*. Still, it continues to inspire considerable devotion.

Cultural contexts provide ego with a ''zone of indifference'' (Barnard 1938, pp. 167–71, 185–99). Each command does not require the use of sanctions. Rather, on the macro tier, ego's right to use specified resources and to intervene in prescribed sectors is taken for granted. Not surprisingly, cultural attributions are made to institutionalized social entities (such as churches, corporations, political parties, and state agencies). Since culture is around for so relatively long, it can hardly provide a reputation for particular individuals who happen on the scene for brief periods. Cultural orientations focus on macro actors with comparable longevity. Political legitimacy, for example, is wasted on concrete persons; it works much better as a moral basis for collectivities who outlive their personnel. Consequently, parties and polities generally have more stable reputations than candidates, officials, or regimes.

What does macropower gain by being a generalized capacity? The principal benefit is enhanced predictability. A stable reputation takes a good deal of guesswork out of power relations. For instance, the 1962 dispute between the federal government under Kennedy and ''Big Steel'' over ''inflationary'' price increases was not an anomic struggle-to-the-death because of predictability. Both sides shared general definitions of what the other's ''rights'' were. Often, this is sufficient to limit the scope of conflict. Knowledge of what resources the other side can roll out also scotches conflict before it gets out of hand.

At first glance, enhanced predictability seems to dilute what power can accomplish. Isn't power's status as an independent variable and a lever for change threatened by predictability? Quite the contrary, for the alternative to predictability is chaos. Imagine if we had no inkling of how much muscle was available to corporations, unions, political parties, and the federal government over an issue. The volume of resources alone makes some predictability imperative. Predictability is also necessary because the range of resources on the macro level is so great. (Macropower often employs several types of resources; see below.) The total absence of predictability creates anomie, that is, complete uncertainty about who can and should do what. Generally, a decline in predictability weakens domination. In short, predictability increases the power of macropower to explain and to mold the world.

Power Plays

The advantages of predictability are particularly sharp in the case of power plays. Predictability opens the door to recurrent power plays or bluffing. The capacity to bluff presents macro actors with enormous opportunities, but it also introduces perils.

A good reputation, according to Blau, "is like a high credit rating . . . which enables a person to obtain benefits that are not available to others" (1964, p. 259). For ego, this means commands do not always call for the spending of resources. The stable reputation of macro actors permits them to dominate repeatedly without digging into assets. The Soviet Union is usually able to order its allies without commitment of economic or military hardware. Most American citizens pay taxes without overt sanctions by the Internal Revenue Service. Management can ordinarily issue new work directives without worrying how to compel workers to accept them.

Macropower becomes increasingly effective because of the institutionalization of bluffing. Ego's gestures of power yield results solely because they emanate from a credible source. Credibility does wondrous things for ego's prospects for domination. For one thing, it produces flexibility in the use of resources. Each threat or promise does not require the depleting of reserves. As Robert Bierstedt writes, "A battleship is even more effective as a symbol of power than it is as an instrument of force'' (1950, p. 738). This, in itself, produces economy in power relations. Overcoming resistance and pursuing goals are then less costly than they seemed on paper. Further, once resources are held back, ego can treat them as a reserve for unexpected events. For example, the Soviet Union's military credibility in Europe allowed it to redeploy manpower and equipment when tension rose along its border with China.

The capacity to substitute reputation for resources permits ego to branch out. With credibility and a reserve of assets, ego may be inspired to move into new sectors or to formulate new goals. Earlier, nation-states focused on warfare and taxation. Today, the state also penetrates health, education, welfare, and science—to name just a few of the domains it touches. The modern state's ability to match a growing reputation to an expanded resource base is a key factor in this branching out. The same is true for many multinational corporations.

Bluffing is beneficial because ego can use credibility to expand resources, reputation, and power. Those who treat this topic draw analogies between power plays and the banking system. (See especially Deutsch 1963; Gamson 1968; and Parsons 1967b, 1967c.) If all depositors descended on the banks at the same time, our economic system would falter. As long as the banks are credible, depositors are unlikely to panic. Consequently, banks use money they do not really have. Most of the assets, at any moment, are out as loans and so on. Nevertheless, banks can invest and grant loans as if the assets were safely in their vaults because there are few calls on the money. The practice allows the banking system to generate new wealth via interest and profits. Macropower wielders are capable of repeatedly investing their reputations through power plays. The propounders of the analogy argue that new power is created in a similar way. Every successful bluff increases macropower wielders' reputations, probably their stockpiles of resources, and possibly their overall power. Hitler's success at dismembering Czechoslovakia through bluffs in 1938 is a prime example of this process.

Regular power plays make macropower more effective, but they also pose pitfalls. The principal danger is escalation. Power plays must be backed occasionally by the spending of resources, or credibility wanes. Alters must, from time to time, be reconfirmed in their view of ego's reputation. Sometimes ego has to "put up or shut up." If power wielders cannot impose goals, they will be considered spendthrifts. They must avoid appearing to be poor credit risks whose commands exceed what they can afford. The USSR's credibility with its satellites grew because of the successful invasions of Hungary (in 1956) and Czechoslovakia (in 1968). Egypt's credibility, on the other hand, suffered as a result of the Six-Day War of 1967.

A nation that strikes a blustering military posture cannot back down too often, or it will not be taken seriously by adversaries. Similarly, a pope who demands orthodoxy must use sanctions against some dissidents or face the erosion of his authority. In both these cases, ego may have to use up resources intended to be held in reserve.

But escalation is more than just an occasional unexpected expense. Once ego's credibility is challenged, alters are likely to call threats or promises more and more often. Power becomes costlier because ego can bluff less often and must spend added resources to salvage credibility. This phenomenon is in the power sector what inflation is in the economic realm. On the international scene, escalation may force a war that no one wants. Why the United States got enmeshed in the Indochina war will be debated endlessly. But our escalating involvement (and failure to extricate ourselves rationally) was due partly to a fear of losing credibility. Within religious organizations, escalation can lead to schism; in national politics, it can promote alienation of supporters; and in business, it may provoke price wars that eat into everyone's profits.

"Put up or shut up" is a thorny problem for macropower. Ironically, although power plays are more routine on this level, micro actors find it easier to come up with the resources when bluffs are called. The reason lies with the differences in reputation for the two provinces. As I have said, microreputation depends more on personal and situational qualities. On the macro level, reputations flow more from cultural orientations. Personal attributions are more readily converted into normative resources. When people are seen as smarter, holier, or more loving, it directly expands their ability to wield love, prestige, acceptance, and esteem in order to persuade. Culture's impact, on the other hand, is indirect. Macro actors, for example, will find legitimacy an unreliable way to increase a resource base. Cultural contexts yield definitions about who has the right to use resources, but these orientations cannot produce assets.

Of course, personal reputation is sometimes important in macrosystems. Cultural definitions are not the sole source of reputation. The choice among candidates in an election involves personal attributions ("Does he *look* presidential?"). However, the institutionalized reputation of political parties is crucial, too. The popularity of an administration is also a form of personal attribution. Citizens judge the competence of incumbents, and these judgments help make or break the latters' reputations. Generally, the popularity of incumbents is more fleeting than the legitimacy of a system. (See chapter 6, pp. 137–38.) Yet, both affect the credibility of macropower. The loss of personal attributions can be disastrous for incumbents in a macrosystem, even when legitimacy remains intact. Jimmy Breslin's account of the Nixon impeachment process is illustrative of how ephemeral personal reputation can be in the polity:

When Tip O'Neill [House Democratic Majority Leader] decided that his primary duty was to make rapid the removal of Richard Nixon he took on great power. Because everybody began to regard him as being quite powerful. And meanwhile, each day, these little pieces of trouble dropped on the floor at Richard Nixon's feet and more and more people noticed it. As the level of regard for Nixon's power dropped, the level of danger for his career rose. At the end, Nixon had not the personal political power of city councilman. He sat in the Oval Office, but he might as well have been in City Hall, in Dayton. (1975, pp. 34–35)

However, the relationship between personal reputation and macropower is never direct. Several factors must intervene before the loss of personal popularity depletes normative assets or before greater popularity is translated into new resources. A macro actor's chances of converting personal reputation into normative resources depends on broader societal factors. Differences between societies are almost as great as between the macro and micro levels. For example, a U.S. president finds it harder than a European prime minister to translate high ratings in public-opinion polls into successful legislative action. Variations in political culture may play an indirect part here. However, the organization of the respective polities explains more. Under a parliamentary system, a popular prime minister can threaten to call elections and thereby increase his legislative strength. Our system of separation of powers and preordained elections gives a president no such option. On the other hand, Nixon was able to linger in office longer than any prime minister—in Europe he would have been removed by a simple vote of no-confidence by parliament.

In sum, institutionalized bluffing makes macropower more effective and economical. Systematic increase in resources, reputation, and power is likely. Yet power plays face the peril of escalation, which forces power wielders into actions they never intended in order to salvage credibility. Moreover, ego is less able to convert reputation into resources when bluffs are called than are micro actors. Even ego's personal reputation is harder to covert on the macro tier.

Multi-resource Base

Micropower frequently rests on a single resource base; macropower usually depends on more than one type of resource. The latter's capacity to marshall a broader array of resources increases the potential scope of domination.

Leadership is critical in small groups. The success of power in microsettings rests mainly on personal qualities. Ego here is someone who relies more on the esteem in which he or she is held and less on the prestige of position. As a consequence, normative assets are often the major resources that are brought to bear. Persuasion is the order of the day. Of course, inducement and constraint are occasionally important in such settings. Friends, as well as congressmen, can be bribed. Loved ones, and not just "the enemy," are sometimes targets of violence. Yet, micropower is capable of getting by for longer periods on normative assets alone. There are two reasons for this: the expressive nature of microbonds; and the fact that such ties tend to be voluntary.

Positive expressive (i.e., "warm") bonds are at the core of microrelations. Most of the time, they are a key purpose of the relationship. For families, work cliques, and "the guys at the corner bar," cohesion is one goal of their interactions, not just an incidental necessity. Neither utilitarian nor coercive assets are suited for forming or sustaining warm feelings. People cannot be paid or bullied to enjoy one another's company. Such tactics are counterproductive, for they only drive people apart; they do not bring them together. Normative resources are most appropriate for nurturing positive expressive linkages.

Membership in many microunits is genuinely voluntary. Friendship groups are the clearest example of this. But the ease of divorce makes family membership today more voluntary too. Secession is the prime threat to voluntary groups. Members must want to remain members or the group will founder. The desire to preserve voluntary relationships disappears if ego regularly tries to constrain or induce other people. Morale is critical. Persuasion via normative assets is less of a danger to morale because it is less alienating. Hence, normative assets are least likely to provoke secession.

Macro actors, on the other hand, control a profusion of utilitarian, coercive, and normative resources. As I indicated in the opening chapter, society's strategic resources occur more regularly and in larger amounts on the macro level. The means of industrial production, nuclear weapons, and the mass media, for instance, are not tied to isolated individuals or small groups. When these resources are discussed, labels like "upper class," "military-industrial complex," and "Eastern media establishment" are invoked. These terms display an awareness that the vehicles for transformation are controlled by macro actors. The resources involved cut across all three of our types.

Normative assets alone are not a good bet for successful domination in the macro world. For example, when King Constantine sought to rally support against the Greek military junta in 1967, he relied heavily on the normative resources of the monarchy to sway doubtful political and military elements. His countercoup failed in the face of the junta's control of the armed forces and the radio, and he was forced into exile.

A multiresource base gives macro actors greater opportunity to operate widely and to make sweeping changes. In particular, diversity of resources is essential for overcoming resistance in these settings. A multiresource base allows varied types of sanctions to be employed. Different types of sanctions can be used on different segments of the population. The need for varied sanctions in macrounits springs from the greater heterogeneity among the membership. (See chapter 5.) For example, a victorious revolutionary movement might try to persuade the workers to go along by offering improved pay, benefits, and working conditions; it might constrain leaders of opposition parties by imprisonment, exile, and execution; and finally, it might attempt to persuade the intellectuals to support the cause via ideological appeals.

Ego must beware of the mixing of resources. Different sanctions applied to the same group may cancel each other out. Normative resources do not work on those who have been previously induced and constrained; utilitarian resources are wasted on the persuaded and constrained; and coercive resources do not reinforce persuasion and inducement. Indeed, the application of resources in each case probably undoes what has been accomplished already. If power wielders are to optimize their chances for success, they must decide how they wish to dominate a group—either to induce, constrain, or persuade it—and then give primacy (although not necessarily exclusive reliance) to mobilization of utilitarian, coercive, or normative resources.

Richard H. McCleery (1957) describes how the introduction of rehabilitation-oriented staff members created havoc in a custodial prison by mixing sanctions. A system built on coercion and constraint was undermined by the introduction of persuasive methods. The short-range consequences were riots and turmoil. The domination of coercion-oriented staff was weakened. Previously constrained prisoners were not won over by power that stressed interior dispositions rather than external control.

On the other hand, the complexity of modern life sometimes forces macropower wielders to mix resources. For example, a government may try to regulate the urban poor by concentrating coercive resources in ghetto areas. But it may also feel the need to persuade them by appeals to common beliefs and values. Finally, it may try to induce them by providing welfare and greater employment opportunities. To ensure that constraint, persuasion, and inducement do not cancel each other out, a regime is advised to structurally differentiate its modes of sanctions. By centering coercive power in the police, it focuses the antipathy on this department. At the same time, other agencies are free to persuade and induce ghetto residents more effectively because they are not burdened by hostility toward police constraint. Persuasion and inducement are also more effectively pursued if they are separated. For instance, persuasion may be best carried out by locally based churches and voluntary associations. The dispensing of utilitarian resources requires considerable technical and administrative competence and often promotes greater alienation than the manipulation of normative resources; thus, utilitarian activities probably are best conducted by external (public or private) social-service agencies.

Piven and Cloward (1971) have argued that governments alternate between inducement and constraint in the regulation of the poor. During times of social unrest, the flow of economic benefits is stepped up; but after things calm down, this tap is turned off and coercion is reimposed. Their theory suggests that effective use of resources as sanctions requires temporal segregation and not just structural differentiation. Yet, whether temporal segregation works as well as the structual mode—whether a regime can reemphasize constraint after a period of inducement (or persuasion) without significant costs—is still, I think, an unanswered question.

Macropower's multiresource base is also a source of difficulty when bluffs are called. Micropower leans heavily on normative resources. Hence, if ego is "called," he or she probably only has to come up with intangible assets (e.g., to say something loving, pious, or smart). Since reputation is more easily translated into normative resources on the micro level, the stresses of calling power plays are not so severe. By contrast, macro actors are doubly disadvantaged. They have a harder time turning attributions into normative resources. And, because they rely more on a multiresource base, even when they convert reputation into normative assets, it does not help them if they are called on to put up coercive or utilitarian assets. For example, the moral support the Dubcek regime received before and after the August 1968 invasion of Czechoslovakia strengthened its hand in dealings with the Soviet invaders. Yet, moral support was no substitute for the military and economic might the Russians brought to the confrontation.

Power wielders, regardless of system-level, are loath to put up tangible resources. They are reticent either because they do have them or because they do not want to deplete stockpiles. Since macropower is more dependent on tangible resources, the problem is especially germane for this area. There is a benefit to relying on normative resources (as micropower wielders are able to do). The use of symbolic assets does not necessarily result in depletion. In fact, judicious mobilization of normative resources may expand personal reputation which, in turn, increases the store of these assets.

Specialized
Informational Capacity

The importance of an informational capacity in our time has led
some to proclaim the birth of a new civilization. They herald the
coming of "postindustrial society." Their chief prophet is Daniel
Bell, who says:

. . . After the Second World War, the scientific capacity of a
country has become a determinant of its potential and power, and
research and development (R & D) has replaced steel as a comparative measure of strength of the [world] powers. For this reason the
nature and kinds of state support for science, the politicization of
science, the sociological problem of the organization of work by
science teams all become central policy issues in a post-industrial
society. (1973, pp. 117–18)

Who can disagree with Bell about the significance of information in advanced societies? I leave it to others to debate whether or
not the change is comparable to the rise of industrial capitalism in
the nineteenth century. We can all agree that modern macro actors
need more information than their predecessors or their contemporaries in microunits. Today, the state and business corporations
rely on an endless stream of data in order to pursue their goals. In
the past, both depended more on received knowledge, including
traditional technologies and long-standing bookkeeping and accounting procedures. Small groups, even now, have fewer informational requirements. The uses of love, for instance, do not
benefit greatly from R & D inputs (the works of Masters and Johnson notwithstanding).

Macroscopic systems vary in the ability to create knowledge
and to make it usable. Differences persist even among those with
specialized R & D units. Variations are evident in all sectors.
There are differences among polities—the United States versus
Luxembourg or Albania. Differences exist among agencies within
the same polity—the CIA versus the Interior Department or the

Civil Rights Commission. Even modern business concerns differ—
International Telephone & Telegraph (ITT) versus R. H. Macy's.

Yet, some competence in generating information is a hallmark of all advanced societies—and of key units in them. The
number of volumes on library shelves is a commonly employed indicator of this capacity. The growth of science and technology,
and of universities, research centers, and the mass media, also attest to the "knowledge explosion." But the exponential expansion
of knowledge does not in itself fill the needs of macropower. An
activist orientation makes modern states insatiable consumers of
information. The same is true of many business organizations. Activism may widen the gap between needed and available data even
while the pool of knowledge is increasing. Moreover, the ability to
create or collect knowledge (and to preserve it) does not necessarily make macropower more rational or effective. "Good" information also must get to centers that make decisions.

Knowledge as it is created or collected and information as it
is used are not the same things. Between collection and use,
knowledge is placed aboard an assembly line where it is reshaped
as it passes from administrator to administrator and from agency to
agency en route to a decision center. Physically, it is condensed.
For example, a several-hundred-page report to the National Institutes of Health on heart disease may end up on the president's desk
as a ten-page recommendation for a crash program to conquer the
disease. In transit, data are not summarized and eliminated strictly
on logical and empirical grounds, but on the basis of the interests,
theories, assumptions, and prejudices of those through whose
hands a report passes. As data are condensed, "value" is being
added. Information is continually being remolded to meet the
needs of intended consumers.[1] If knowledge is to become useful,
processing is inevitable. The danger of decomposing into mere
ideology is a real one. Yet, decision makers cannot avail themselves of data, regardless of how scientifically impeccable, unless
value adding has occurred. Facts cannot and do not help make policy; only processed information can.

What structural factors block the delivery of information to decision-making centers? Harold L. Wilensky suggests that the undue reliance on three arrangements impedes the use of what he calls "organizational intelligence." The three are hierarchy, specialization, and centralization (1967, pp. 41–62). Without some organizational routine—some hierarchy, specialization, and centralization—knowledge could not be converted into information. Nevertheless, an excessive zeal for each has dysfunctions for the process.

Wilensky says that the shape of the hierarchy (the number of ranks and the number of persons on each level) affects the flow of organizational intelligence. If an organizational pyramid is tall and narrows sharply at the top, there is "a long promotion ladder for a few" (p. 45). Those on lower ranks have neither information nor the motive to obtain it. Moreover, among nonmobile, middle-level staff, "defensive cliques" develop that restrict information in order to prevent change. They resist change, Wilensky argues, out of resentment of their mobile colleagues. The flow of intelligence is also stifled by the ambitious and mobile, who pool information but pass on only the portions that enhance their own careers. Wilensky feels that "the optimal shape of the hierarchy would be relatively flat (few ranks permit a speedier diffusion of more accurate information) with a bulge in the middle (more specialists who have information and more potential managers motivated to command it)" (p. 45). He cites the modern military—with its shift from a rigid pyramid to a flexible demand-shape organization— as an organization reshaped to enhance the flow of intelligence.

Wilensky suggests that the effects of specialization are even more disruptive for the processing of information. Specialization is essential, for technical competence is necessary to create and to appreciate knowledge. But it may be inimical to the creative interpretation needed for policy formation. Specialization foments interunit rivalry, which blocks the sharing of information. "The primary cost of specialization," says Wilensky, "is parochialism—the production of misleading or irrelevant information, a product of the familiar limitations of the expert" (p. 49). Yet, he also sees a constructive rivalry. This form allows the clarification of alternatives and the airing of opposing cases. Wilensky's major example of the dysfunctions of specialization is the failure to transmit the signals of an impending Japanese attack to the chief executive in late 1941. Various bits of telltale data lay scattered among rival intelligence agencies. Formally, communication lines were mandated but crucial messages never flowed across these lines, let alone upward to the president.

The principal liability of centralization, according to Wilensky, occurs when "intelligence is lodged at the top, too few officials and experts with too little accurate and relevant information are too far out of touch and too overloaded to function effectively . . ." (p. 58). Yet, excessive decentralization may promote dysfunctional competition and delay decision. "More simply, plans are manageable only if we delegate; plans are coordinated only if we centralize" (p. 58).

The CIA was created specifically to promote higher-level coordination in order to prevent future Pearl Harbors. Nevertheless, Wilensky points out: "After administrative reform, a more unified, centralized intelligence agency, producing a unified consensual judgment, then fosters the illusion of security, of reliable intelligence, which, as the Bay of Pigs invasion illustrates, can conceal fantasies at the highest level" (p. 58).

Cultural factors also bear on informational capacities (although their impact is probably more indirect). Wilensky, for instance, points out that intelligence distortions sometimes occur because of differing "doctrines of intelligence." Some knowledge units favor the collection of raw data at the expense of evaluation; other units minimize data collection and put great stress on evaluation. The first kind of bias overloads a system with more unprocessed information than it can absorb; the latter bias is likely to disseminate theories and preconceptions that have not faced empirical scrutiny as facts. (See Etzioni 1968, pp. 144–46.)

The scientific values of experts in the knowledge system are influential, too. Researchers never collect all facts, only selected ones. Which bits of data are collected and which are ignored is decided in part by which scientific paradigm a researcher is working under. (See Kuhn 1970.)

Ego's power potential rises when muscles and nerves are synchronized to overcome resistance and implement goals. Examples from government and the military are the most visible ones, but the benefit of infusing power with information applies to all sectors of macrosocial life. However, increasing dependence of informational capabilities is not without drawbacks. I have alluded to the most obvious of these previously. Dependence on information is addictive: larger and larger doses are needed to keep the user content. Our reliance on processed knowledge reinforces an emphasis on rationality in power relations. Macro actors are now less willing to rely on muscle or bluff. They want to know as much as possible about a situation, and how well the resources they control will work in a situation. They expect R & D units to produce this type of information. Thus, the informational capacity of the modern world is expanding, but it seems to have difficulties keeping up with the exigencies of a macropower yearning to be more sophisticated.

Conflict between experts and power wielders is another problem springing from the addiction to information. The grounds for such a struggle are not new to students of complex organizations, who have known for some time about the contradictions of "line versus staff" and "the professional versus the bureaucrat." We are now conscious that these strains exist for polity and society as well. We know that science cannot save us. Transformation requires the remolding of scientific knowledge for policy purposes—that is, knowledge for knowledge's sake must be "distorted" before it can help make policy. The creators of knowledge do not take kindly to distortion, but they also resent the lack of power in affecting the direction of the distortion. The needs and values of experts and of information consumers are difficult to reconcile. Tension exists between technicians and politicians in all advanced societies. The plight of Soviet dissident intellectuals should not blind us to the occasions for strain in democratic societies. A remolding of knowledge that satisfies both expert and power wielder will never be easy. Some have seen this conflict as the pivotal one in so-called postindustrial society. (See, for example, Touraine 1971.)

Yet, there is profit in conflict too. The prospect for a viable democratic society declines when experts are stripped of autonomy and their role as critics. Fusing information and decision centers is misguided. Macropower wielders will only hear what they want to hear. The quality of information will be impaired unless reports are allowed to contain "heretical" proposals, and this cannot occur within the bosom of macropower. The autonomy of knowledge centers, and their tolerance of diversity, are safeguards against the oppression of "static utopias." (See Moore 1972, ch. 5.)

The Separation
of Systemic Power
from Intermember Power

Systemic power is more "real" on the macro level. The rise of units specializing in collective goals makes this sphere the place where important things are done. The separation of systemic power from intermember power is one of the key divisions of labor marking modern society. Two of the many others that have been vital are the differentiation of economic activities from kinship networks and the breaking away of educational structures from the religious nexus.

But the development of systemic power is a different kind of specialization. Most divisions of labor, including the rise of the economic and educational sectors, are cases of horizontal specialization. The development of systemic power is vertical, however. A horizontal division leads to separate units whose interactions can be traced without added theoretical assumptions. The relationship between the occupational sphere and the family is illustrative of this pattern. On the other hand, a vertical division means that new tiers develop within a social system. These tiers deal with activities for which there were previously no specialized units—a trait common to all divisions of labor. In addition, the higher tiers encompass the lower-order ones and set limits on their conduct. The modern polity, as we shall see in chapter 6, operates on such a plane. It is on a higher level, it "contains" other societal actors, and, to a degree, it limits what they can and cannot do.

Macrosystems generally have more tiers than microsystems. When sociologists analyze the vertical differentiation of microsystems, they are usually talking about analytical constructs. Concrete activities are fused and the differences are abstractions superimposed by an observer for the sake of analysis. In contrast, the tiers in macrosystems are both more plentiful and more visible. The language of the observer traces real configurations of the social terrain.

Macrosystems are fruitfully seen as "Chinese nesting boxes" (Parsons 1967b, p. 322). They are nested in larger units (suprasystems) and themselves encompass smaller ones (subsystems). The nature of the larger system constrains what happens in the units they contain. For example, the performance of a single hospital is not fully understood in terms of intraorganizational dynamics. When we see hospitals as part of the broader medical, economic, and political systems, we understand much more of what occurs. Clearly, the failure by hospitals to control costs cannot be explained by internal processes alone.

The emergence of centers of systemic power is the most important example of tier formation. Prior to breaking away, a group's systemic power potential is enmeshed in its patterns of intermember power. The pursuit of collective goals here is a by-product of the competition over resources. European feudalism approximated such a situation. The foci of identification and integration for the key macro actors (fiefs, baronies, duchies, and so on) were inward rather than directed toward a center of systemic power (the monarchy). The state apparatus was weak, perhaps nonexistent. The most powerful members saw their particular goals and the interests of the larger system as identical. Feudal lords pursued both within a framework of power that was heavily intermember in focus.

Systemic power is more explicitly macrosociological than intermember power. Both occur in this domain. Yet, systemic power is only likely to shake free from the web of intermember power after we leave the microsocial realm. Although collective goals occur in small groups, acts geared to these ends are difficult to separate from the competition over resources. For instance, normative resources are central in microsystems, but their deployment for collective purposes is hard to disentangle from the competition over their allocations. The family provides a case in point—it is usually impossible to tell when parents use love to socialize their children and when love is a scarce resource sought by all the members.

Complex organizations are the species of macrosystem that exhibits a separate systemic component most regularly. This pattern is no accident, since the defining feature of complex organizations is a specialization in collective goals. Two divisions of labor stand out sharply in these units. Herbert Simon (1957) was the first one to call attention to their difference. He recognized a traditional horizontal division of labor in organizations, which divided work and subunits by discrete tasks. In addition, he pointed to a vertical specialization based on power. Activities in the latter realm focus on the organization of the decision-making process rather than on work performances. Simon's insight is invaluable for organizational analysis. An observer has little difficulty in distinguishing the struggle over budgetary allocations among departments in an industrial organization from the activities of the central administration. Even organizations that ostensibly give primacy to intermember power tend to develop vertical administrative structures. For example, Harrison's (1959) study of the American Baptist Convention found that responsibility and resources were initially in the hands of local congregations. Yet, despite values favoring local autonomy, the central administration gradually acquired its own resource base, a greater control of intracongregational activities, and a grudging right to set denomination-wide policy.[2]

Networks of organizations are less likely to have specialized centers of systemic power than are single organizations. For every interorganizational field with centralized coordination, there are many more where systemic power remains diffused among the member units. (See Lehman 1975.) For example, ties among hospitals in most communities are intermittent, informal, and concerned with such activities as the exchange of specimens and diagnoses or the sharing of laundry services. Up to now, interorganizational fields have been less mobilized for shaping their destinies than intraorganizational structures.

Variations also are found among societies. Differentiated systemic power centers exist more often in modern societies than in earlier ones. However, Imperial China and ancient Egypt at their peaks had stronger capabilities than did European feudal societies.

The term "political power" is usually employed when discussing systemic power in society. (See, for example, Parsons 1967b.) I will use this term in the rest of the book. It alerts us that the pursuit of collective goals for societies is a crucial political act. Yet, society's network of intermember power also has political overtones which employing the term "political power" must not obscure. An appreciation of political life requires that both power networks be understood.

The *political system*—or *polity*—is society's network of political power. The organs specializing in political power are commonly called *the state*. State and polity are overlapping phenomena. (Their relationship is detailed in chapter 6.) Yet, intermember power remains an important force even in societies with potent states. Many Power Elite theorists and Pluralists continue to emphasize intermember power at the expense of political power. Power Elite critics of American society suggest that some members (e.g., the "military-industrial complex") are so dominant that political power merely reflects skewed intermember power (Mills 1956; Domhoff 1967, 1970). Some Pluralists also presume that political power mirrors intermember power. They depart from the Power Elite view only because they see intermember power as more equitably distributed. (See, for example, Riesman 1950.)[3] On the other hand, theorists of totalitarian society reverse the imagery. They argue that the modern totalitarian regime is so strong that political power wholly swamps intermember power. (See Friedrich and Brzezinski 1965; Arendt 1966.)

Tracing the interplay of political power and intermember power is never easy. The relationship is not self-evident or a matter for theoretical assertion; detailed research is always required. On the one hand, the states of advanced societies have special access to resources, information, and reputation. They control normative, utilitarian, and coercive resources and a burgeoning R & D capability. Power plays are a fact of daily life. Thus, the modern state is rarely a passive instrument of intermember power. Even contemporary Marxians acknowledge the partial autonomy of the state. (See, for example, O'Connor 1973; Offe 1974; Miliband 1969; Poulantzas 1973.) On the other hand, it is also unlikely to be able to negate intermember power entirely; the diversity within contemporary societies makes such domination too costly in the long run. Indeed, the Soviet Union despite its totalitarian proclivities has felt the need to abandon undiluted Stalinism.

Researchers who venture in this area must move with caution. As I noted in the previous chapter, classification into the two spheres is relative. Power is never unequivocally political or intermember for two reasons: one, empirical; the other, theoretical. Empirically, the state is not *sui generis*. At times, it is just another competitor for societal resources. Political authorities develop vested interests (such as maintaining themselves in office) and often pursue ends for this reason. As a result, some policies of the state are better viewed as involving particular as well as collective goals. The actions of regimes in election years are noted for taking on such a tinge. From a theoretical vantage point, the classification of power is relative because the system of reference must be specified. What is systemic or political power on one tier is intermember power on the next higher one. I used military expenditures on the national and international scenes to illustrate this point in chapter 3. Similarly, a corporation seeking profit is exercising systemic power in its intraorganizational system, but is engaged in intermember power from the perspective of interorganizational or intrasocietal analysis.

The complexities of modern life make it improbable that intermember power is an automatic guarantee of political power or vice versa. Political power resides largely in the machinery of the state, not in society's other members. The ability of the latter to gain access to the former requires mobilization via a complex set of social processes. The outcome is never assured. Following Parsons (1967a), I subsume these mechanisms under the heading of *influence*. This concept refers to "upward" processes through which society's members strive to convert intermember power into an ability to affect the decisions of the state. Use of the concept of influence changes the question of "who governs?" The answer to that question is: the government governs—that is, political power today is found principally in the organs of state. The more telling question is: "For whom does it govern?" This query directs our attention to the mechanisms of influence. It makes us realize that getting the state to do what we want is not the same as intermember power (e.g., being rich) or political power (e.g., occupying positions in the state)—although it is affected by the first and seeks to impinge on the second.

Influence refers to upward processes. Subunits struggle to shape the actions of higher tiers, in this case, the centers of political power. The comparable downward processes are called *social control*.[4] Here the issue is how well the state uses its muscle and reputation to penetrate intermember power. Weak political power results in little social control. When political power is employed to coincide with existing intermember power, social control also remains minimal. This occurs when the state's commands are not intended to disrupt a society's arrangement of power and privilege. Social control is high when political power seeks access to the intermember power-privilege cycle and aims to move the system profoundly. Social control in the United States was low until the

1930s. The Soviet Union under Stalin probably is the best approximation of high social control. The state (or perhaps more accurately, the Party) made intermember power virtually irrelevant because of the scope and intensity of its penetration of society. (How influence and social control promote the viability of the polity is a central topic of chapter 6.)

Political power and intermember power differ in two other respects: the character of backing for power plays and their need for hierarchical organization. Earlier I noted that bluffing behavior is more common in macropower relations. Macro actors find it especially vexing to come up with the appropriate resource backing if commands are called. Analysts fond of analogies between economic and political life assert that coercive resources are the polity's counterpart of the gold standard. (See, for instance, Parsons 1967c.) They suggest that when political power plays are called, commands must be backed by possible violence in much the same way as gold backs currency and credit.

How useful is the analogy? Its principal benefit, I think, is that it calls attention to the status of coercive resources in political systems. There is value in seeing coercive resources as an ultimate backing for political power so long as we remember that the state's power is based on normative and utilitarian resources too. The gold standard analogy is beneficial because modern states have a monopoly over the means of macroviolence. Other actors, for instance, do not ordinarily have private armies. (Weimar Germany was an instructive deviant case in this regard.) Nor do member units control the major means of destruction (e.g., nuclear weapons). Urban guerrillas and gangsters are no threat to the state's monopoly, only to its credibility.

The notion of ultimate backing is also useful because of heterogeneity in advanced society. The state is unable to persuade or induce all of the members all of the time because members are so different. Unless the state is able to constrain members who refuse to go along, it may find its effectiveness as a goal attainer eroded. I do not suggest that the state ought to maximize its reliance on force. States that rely less on violence are more viable than those that put too great a stress on coercion. Nevertheless, no regime depends solely on reputation or on utilitarian and normative assets—although these are less alienating and more efficient for developing the attributions of power and the acquiescence to commands. A successful state must have the prospect of falling back on coercion, if only as a last resort.

The notion of ultimate backing is less applicable to the intermember sphere. No resource type in this domain is analogous to the gold standard in the economy. However, utilitarian resources are probably used most to bolster intermember credibility. This is particularly true if more than a show of normative assets is required, this is, if tangible assets have to be put on the line. Utilitarian resources are commonly the principal weapon and the prize of intermember struggles. Moreover, economic assets may be key weapons even in mainly normative struggles. Weber helped us to recognize that economic privilege (control of wealth, jobs, and so on) provides an indispensable basis for systems of "honor." (See Gerth and Mills 1946, pp. 180–86.) The state's monopoly on violence also confines intermember struggles to utilitarian resources. Corporations wage economic warfare because they cannot bomb their competitors. Finally, utilitarian resources are more sought after because they are sources of gratification (e.g., goods and services). Coercive resources are not ends in themselves. Rather, their use creates deprivation (e.g., pain and anxiety).

Hierarchy also plays a different role for political and intermember powers. The pursuit of collective goals demands mobilization. A vast array of resources and information may have to be acquired and allocated. Without some hierarchy of decision making, mobilization would not be possible. No comparable requisite exists in the case of intermember power. True, intermember power often has been distributed more unequally than political power throughout history. The privilege of wealthy and the revered has been at least as great as the state's control of the public. But there are several reasons for reducing intermember differentials. Certainly, if we seek greater justice and less alienation, more equality is required. Increased democracy also calls for greater intermember equality. Equalizing influence appears hard to accomplish unless we first reduce intermember inequality. These aims are not necessarily utopian or destructive of societal order. On the other hand, any attempt to organize political power nonhierarchically makes the pursuit of collective goals impossible.

Conclusions

The five correlates of macropower clarify why it is a good organizing concept.

In macrosystems, power is more often a generalized capacity because a stable reputation promotes predictability in power relations. Enhanced predictability may seem to be a burden for power. Yet, predictability is essential for the effective wielding of macropower, given the volume of resources involved. Predictability is also urgent because macropower generally rests on more than one type of resource. If there were no way of anticipating who possessed or was entitled to which resources, the ensuing chaos might approximate the "war of all against all." At the very least, it would generate uncertainty about who had the right and the ability to issue commands. Neither situation is conducive for the rational and effective attainment of collective goals.

"Power plays" are more routine in macrosystems. The pitfalls of escalation are real. But judicious power plays increase ego's reputation, resources, and power, and, hence, the prospects for expanded domination.

Macropower is more likely to be based on a combination of normative, utilitarian, and coercive resources, while micropower wielders are bound more to normative resources alone. The array of resources on the macro level makes possible a spectrum of goals not ordinarily found on the micro level. It also increases the chances that recalcitrants can be sanctioned successfully.

The wielders of macropower are more likely to be served by units providing an informational capability. R & D units increase the prospects that resources will be used intelligently. This, in turn, promotes greater effectiveness in pursuing goals and neutralizing resistance.

Finally, systemic power represents macropower *par excellence*. The more macroscopic a group is, the greater the probability that units specializing in systemic power have broken away from intermember power. As a result, two capabilities are optimized: the pursuit of collective goals; and the ability to restrict an otherwise uncontrolled struggle for intermember power and privilege. These capabilities are vital for checking spiralling societal inequality and the miseries that spring from it. Yet, they are double-edged, for political power represents the surest way to protect the status quo or to expand privilege.

In short, power on the societal level has a far greater chance for effective use. Not all macropower is equally effective for directing societal processes—since political power is better than intermember power. In chapter 5 and 6, I examine the morphologies of these two power networks.

Yet, as I just indicated, political power is double-edged. It is as likely to promote destructive ends as transforming ones. As Lewis Coser points out, "Adolf Hitler and Joseph Stalin may indeed have been instrumental in increasing the collective power resources of their respective societies, but they did a good deal of other things besides" (1976, p. 160). Political power must bend to member needs while still retaining effectiveness if it hopes to be humane. This is no easy task. Further, while political power is more effective than micropower, polities are not necessarily successful or viable. Chapters 6 and 7 explore the problems of responsiveness and political viability.

Part Three

Societal Power

All societies have two realms of power, the political and the inter-member; however, they vary dramatically in how much these are structurally separated. Only in the modern, industrially advanced world do we regularly find a distinct layer concerned with collective goals which makes itself felt over and above the immemorial struggle for valued resources. Still, intermember power must always be explored if political life is to be understood. This exploration is necessary regardless of whether a society's system of intermember power is fused with or absorbs political power (as in most premodern situations) or is separate from but deeply penetrated by the latter (as in advanced nation-states).

In chapter 5, I examine the morphology of intermember power and suggest that the arrangement of this capacity provides the groundwork for a macroscopic view of inequality, which remains as a paramount source of societal misery and discontent. Chapter 6 considers the morphology of political power as well as the principal political processes linking the two types of power networks.

chapter five

The Morphology of Intermember Power

IF left unchecked, the cycle of intermember power and privilege inexorably widens inequality. Inequality inches modern society toward chaos either through the misery or the discontent that it spawns. This chapter investigates the nature of societal stratification in an effort to gauge the future of inequality. I provide a macrosociological view of inequality. Such an approach departs from much of American social-stratification theory.[1] It focuses not on the ranking of individuals, statuses, and roles, families or statistical constructs, but on the inequality among the major groups that make up a society.

More precisely, this chapter presents the elements for a macrosociological mapping of societal inequality. I begin by arguing that this task requires a profile of the recipients as well as the resources in intermember power networks. The recipients are called *macrosolidary groups* because modern societies rarely consist of "pure" classes or "pure" status groups. Another characteristic of modern stratification systems is their fluidity, or looseness. The factors behind fluidity are probed. Particular attention is given to the fluid nature of American inequality and whether our system is drifting in a classlike direction. Contemporary systems of intermember power are also more indeterminate; boundaries among recipients are blurring. The question of indeterminacy resurrects the old debate over how "real" recipients are. But indeterminacy has practical implications as well. It is at the heart of today's struggle for more equality; but it is also an impetus for the striving and discontent that Tocqueville spoke of over a century ago. The chapter concludes with a discussion of the future of inequality and why this question is now a political-power issue and not exclusively a topic of intermember power.

Social Stratification

The study of inequality is sometimes called "social stratification." To view social stratification in macroscopic terms does not stop us from asking why people are treated unequally, why society's statuses and roles receive different rewards, and whether all men and women, someday, will be equal in every respect. A focus on macroinequality brackets these questions; to a degree it premises their resolution on elaborating the nature and consequences of differential privilege and power among society's principal members.

Let us recall that "privilege" here refers to the possession of a certain slice of a society's resources; and that the term "power" (used in its intermember aspects) considers the prospects for increasing the size of one's slice in the future despite resistance. Chapters 3 and 4 discussed why present access to resources is one basis for this potential. I noted that privilege and power are reciprocal phenomena. All other things being equal, privilege expands intermember power, which then generates greater privilege, *ad infinitum*. (See Lenski 1966.)

Hence, the discussion of inequality in societies begins with two dimensions: We must consider which groups are significant in the allocative process (the *recipients*); and we must examine what is being distributed (the *resources*). [2]

Recipients

I refer to the recipients as "macrosolidary groups." (See Lehman
and Lehman 1975.) Other authors have pointed to similar phenomena, using such terms as "collectivities" (Parsons 1951; Etzioni
1968); "solidary groups" (Parsons 1967a; Gamson 1968);
"classes" (Dahrendorf 1959; Giddens 1973; Lenski 1966); and
"ethclasses" (Gordon 1964). I resort to a neologism because alternative terms are ambiguous. "Collectivity," apart from Parsons
and Etzioni, is used too loosely; sometimes it even refers to statistical aggregations. The term "solidary group" does not make clear
how the objects of study differ from cohesive small groups (such
as cliques in complex organizations). Over the years, "class" has
taken on an overwhelmingly economic connotation; to employ it
more broadly now fosters confusion. Finally, the notion of ethclass
intimates that only ethnic and economic factors can shape society's
intermember power.

What is a solidary group and what makes it macroscopic? A
solidary group is a collection of social actors who have similar
characteristics, who feel affected by what happens to one another,
and who share networks of social relationships. It is not sustained
primarily by self-interest or by fear: these factors play some role,
but the key ingredient binding participants to the group is common
identification, a feeling of "we." Actors who perceive a shared
fate want to form warm bonds with one another. Families are
solidary groups; so were the cliques in the Bank Wiring Observation Room. Yet neither is macroscopic.

A solidary group becomes increasingly macroscopic when:
(1) its members share more than one attribute; (2) the group transcends local boundaries; (3) it is marked by a common style of
life; and (4) its members are woven together by associations and
organizations.

Multiattribute groups The cohesion of any group requires the
possession and recognition of common attributes. Most Americans
feel they can "spot" Catholics, blacks, Jews, members of the

upper class, and so on by their social characteristics (such as physical qualities, name, speech, attire) or by common activities
(schooling, worship, jobs, recreational patterns). However, shared
traits only guarantee the existence of social aggregates or "quasi
groups." (See, for example, Dahrendorf 1959; Gamson 1968; and
Ginsberg 1953.) For a solidary group to exist, "the persons in the
aggregate must take account of the perspectives of the others,
identify with the others, be interested in their interests. There is
not merely a number of egos making the same demand, but the
demand is made in behalf of a self including the various egos"
(Lasswell and Kaplan 1950, p. 30).

Membership in macrosolidary groups is based on more than a
single attribute. Often one is economic but others may be educational, religious, ethnic, territorial, or based on lineage. For example, to be an Irish-American entails being a Roman Catholic,
and in the past also implied urban residence, working-class position, a lack of college education (especially at secular schools),
and allegiance to the Democratic Party. Thus, a macrosolidary
group is found at the empirical intersection of two or more social
categories such as race, ethnicity, religion, education, or class (in
the strictly economic sense). Although a macrosolidary group falls
near such intersections, not every trait has the same importance.
For Irish-Americans, ethnicity and religion have been more salient
than class. Moreover, the modern world is marked by growing heterogeneity within macrosolidary groups. Not all the parts have
each attribute in common.

Multilocal groups The principal members of macrosolidary
groups are other groups and not individuals. These subgroups are
localities. However, most macrosolidary groups in modern societies are not localities. Although there is some common territo-
riality, the overall group is not bound to a single geographic zone.
For example, even if Harlem, Bedford-Stuyvesant, and Watts are
geographic units, the overarching black American community is
not; its sense of "we" transcends specific physical boundaries.

In simpler, traditional societies, some macrosolidary groups have a geographic core. Once societies become large and internally diverse, macrosolidary groups move beyond purely local significance. This is especially true of advanced societies. But some traditional societies, such as classical Hindu India, display this pattern too. India is often portrayed in terms of four main castes (*varna*) which are society-wide. However, some argue that these cannot be reckoned as authentic macrosolidary groups. Traditional India, they say, really consists of some 2,000 locally based castes (*jati*). About four-fifths of the Indian population lives in rural settings where *jatis* are visible and unambiguously ranked. The integration of *jatis* into *varnas* is not at all clear. For example, although most *jatis* using the Brahman label are at the top of the stratification system, some Brahman groups are close to the bottom.[3]

The relation of localities to macrosolidary groups is difficult enough to assess in traditional societies; it is even harder in advanced societies, particularly for the United States. In our society, localities are primarily residential and do not carry the vocational connotations of India's *jatis*. Geographic subgroups in the United States provide mainly the home base—a dormitory—for family units.[4] They are rarely occupational settings. Because the residential base is a center of kinship ties, expressive bonds are of paramount importance there. Ample sociological evidence exists that "like attracts like" in modern residential communities. Glazer and Moynihan, for instance, in their study of New York's five main ethnic groups, present data on the particular strength of this pattern among Jews (1963, pp. 159–66).

But this tendency is not restricted to any one group. The desire to reside with others like ourselves is ubiquitous and strong. The chances are good that residential communities are more homogeneous than their overarching macrosolidary groups. That is, the families that make up localities are more similar than are the localities that form a macrosolidary group. For example, there are suburban neighborhoods composed of the families of college-educated, black executives and professionals, most of whom belong to the same local church. These families have little desire to live in Harlem. Nevertheless, they are part of the black American macrosolidary group.

Since localities have different characteristics, they may have different ranks. The result is that contemporary stratification systems are "unbalanced." (See Etzioni 1968, pp. 432–56.) Macrosolidary groups can still be compared and ranked broadly on a scale of high to low. The American upper class, for example, is ranked higher than blacks or Chicanos. But particular localities depart from these rankings. For example, a middle-income Chicano neighborhood may contain families with attributes similar in rank to families in an adjacent Anglo community. But the larger systems these two localities are hooked into do not have the same overall rank.

Unbalanced ranking will probably be a permanent feature of societal inequality. As long as social and geographic mobility continues, variations in rank among subgroups (localities) will have to be considered in the study of social stratification. (Two consequences of unbalanced rank—fluidity and indeterminacy—are examined later in this chapter.)

Styles of life Shared symbols also help to define macrosolidary groups. Such orientations promote common ways of thinking, feeling, and acting which, in turn, heighten the members' sense of "we" and their interactions. Moreover, the nonmaterial character of symbols gives them major macroscopic potential because they do not have the same spatial and temporal limitations as face-to-face bonds. Symbols can bind together people who do not interact, who do not know each other, and who live at different points in history.

All this is ordinarily treated in social-stratification texts under the rubric of "style of life." These books point out that people in macrosolidary groups resemble each other in dress, etiquette, speech, recreation and consumption patterns, and so on. However, symbols also play a dynamic role in promoting cohesion. Values provide a source of the collective goals that a group (or its organizational arm) strives to implement. Philanthropic values among

Jews, for instance, have led to the creation of numerous agencies pursuing welfare, health, and social-service goals. These agencies are more decisive for macrocohesion than are values alone.

Associations and organizations In isolation, symbols are not a sufficient basis for macrocohesion. The critical grounding for modern macrosolidary groups comes from their tendency to develop agencies to promote self-awareness, solidarity, and mobilization. These agencies usually contain only a minority of the members. Their goals push in one of two directions: either expressive or instrumental. Following Etzioni (1968, pp. 100–102), I distinguish between associations and organizations in this regard. *Associations* are agencies that seek to heighten solidarity and group consciousness—churches, fraternities, schools, and social clubs are examples. *Organizations* are created to mobilize members in the pursuit of special interests—examples include business corporations, the NAACP, labor unions, lobbies, and the National Association of Manufacturers.[5]

Although solidarity is not the official purpose of organizations, it is a frequent outcome of efforts to arouse members. For example, a labor union may be oriented toward improving the economic lot of the rank-and-file, but it may also increase class-consciousness and solidarity. In addtion, agencies sometimes serve both associational and organizational purposes; hence an either-or categorization is not always easy, possible, or desirable.

The pressures on associations and organizations are tremendous. Today's macrosolidary groups are geographically scattered and internally diverse. The task of weaving them together is thus increasingly difficult.

Associations and organizations now have to do more than awaken, integrate, and represent one locality; they must arouse and mobilize actors in dispersed localities. The modern mass media also provide this service, since they impart information to local units. By making us aware of events in distant places, we are able to respond to the distress of a "brother" even without interaction taking place. Black Americans in the Bronx are able to learn

of injustices toward fellow group members in Chicago or Missis-
sippi solely on the basis of television and newspaper reports. But,
at times, members doubt the reliability of the mass media. Hence,
modern macrosolidary groups—or, more accurately, their associations and organizational arms—sometimes generate their own informational capacity. That is, they may create communication
channels in order to promote consciousness, solidarity, and shared
interests. The ethnic press in the United States (as well as segments of the general press that cater to a particular clientele) provide examples of such an informational capacity.

Internal diversity also breeds problems for associations and
organizations. If agencies intend to encompass an entire macrosolidary group, they must try to weave together components which,
despite some similarities, are also marked by differences in traits,
resources, and interests. Not all continue the effort to be all-
embracing. Some settle for representing selected subgroups (for
example, in the 1960s, the Black Panther Party claimed to speak
for ghetto blacks). Other associations and organizations seek to act
for all those with shared attributes across existing groups and subgroups (for example, consumer groups and the women's movement). Finally, some aim to forge new linkages among localities
and thus to create new macrosolidary groups (such as radical
movements hoping to build an American proletariat).

Resources

In chapter 3, resources were classified as coercive, utilitarian, and
normative. Each manifestation of power and privilege uses one of
these types or some combination of them. Generally, macrosolidary groups (like individuals) have a consistent access to resources: Privileged access to one resource increases the probability
of privileged access to others. For example, access to higher education in our society increases chances for high income and pres-
tigious occupations. (On this matter, see especially Collins 1971;
Milner 1972.) However, there are also instances throughout his-

tory of groups with inconsistent access. Probably the most cele-brated cases are the rising bourgeoisie with high access to utilitar-ian resources and low access to normative resources; and the declining aristocracy, which has the reverse pattern. (For the case of France, see Barber 1955.) Jewish merchants and bankers in me-dieval Europe displayed a "profile" similar to the emerging bourgeoisie.

The role of recipients with inconsistent access to resources (high privilege on some; low on others) is noteworthy. These pat-terns may tell us a good deal about what is really going on just be-neath the surface of intermember power. Frequently, inconsistency points to strategic power shifts or to potential conflicts. For ex-ample, "sumptuary legislation" in the late Middle Ages provides evidence of growing tensions between established nobles and the new bourgeoisie. These laws attempted to limit access of specific groups to certain types of apparel. Ermine and gold cloth, for in-stance, were to be sold only to aristocrats. Sale to or purchase by commoners was a punishable offense. Similarly, efforts were made to prevent affluent commoners from acquiring coats-of-arms. Laws were passed in Britain and on the Continent confining use of coats-of-arms to old noble families. Needless to say, violations of both prohibitions were frequent. (see Barber 1957, pp. 160–61.)

Resource primacy and resource ambiguity Intermember power systems vary by which type of resource is most important. Marx-ian theory asserts the primacy of utilitarian resources; Structural-Functional theory, the primacy of normative ones. However, which type is more important is shaped (to some degree) by the nature of the recipients (macrosolidary groups and localities). Where the re-cipients are classlike (in Marx's sense), utilitarian resources tend to have priority; that is, they are most valued and their control af-fects access to other types. Where the recipients look like status groups (in Weber's sense), normative resources are commonly central. Most stratification systems contain recipients somewhere between pure classes and pure status groups. Thus, the specific relationship between recipients and resources is not always easy to predict. Both types of resources play some role in all distributive processes.

The fact that recipients are rarely pure classes or status groups is an important reason for ambiguity in the allocation of resources. But there are other reasons too. The proliferation of resources is another factor. Our typology is an analytical one; concretely, a vast array of assets is distributed in systems of inequality, not just three types. Many of these are blendings of analytical types so that it is difficult for an observer to make a precise determination about resource priorities. For instance, the hardware of the mass media (TV technology, printing presses) are both normative and utilitarian. They are normative because they create and transmit symbols. They are utilitarian since they are part of a society's technological capabilities.

Even if a resource is analytically pure, it represents only one of many that fall under a given heading. Utilitarian resources, for example, are not exhausted by material objects (since they also include such things as services, and technical and administrative know-how). Nor are economic resources unidimensional. Norbert Wiley reminds us that Max Weber saw the economy divided into three distinct resource markets: labor, credit, and commodity. Wiley argues that although there is a tendency for a group with high access to one (e.g., the labor market) to have high access to others (e.g., the credit and commodities markets), some groups are high in some and low in others.[6]

Thus, the actual flow of resources among recipients is more complex than an analytical classification implies. No two groups will receive the same resources in precisely the same quantities. The concrete richness of resources in the allocative process heightens ambiguity because perfect consistency in access is improbable. Recipients' intakes of resources will never be exactly on the same level of privilege, even when there is a rough parity (e.g., in income, education).

In the face of the multiplicity of resources, perfect consistency of access would require clear standards for comparing resources. Yet, a social calculus to calibrate all assets is an impossibility (Parsons 1954, pp. 386–439). How can we compare the exact worth of different resources which appear in varying "chunks" and amounts? For instance, which provides more power and privilege: a ton of gold or a monopoly on the means of salvation? How convertible is one to the other? Since no two groups receive the same resources in the same quantities, the precise power and privilege of groups is difficult to gauge. Moreover, the changing supply of any resource alters its value over time. Generally, the greater the availability of a resource, the less each of its chunks is worth. Milner (1972) argues that this tendency is as applicable to normative as to utilitarian resources and treats the issue as one of "status inflation."

The inability to calibrate all resources is a dilemma for scientific observers and for recipients alike. For observers, it raises a methodological challenge. For recipients, it introduces wariness and "mutual respect" into intergroup life; but, as I suggest below, it does not necessarily yield equality or contentment.

The case of coercive resources The reader may wonder why I have not spoken of settings where coercive resources have priority. Actually, such stratification systems are rare. Coercive resources may play an important role in the formative stages of a system of inequality. For example, the military prowess of the lord and his protection and domination over the peasants helped stabilize the feudal system in Europe. However, control of coercive resources provides a weak basis of stability once dominance has taken root. Pure coercive resources are aimed at constraint: they engender deprivations and are not a source of gratification, even for the users. Actors who have attained a position of dominance are unlikely to be satisfied with a superior command of arms. They will want to savor the fruits of their triumph and so will seek to widen their resource base to give centrality to more gratifying factors.[7]

Another reason for the shift from coercive resources is that they are far more alienating for those being dominated. A system of intermember power, like any social arrangement, is more stable if it is seen as legitimate—plausible, morally correct, and soon. (See chapter 2.) Reliance on resources that promote subservience, apathy, or resistance weakens the chances for pervasive legitimation and hence the prospects for a stable stratification system. Therefore, systems resting initially on violence tend to shift priority to less alienating assets. The descendants of warriors and warlords become a hereditary aristocracy whose position rests more on rights to diffuse deference and income than on the wielding of weapons. In the case of European feudalism, an estate system evolved that divided the population into legally defined segments, each with distinctive prerogatives, duties, and powers established by law.

The state's control of the means of violence also limits the role of coercive resources. As I noted in chapter 4, the state, the center of political power, has a relative monopoly over macroscopic coercive resources in most modern societies. It has so restricted access to these resources that they cannot play a decisive role in today's struggles for intermember power. Two long-range consequences take shape. First, the state's credibility to threaten intervention among member units has been strengthened. Its mastery of violence means it can obtain acquiescence with less overt constraint than in the past, because real resistance is impossible. Second, removing the most alienating and destructive resources from the struggle helps stave off the Hobbesian nightmare—at least in the intermember realm.

Recipients:
Classes versus Status Groups

Who are the main recipients in systems of intermember power? Weber's division of macrosolidary groups into classes and status groups provides a starting-point, although there are few pristine instances of either. Most recipients contain elements of both. Nevertheless, groups and entire stratification systems can be compared by which type predominates and by how much. Two factors are important in moving systems in class or status-group directions: the preexisting organization of intermember power; and how human beings are disbursed under the prevailing division of labor—that is, how people and groups are matched to a society's most strategic activities, notably in the economic sphere.

Preexisting
Intermember Power

The term "historical factors" has usually served as an umbrella concept for the effects of preexisting intermember power. How power and privilege have been organized in the past limits present and future options. The thesis of Barrington Moore's *Social Origins of Dictatorship and Democracy* (1967) is that the modern world has been formed by the interplay of monarchs, feudal lords, peasants, and the urban bourgeoisie. Three kinds of "modernizing revolutions" are possible, according to Moore, depending on the past relations among these actors: bourgeois democracy, fascism (feudal-bourgeois coalitions), and communism (peasant revolutions). He offers Great Britain, the United States, and France as examples of societies that underwent bourgeois revolutions; Germany and Japan as instances of the fascist type; and Russia and China as examples of communist societies. Moore also applies his formula to differences within societies. For example, he explains the rapid triumph of industrial capitalism in the United States outside of the South largely in terms of the absence of a landed ("feudal") aristocracy north of the Mason-Dixon line. Moreover, he sees the Civil War as a bourgeois revolution imposed by the North (pp. 111–61).

Lenski's hypothesis on the interaction of power and privilege provides the implicit theoretical underpinnings for Moore's thesis. If Lenski's hypothesis is valid, then a recipient's past edge provides a basis for present power and privilege—and also shapes the nature of future challenges and opposition.

The impact of resource priorities can also be treated under the heading of historical factors. The relationship between recipients and resources is not one-way: Resource priorities help mold recipients (making them more classlike or more status-group-like) and not just vice versa. Therefore, prevailing priorities limit or accelerate the alteration of stratification systems. The centrality of normative resources may inhibit movement in a class direction. For instance, the importance of ritual purity and diffuse deference in India may be one factor explaining the tenacity of caste distinctions despite their official abolition. Conversely, I shall suggest that our focus on utilitarian assets is one reason why I expect the "ethnic factor" to decline in America.

Personnel Allocations

The character of intermember power is more immediately expressed by how personnel are matched to strategic tasks. These activities are generally occupational once economic life ceases to be a local matter and market relations become society-wide. (See Giddens 1973, pp. 82–91, 132–35.) Michael Hechter (1974; 1975) treats this issue in terms of the persistence of a "cultural division of labor." In his research on the survival of ethnic conflict in Great Britain's "Celtic fringe" (Wales, Scotland, and Northern Ireland), he inquired whether or not ethnic, religious, or linguistic criteria still affect who performs in different economic sectors. His qualified conclusion is that these criteria remain important.

Studies of the "cultural division of labor" come down to asking whether universalistic or particularistic standards prevail when a society assigns its personnel. Which type is operative goes a long way in determining the recipients in the stratification system. Allocation of personnel on the basis of general assumptions about competence—based on training, ability, performance (universalistic criteria)—helps create one set of macrosolidary groups; emphasis on predetermined, "immutable," and "irrelevant" qualities (particularistic criteria) promotes a different set of groups. American society, with its rules about equality of opportunity and individual initiative, is closer to the universalistic end of the continuum; classical Hindu India, with its stress on fixed caste position, is nearer the particularistic end.

Systems using particularistic criteria are marked by macrosolidary groups in which membership is an inherited quality (estates, castes, ethnic and religious groups). Systems that stress universalism have macrosolidary groups in which membership is less ascribed (such as the American business elite), although some ascriptive groupings may persist. Here, intermember power is more often composed of groups who cannot monopolize economic positions on hereditary grounds; abilities and performances are expected to play a role. Economic achievements are likely to be a major basis of privilege in universalistic systems; in particularistic ones, economic activities remain submerged in tribal, ethnic, religious, or familial structures.

Most modern societies give primacy to universalistic criteria. Therefore, occupational and economic achievements often provide a key basis for group formation in such systems of inequality. Premodern societies rely on particularistic standards; hence inequality takes on more of an ethnic, religious, or tribal tinge.

I do not deny the importance of economic activities in premodern societies. All societies must produce goods and services. Should this capacity falter, even the most ethnically—or religiously—oriented system may disappear. The question is one of the relative emancipation of these activities from a particularistic "cultural division of labor." The Hindu castes are set off from one another by economic activity; still, these activities are not assigned on universalistic grounds, but are hereditary. Castes are mainly noneconomic groups who share economic tasks. The stress on universalism and economic achievement is more central for advanced societies. Class factors, therefore, play a key role in the organization of inequality. Yet even the most advanced society has particularistic pockets, as shown by the survival of the ethnic factor and racism in the United States.[8]

The Mixed Nature
of Recipients

When universalistic criteria are decisive, macrosolidary groups approximate classes; when criteria are particularistic, the recipients look more like status groups. Yet, to speak of specific groups as either classes or status groups is a gross distortion. Without question, Marx attempted to apply the notion of class to concrete social entities—notably nineteenth-century capitalists and workers. But the European bourgeoisie and proletariat are only partially classes because particularistic criteria have not completely disappeared. Indeed, no concrete "class" has ever been bound totally by universalistic standards. For instance, one thrust of Baltzell's (1964) critique of the current American upper class is that it has a negative impact on our society, since membership is based too heavily on origins, and the highest achievers from other sectors find it hard to enter.

Weber was ambivalent about whether class and status group are concrete or analytical categories. (See Heller 1969, pp. 9–11.) Still, in his treatment of the Indian caste system, he recognized that although castes come close to status groups, they also have class features. Thus, it seems fruitless to debate whether Indian castes or the nineteenth-century British bourgeoisie or the twentieth-century black Americans are really classes or not. Sociological knowledge advances further if either-or classifications are abandoned in favor of an ongoing examination of the collision of class and status-group elements. An adequate description of recipients in intermember power systems requires a treatment of how both ingredients are melded.[9]

Fluidity
among Localities

Additional difficulties face those wishing to chart stratification systems. I have alluded to perhaps the most critical of these: the unbalanced character of modern intermember power. Localities are more homogeneous than the macrosolidary groups they hook into. Thus, while overarching groups are capable of being ranked roughly on a scale of high to low, some local members depart from that ranking. Greater similarity on the local level means that cohesion also will be greater there. Modern stratification systems are marked by strong local cohesion combined with more fluidity among localities.

Fluidity is a characteristic of all contemporary stratification systems. The weakening of ties across localities makes it difficult to predict the future. Marx would never believe the complexity of today's European working classes. They are still riven by ethnic, religious, and regional cleavages (as most Irish Catholics, Scots, Walloons, and Calabrians will testify). But they also remain divided by economic factors—type of industry, skilled versus unskilled work, and so on.

The fluidity within macrosolidary groups is even greater in the United States. Sitting atop the system is an upper class, which Domhoff sees as woven together by "a set of social institutions which are its backbone—private schools, elite universities, the 'right' fraternities and sororities, gentlemen's clubs, debutante balls, summer resorts, charitable and cultural organizations, and such recreational activities as foxhunts, polo matches, and yachting" (1967, p. 16). Domhoff's "social institutions" have here been called "associational webs." He also cites the importance of intragroup marriage as another key source of upper-class cohesion. (It is probably not farfetched to view the endogamy of macrosolidary groups as an extension of their associational life.) Domhoff, however, is less convincing in showing that this class is politically united by organizational arms pursuing consistent class interests. Aside from its common interest in the prevailing order of power and privilege, the American upper class is characterized by internal diversity and competition.[10]

Below the upper class, the American stratification system contains components with more status-group ingredients. (Of course, the frequently attached prefix "WASP" reminds us that

the upper class has status-group traits too.) Our ethnically dominated macrosolidary groups, spawned mainly by immigration, are
now fissured by economic mobility. The overarching group is still
typified by ethnic and religious similarities, but localities are divided along economic lines (and by education as well, insofar as it
correlates with economic position).

The old associational webs no longer seem to work.
Churches, lodges, and fraternal orders were better able to bind
together localities during more homogeneous times. Social mobility has made this task difficult. The most affluent families and
localities are abandoning traditional associational affiliations. They
are looking for better schools for their children, different centers of
recreation, new clubs, and sometimes even other religions.

As economic divisions grow, differences in interests intensify. The most tangible indicator is the increased percentage of
Republican voting among the economically mobile elements of
ethnic groups. Even the Jews who share the impact of Hitlerism
and Israel's struggle for survival are becoming internally divided
over issues that run along class lines. (See especially Rosenberg
and Howe 1974; also Levy and Kramer 1973.)

In America, the dispute over the survival of ethnicity has
become as much a debate over *praxis* as a scholarly disagreement
about the evidence. Those who say class will triumph prefer
America to be organized along class lines; those who say ethnicity,
advocate ethnic revivalism.[11] The truth of the matter is that the
overall U.S. system of inequality is much more difficult to describe than a generation ago precisely because the most cohesive
units are local communities, while the larger groups are more
fluid.

For instance, it is fruitless to wrangle over whether life in
Boston's West End is the product of the working-class character or
the Italian background of the inhabitants.[12] It is the product of
both, and, in the end, the two factors are so intertwined as to make
the direct effects empirically indistinguishable. The separate effects of class and ethnicity can only be discerned when we move
from more homogeneous localities to the more heterogeneous net-

works they combine to form. But it is precisely the nature of these larger networks that is now in question.

Contemporary American communities can move in one of two general paths: they can link up along class lines more than they have in the past; or they can strengthen status-group ties, notably those dealing with ethnicity or religion. In other words, the residents of the West End can, in time, become part of a new American working class; they can remain part of an Italian-American macrosolidary group, or join a Catholic macrosolidary group. At the moment, associational webs and organizational arms exist with the ability to bind them to all three. It is possible that this locality (and others like it) may serve simultaneously as a subgroup for two or more macrosolidary groups for a time. Whether such overlapping affiliations are viable over a protracted period is uncertain. Can the West End be part of an emerging working class and remain part of an Italian-American community—or are the exigencies of class and ethnic mobilization too antithetical?

Despite talk of ethnic revival, I think the prospect for ethnic cohesiveness in America is weaker than a generation ago. The fluidity of the American stratification system is the principal reason for this. Yet, increased class mobilization is not an historically necessary outcome. I cannot forecast with total certainty that, a century from now, we will be much closer to a class system. But I have two reasons for believing this to be the case. The first has to do with the continuing decline of the "cultural division of labor." As universalistic criteria are employed more pervasively, economic standards will shape group formation to a greater degree. Thus, macrosolidary groups should look more and more like classes. My second reason has to do with the priority given to utilitarian resources in the American system. If there is an association between type of recipient and the dominant type of resource (and the causality is not one-way), then preference for utilitarian resources should push the stratification system further in a class direction.

Historical factors provide the major complication for this

scenario. In Europe, feudal remnants and the survival of ethnic, religious, or cultural minorities have been the principal historical factors impeding class reorganization. In America, the key historical factors have been the waves of European immigration and the legacy of slavery. These events created macrosolidary groups that were built around ethnicity insofar as this attribute was the dominant one shaping the remainder of the members' traits.

But American ethnic groups never looked like India's castes; they were always closer to the class end of a class-status continuum. American society always officially endorsed universalism. The original homogeneity within ethnic groups (in terms of economic, educational, and regional attributes) was impossible to maintain over several generations. The primacy of utilitarian resources also stimulated classlike tendencies. The result was a growing diversity within these macrosolidary groups. An expanding economy helped these processes but by itself could not have instigated them. Moreover, the "cultural division of labor" is still eroding, and the primacy of utilitarian resources persists. Thus, the undermining of the ethnic factor continues, making the long-range prospects for an ethnic America bleak.

I understand the moral and emotional pulls of ethnicity. Especially during times of rapid change, ethnic revivals are likely to be with us. Glazer and Moynihan (1974) point out that it is still easier to mobilize groups with ethnic appeals. Ethnic labels, such as Polish, Greek, black, do not carry the invidious implications (at least for the subjects) of such economic categories as "poor," "lower class," or "working class"—it is easier to cry "Black is beautiful" than "Poor is beautiful." Yet, how useful these appeals will be for the pursuit of utilitarian resources is doubtful. Class organization lends itself more readily to this task.

Ethnic revivals will resemble past religious revivals in American history. The history of religion in America has been one of progressive secularization, interrupted by short bursts of sectarian intensity. The movement to a classlike system likewise will be interrupted by bursts of ethnic enthusiasm. Further, as churches become more heterodox and secular (as with post-Vatican II Catholicism), ethnicity may be more capable of touching deep emotional wellsprings than modern religion.

These guesses about the future of ethnicity are, of course, couched in the language of *ceteris paribus* (all else equal). For now, the macrosolidary groups below the American upper class are still shaped mainly by status-group considerations (of which ethnicity is the most salient). Yet these groups are fluid; their cohesiveness is diminishing because their local components differ in economic and educational attributes. As I have said, the future is not inevitable. Indeed, there is a good deal of voluntarism, but of an administrative nature. The course of the American inequality will be set, to some degree, by the new or existing associations and organizations. How clever and powerful their agencies are will determine whether new recipients emerge, old ones are strengthened, or fluidity continues.

Indeterminacy
among Recipients

Fluidity within macrosolidary groups is not the only product of unbalanced rankings. Indeterminacy is also fostered among recipients. Unbalanced ranks result in similarities among localities which are at least as great across macrosolidary groups as within them. An upper-middle class Jewish suburban community, for example, now has more in common with a comparable white Protestant community than with a Hasidic enclave in Brooklyn. These developments yield a blurring of boundaries among the recipients in networks of intermember power.

Indeterminacy is also furthered by fluidity and by the ambiguities of resource allocation. The decline of interlocality cohesion helps make macrosolidary group boundaries fuzzy. Indeed, the preceding discussion suggested that the future nature of recipients is "up for grabs." The fact that no two groups receive the same resources or have the exact same levels of privilege also blurs the focus of stratification systems because it becomes impossible to estimate precise differences in privilege.

Indeterminacy has methodological and substantive significance. Methodologically, it raises doubt about a realist perspective on macroinequality and seems to encourage a nominalist view. Substantively, indeterminacy provides an impetus for the current push for more equality.

"Realism" versus "Nominalism"

Students of social stratification are concerned with the "reality" of the units of analysis: Are recipients actual groups in society or are they arbitrary labels imposed by observers? (See Ossowski 1963; Wrong 1964.) To make a topographic analogy: Are those who chart intermember power drawing contour lines or grid lines? Contour lines are representations on a map describing vertical configuration of the terrain; grid lines are conventions accepted by mapmakers allowing them to locate points on a map. Contour lines describe something that exists, a hill or a valley. Grid lines have no existential basis but are artificial markings which make using the map easier but say nothing about the terrain.

My characterization of recipients at the beginning of this chapter espoused a realist perspective on macroinequality; thus my imagery was one of contour lines. But some of the things I have said in subsequent sections require that this realism be tempered. In particular, how real are recipients whose ranks are unbalanced, whose cohesion is fluid, and whose access to privileged resources is ambiguous? Or, to put it differently: Does indeterminacy in modern stratification systems require a nominalist (grid-line) view of macroinequality?

I think the answer is no. All macrosolidary groups and localities are real, but some are more real. Others are closer to aggregates or quasi groups. Yet, they are set off from the latter by minimal levels of consciousness, cohesion, and mobilization. That is, they display some self-awareness, some positive expressive bonds, and some arousal for common interests. Nevertheless, variation is considerable. Some recipients are relatively dormant, almost like quasi groups (American blacks before the Supreme Court school-desegregation decision of 1954); others occasionally resemble large-scale organizations in their degree of activation (American Jews when Israel is at war).

Associations and organizations play indispensable roles in consciousness, cohesion, and mobilization. As indeterminacy has increased, these agencies have become even more pivotal. This has led some to assume that administrative entities are the real actors in modern macroinequality, especially business corporations as the new upper class. (See, for example, Hacker 1975.) Unquestionably, such units are crucial in the contemporary world. However, their main relevance for intermember power derives from how well they activate and represent a society's natural solidaristic units. (See Zeitlin 1974.) The indeterminacy of the latter (macrosolidary groups and localities) is a fact of life today. But its importance or permanence should not be overstated.

Simply because recipients in stratification systems have blurred boundaries does not mean that they are not real; it only means that some are more loosely integrated and weakly mobilized than others. No one should be disturbed by this except those committed to an organismic (highly integrated) view of social reality. In the language of contour lines, some terrain features are very visible and their features rise and fall precipitously; other parts of the terrain roll more gently, perhaps imperceptibly. But the latter characteristics are just as real as the former.

Indeterminacy
and More Equality

The indeterminacy of intermember power does more than pose problems for macrosociological mapmakers. It also fuels the modern quest for more equality (Gans 1973).

Indeterminacy blunts the sharp edge of inequality by reducing the visibility of barriers. Such blurring, as I suggested in the discussion of ambiguities in allocative patterns, may introduce wariness and mutual respect to intergroup life. Yet, as Tocqueville (1954 ed.) first observed, the blurring of barriers does not lead to domestic tranquillity but to greater striving, to a "brooding over advantages they do not possess," and to a push to unearth and topple additional inequities. Tocqueville generally spoke of the dilemma in microsocial terms. More recent commentators, enlarging upon his insight, lodge the dilemma in national character or culture, on the one hand (Lipset 1963; Milner 1972), or in social psychology, on the other (Sennett 1976). But the "Tocqueville dilemma" has macrostructural dimensions, too, and it is on these that I focus here.

Paradoxically, as boundaries between recipients become fuzzier, some groups (or their associational and organizational arms) exaggerate recipient distinctiveness and cohesion. As the uniqueness of one's own group diminishes, the need to stress its special character sometimes grows along with a need to disparage the attributes of (what we used to call) outgroups. (If "Italian is beautiful," then Polish has to be less beautiful, or even ugly.) The propensity to exaggerate the uniqueness of one's own group is one of the sources of our present ethnic revival, since (as I noted above) it is still easier to arouse commitment with ethnic appeals than with class-oriented ones. Yet, as suggested earlier, such revivals are destined to be episodic and short-lived.

Exaggeration of group distinctiveness and cohesion also propels the pursuit of more equality. An oversimplified view of recipients prevents mutual respect from leading to accommodation. Just as differences in attributes are emphasized at the expense of similarities, so differentials in privilege are also stressed. Groups are likely to be concerned with what the business elite is getting or what the blacks or the Jews are getting—and what "we're not getting but deserve too." Thus, at a time when resource allocations are becoming more ambiguous, concern over and exaggeration of differential privilege grows. This tendency exists over and above the discontent generated by objective inequalities.

The indeterminacy of intermember power allows for no closure in the quest for more equality. As Tocqueville noted, the blurring of rank and boundaries generates unquenchable anxiety and striving. The successful storming of one bastion of privilege means that new pockets of privilege are searched for and discovered. Victories create a need for more achievement and more competition. "To conceive of men remaining forever unequal upon a single point, yet equal on all others," he wrote, "is impossible; they must come in the end to be equal upon all" (1954 ed., 1:55). However, as I indicate below, each triumph over inequality does not guarantee that past conquests are permanent. There is always the detection of a new inequity to be overcome *and* the welling-up of old inequities.

Of course, the struggle for more equality in America has not always taken a political turn. There has been stress on personal achievement as well as on governmental intervention. On the face of it, these two solutions seem antithetical. Historically, a compromise has emerged: equality of opportunity has been emphasized and not equality of condition or result. Yes, the government should intervene, this solution says, but only to allow each person a comparable chance to achieve.

Regardless of what equality of opportunity may have done for individuals, it has failed to promote equality among groups. The strategies of equality of opportunity—of which affirmative action is only the most recent manifestation—are reductionist. They generally work on the basis of one attribute at a time (being black, Spanish-surnamed, or a woman), whereas underprivileged macrosolidary groups are deprived on the basis of several attributes at once. The one-attribute-at-a-time approach is likely to be ineffective because the beneficiaries are probably the more privileged individuals and the more privileged subgroups (for example, "middle-class" blacks). Macroscopic inequalities are merely transferred from macrosolidary groups to among lower-level units.[13] Given that the modern stratification systems are in flux anyway, this amounts, at best, to no real change, and, at worst, to needlessly burdening tomorrow's intermember power with "excess" inequality.

In the final analysis, remedies such as quotas are a micro-scopic solution. They entail a strategy of wrenching single attri-butes out of context. The most this can accomplish is to promote the life chances of individuals; but in the process it may exacerbate macro- (intergroup) inequalities. Groups (as well as localities, as-sociations, and organizations) that are better able to reward partici-pants (because they "own" more resources) can make themselves more attractive to the talented and ambitious. The most powerful social entities, in such circumstances, will only increase their edge by inducing the highly qualified to join their ranks. Armed with this advantage in talent, a group will probably improve its power and privilege position.[14]

In practice, emphasizing either equalities of opportunity or of result rests on seeing intermember power in microscopic or in macroscopic terms. On the macro level, the former distinction is only an analytical one. History suggests you cannot have one without the other. Any strategy that concentrates on opportunities among macrosolidary groups must begin by improving conditions for the most deprived recipients; there can be no true macroequal-ity of opportunity without a prior adjustment in macroequality of result.

In short, America's microsociological equality of opportunity strategies may reconcile the calls for achievement and govern-mental intervention; but they only intensify the "Tocqueville di-lemma." The continuing promise of more equality in the face of persistent intergroup disparities in power and privilege foments macrosocial struggle and discontent.

Conclusions:
The Future of Inequality[15]

One purpose of this chapter has been to show that macroinequality and microinequality are not the same. Consequently, a reduction in one does not guarantee a decline in the other. I can conceive of a program that levels privilege and power among macrosolidary groups (as well as among localities); but such a program may not affect the disparities *within* these groupings. The span between the most privileged individuals and families in society and the least privileged ones could remain unaltered even when the span for overarching groups has been narrowed. Conversely, I have argued that programs for microequality seem to leave macroinequality untouched, and, indeed, may inadvertently increase differences.

In the long run, however, more macroequality is a necessary (if not sufficient) condition for greater equality among individuals, status and roles (such as occupations), and statistical aggregations (such as income categories). The principal centers for accruing, stockpiling, and passing along privilege and power fall on the macrosocial level. Particular persons and interpersonal bonds are not reliable loci for creating or protecting intermember power and privilege. Kinship units, communities, classes, ethnic and religious groups, and associations and organizations have a built-in advantage in gaining and mobilizing resources and transmitting them across generations. If for no other reason, this is so because they possess more resources and have been around much longer than specific men and women or particular microbonds. They provide the structural continuity that is the stuff of history. Thus, if we are concerned with reducing *systematic* inequality (either macro or micro), we must tackle the long-term sources of inequality which are entrenched in the system. These fall mainly on the macrosocial plane.

In the previous section, I spoke of how indeterminacy fuels the quest for equality among macrosolidary groups. There I alluded to the discontent more equality can bring (endless striving, anxiety, intergroup tensions). But the costs of failing to reduce inequality are far greater than the costs of the struggle for more equality.

The primary effects of blurring in stratification systems are subjective in that they promote restlessness and a discontent with current intermember power and privilege. Yet, the struggle to reduce inequality is not built on an illusion. Striving and dissatis-

faction have objective bases as well. These flow from the drift
toward more inequality through most of human history. The drift
is propelled by the power-privilege cycle. There is no doubt that
the unchecked workings of this cycle have done more to foster
human misery down through the ages than has the link between the
indeterminacy and the "brooding over advantages they do not possess."

Lenski, however, sees a slowing of the cycle. He suggests
that one important factor accounting for this slowing in late industrial societies is the rise of specialized centers of political power.
These are, to some degree, committed to advancing the well-being
of the society as a whole. The modern state penetrates the operation of intermember power and thus undermines its direct impact
on privilege. The intervention of all contemporary governments in
the economic sector to control an otherwise independent "market"
is only one—but the most obvious—example of this development.
The state now shapes privilege too; privilege is no longer explained completely by the dynamics of intermember power.

Yet, the power-privilege cycle is so strong that intervention
cannot be halfhearted or intermittent. It cannot be halfhearted because it then fails to check the cycle in the first place. Efforts to arrest the drift cannot be intermittent because more equality, although once instituted, is quickly reversed. Let us presume a
greater parity in power and privilege has been attained. Both the
nature of recipients and of resources are likely to sabotage it. It is
difficult to imagine a situation where all the recipients are equally
"modern," rational, or skillful in using the resources allocated to
them. Thus, regardless of the equalization in privilege, disparities
in the ability to convert these into power remain inevitable. The
special interest of kinship units to pass advantages across generations accelerates the trend.

Renewed inequality stems also from the multiplicity of resources being allocated. As noted earlier, macrosolidary groups
never receive exactly the same assets or the same amounts. The
fact that no two groups have the same "resource profiles"
suggests that, even when they possess roughly equal privilege,

their stockpiles will never have the same liquidity. Consequently, at any given moment, some recipients always have more usable resources at hand; these groups have an edge in power and hence ultimately may have greater and greater privilege.

In the modern world, only state intervention can permanently arrest the power-privilege cycle. However, intervention in the capitalist democracies has failed to alter the existing intergroup inequities significantly. The failure to deliver (perceived and actual) in these states has influenced the macrosocial aspects of the "Tocqueville dilemma."

On the other hand, Giddens (1973) has argued that the state socialist societies have made major inroads on macroinequality. They have done so by eliminating the upper class which still characterizes capitalist democracies. While micro- and macrodisparities still exist (the "New Class"), the hub of classical privilege has been uprooted. This has been accomplished through strict controls against backsliding—that is, there are massive controls to prevent the emergence of social types ("the trader") or macrosolidaristic combinations which could evolve into a capitalist upper class. The cost of increased macroequality, Giddens tell us, has been a fearful one. Exploitation has been moved from the realm of intermember relations to the political sphere. Thus, whatever macroequality state socialist societies have achieved has been purchased through political oppression. For many of us, this price is too high.

In sum, it is only in modern societies that the power-privilege cycle is capable of being arrested. The fact that intervention can now slow the "free" workings of what has been the most important macrosocial process in human history (at least until now) is a monumental accomplishment. Unhappily, to date, intervention either has favored the most privileged (in capitalist democracies) or has been built on political repression (in state socialist systems). Nevertheless, for those of us concerned with *praxis,* the realm of political power requires attention, for only there will most of future history be made. The course of intermember power is now a problem for political power.

chapter six

The Morphology of Political Power

WITHOUT autonomous centers of political power, industrially advanced societies cannot contain a growing disparity in intermember power and privilege. Unless the state (or an alternative agency) intervenes, weaker units are always at the mercy of the stronger ones. Contemporary society finds political power, the political "manager," and the state indispensable. Yet, this ascendancy is far from an unmixed blessing. Unalloyed political power has often been slanted in favor of society's powerful members. Further, in the twentieth century, it has been both the most potent mechanism for alleviating misery and a principal contributor to human suffering. Still, as David Calleo and Benjamin Rowland write: "The nation-state may all too seldom speak the voice of reason. But it remains the only serious alternative to chaos" (1973, p. 191).

The organization of political power is the preeminent issue in the macrosociological study of modern societies. Empirically, political power has become a dominant factor only recently, but analytically, its importance cuts across historical epochs. Our understanding of *all* societies improves by distinguishing between political and intermember powers. This distinction applies as much to the premodern, so-called acephalous (or stateless) societies[1] as it does to today's nation-states. It reminds us that conduct directed toward collective goals appears in every society, whether or not it is fused with the battle over valued resources.

This chapter deals with the political systems of our own time, not those of the past or the future. My interest lies in societies having recognizable states and differentiated political roles. I do not dwell on the debate over the past existence of or the future prospects for "stateless" societies. I presume that political power is present in all societies. The basic issue is the magnitude of the political division of labor. Premodern societies, with few exceptions (ancient Egypt, Imperial China), have low political divisions of labor. Societal actors rarely perform political roles separated from other societal roles. (The latter thrive mainly in geographically bound solidary groups.) Powerful local, ascriptive groups (such as the higher castes in traditional Hindu India) ordinarily perform the routine political tasks that happen to exist. But these units are not political in the contemporary sense. (See Eisenstadt 1968.) As for future societies—real societies in the real world, not utopias—if they are marked by specialization and rationality, then something akin to a state is bound to exist. The "withering away of the state" is not at hand.

My primary focus is on the ingredients of a viable political system in the modern world. I examine the key factors that promote or hinder "stable" political life. I prefer the term "viable" to the more often used "stable," however, because it is less burdened by connotations of inflexibility and resistance to change. A truly successful system of political power is more than stable. It aims beyond maintaining or streamlining the existing arrangements of the state, for to do only that is potentially unstable and may reflect a failure to come to grips with crucial problems besetting society (inequality, the scarcity of critical resources, damage to the environment, alienation). Rather, a viable polity is one that can adapt and transform itself and the entire society in the face of misery and discontent.

The Ingredients
of Viable Political Systems

State and Polity

Discussion of the morphology of political power requires the study of both the state and the political system (or polity, for short). These concepts are not interchangeable: the state is often the most important component of the political system, but it is not coextensive with it. The notion of polity refers to a broader array of phenomena.

What is the state? Max Weber defined it as that social agency which successfully claims a monopoly of the legitimate means of violence over a given territory (1947, p. 156). With some modification, this definition is acceptable to most students of political behavior.[2] I have only two caveats. First, the distinguishing feature of the state is its right and ability to wield political power. Monopoly of legitimate violence is but a secondary characteristic. The responsibility and capacity to set, pursue, and implement collective goals for a given territory is the hallmark of the state. Access to coercive resources may serve as the ultimate backing for political power, but it is neither the *differentia specifica* of the state nor the only type of resource needed for success.

My second caveat is that Weber's definition may lead us to an overly constricted view of the state. The most likely tendency is to equate a state with the executive branch of a national government. The state, however, consists of a broader web of political power. Ralph Miliband (1969, pp. 49–53), for instance, criticizes those who equate the state with the national executive. He argues that the former has six "institutions" or "elements": the government, the administration, the military and police, the judiciary, the "subcentral" government, and parliamentary assemblies.

The government or national executive, says Miliband, is often confused with the state because "it is government which speaks on the state's behalf" (p. 49). The second component of the state, the administrative, today includes more than the bureaucracy of the state in the conventional sense. It encompasses sets of agencies "often related to particular ministerial departments, or enjoying a greater or lesser degree of autonomy—public corporations, central banks, regulatory commissions, etc.—and concerned with the management of the economic, social, cultural and other activities in which the state is now directly or indirectly involved" (p. 50).

The third element, according to Miliband, is the military and police. This "institution" includes such components as the armed forces, as well as the paramilitary, security, and police forces of the state, "which together form the branch of it mainly concerned with the 'management of violence' " (p. 51). Both the administrative and military elements are constitutionally subordinated to the governmental branch. However, their actual autonomy from a national executive and their accountability to elected officials varies strikingly from state to state and from era to era.

Whereas administrative and military elements are officially bound to the government, the fourth element, the judiciary, is usually expected to stand apart. Miliband says that "it is not the formal constitutional duty of judges, at least in Western-type political systems, to serve the purposes of their governments. They are constitutionally independent of the political executive and protected from it by security of tenure and other guarantees" (p. 52). Of course, how free a judicial branch actually is from executive domination differs by period and by polity.

Miliband's fifth component contains the units of subcentral government. In some political systems (such as France) this element is an extension of the national executive and the administrative branch, "the latter's antennae or tentacles" (p. 52). In other systems (the United States, Canada, West Germany, and Switzerland, with federal patterns), the subcentral governments enjoy considerable autonomy.

Miliband's final element is the parliamentary assembly or legislature. Like the subcentral governments, the relationship of assemblies to the national executive is one of conflict and coopera-

tion, even in systems (such as the United States) where they have
constitutionally distinctive mandates. Miliband argues that this am-
bivalence exists for both the progrovernment and antigovernment
sides of the aisle. Opposition parties are not wholly uncooperative,
for in entering legislative competition they help make the ongoing
political game possible. On the other hand, government parties
rarely provide blanket support to the national executive. Miliband
concludes: "It is in the constitutionally-sanctioned performance of
this critical and cooperative function that legislative assemblies
have a share in the exercise of state power" (p. 53).

Miliband's list is not logically exhaustive; nor is it intended to
tell us about the organization of the elements. The first point
makes us aware that other actors may also constitute the state,
such as *the* Party in totalitarian systems. The second point alerts us
to the fact that the character" or "style" of a state derives less
from the elements taken singly than from the network of relationships among them. Merely knowing which elements exist tells
little about the state's organization. States range from monocra-
tically organized systems in which one of the elements (usually the
national executive but sometimes other entities, such as the military) exercises extensive domination over the others, all the way to
systems of "state feudalism" where the elements maintain significant independence and none of them dominates in all or most
areas.

The polity is not the same thing as the state. The enveloping
system of political power embraces more than Miliband's six elements or any other bodies we decide to add to his list. The concept
of "state" focuses our attention only on the bureaucratized agents
of political power. Of course, the state is charged with social control; but who are the targets of control? The concept of "polity"
broadens our perspective beyond the formal boundaries of the
state. It helps us locate the political roles that are lodged elsewhere
in a society. A distinctive quality of the modern world is the multiplication of specialized political roles for both individuals and
groups. Even such unlikely actors as research institutes, hospitals,

and universities have discernible political roles today. The existence of specialized political roles among economic actors was recognized much earlier.

How do we identify political roles? Three factors are crucial; two have to do with the state's capacity for social control and the third with the political influence of the targets of control. Social actors tend to have political roles when they are recipients of the state's commands, and when these commands require significant role performances from them. The modern state's penetration of economics, health, education, and welfare has created political roles where there were none before. Social actors also tend to develop political roles when they struggle to influence state policy. Universal suffrage has been a major impetus for the rise of identifiable political roles. The targets of downward processes and the initiators of upward ones have been treated under the rubric of "citizenship" by T. H. Marshall (1950), who called attention to the extension of the citizenship role in the modern world. He saw this expansion largely as the result of the state penetration of previously "nonpolitical" sectors as well as of broadened democracy, which permits more and more groups to engage in political influence.

The notion of citizenship carries an unnecessarily microsociological connotation. Citizenship applies to more than one status in the status-sets of society's individual participants. With today's struggles over political power and political influence, a wide spectrum of macroscopic actors may be said to have a specialized citizenship role. These include macrosolidary groups and localities, but especially the associations that bind them together and the organizational arms that represent them. Political parties have a place here too.

The polity is not a fixed portion of society. A growing segment of society is subsumed under the political system. The bureaucratic elaboration of the state is one cause of this—and the one receiving the most public attention. But the expansion of political roles in the rest of society is equally important. Many critics give lip-service to reducing the size of the state, yet few express a desire to surrender or shrink their own citizenship roles. In any event, neither diminution of the state nor of macro citizen roles appears likely in the foreseeable future. Both will continue to grow, and thus so will the polity.

Effectiveness, Efficiency, and Legitimacy

A viable political system needs more than an effective state that successfully organizes its elements to impose social control. It also requires groups and mechanisms that allow for the efficient incorporation of influence. Chester I. Barnard's (1938) language of effectiveness and efficiency is used here deliberately because his insights on the ingredients for the smooth functioning of complex organizations are applicable to political systems. Barnard argued that a successful organization is not only effective, that is, able to obtain its goals, but also efficient, that is, able to produce the organization's product at an acceptable cost per unit of output. The cardinal question of efficiency for Barnard and his chief follower, Herbert A. Simon (1957), is the cost of inducing participants to contribute their services to the organization. For the study of political life, this perspective suggests that efficient political systems need contributions (or inputs) from the major macrosolidary groups, localities, associations, and organizations, in society; but that contributions must not be elicited so as to drain off inordinate amounts of resources needed for goal-attainment activities.

Besides effectiveness and efficiency, a third ingredient is essential for viable political systems. Groups must want to play the political game, but they must also view the rules of the game (the political institutions) as integrated, plausible, and morally appropriate. In chapter 2, this factor was labeled as legitimacy, and at several points in earlier chapters I argued that its absence poses serious problems for the success of a polity. A weakly legitimated (or illegitimate) set of political institutions is unlikely to yield sufficient trust in commands. Low legitimacy thus tends to provoke an alienative application of state power which only weakens the effectiveness of social control. A state that spends too much time and energy making sure its commands are obeyed is likely to be less successful at implementing goals; or it may be pushed to have fewer goals or more pedestrian ones. Similarly, a state that emphasizes constraint more, and persuasion and inducement less, is probably inefficient at eliciting contributions from the public. The steady application of coercive sanctions increases alienation and the chances that the public will perform only elementary citizen activities. Under these circumstances, when the state needs to mobilize the public, it tends to fall back on constraint. Such a strategy leads to a vicious circle of escalating constraint and alienation and hence imposes formidable barriers to the efficient upward flow of political influence.

In sum, viable political systems have three classes of ingredients: effective social control, efficiently incorporated influence, and legitimate "rules of the game." Let us look more closely at each of these.

Effective Social Control: The Need for Payoff

Chapter 4 explored how political power leads to effective social control in macrosystems, notably in societies. To provide a backdrop for the present discussion, let me quickly recapitulate the main points. Social control, as used here, refers to ego's ability to penetrate the intermember power nexus to attain collective goals even against resistance. This capacity is enhanced when a specialized agency appears with both the resources and the generalized responsibility to act for the entire system. This agency (usually the state on the societal level) must be able to dominate member units via persuasion, inducement, and constraint; thus it needs normative, utilitarian, and coercive resources, else goal attainment and the neutralization of recalcitrants will falter. Each type of domination is easier to attain by subunits specializing in one kind of power; but the ultimate backing of political power is provided by coercive resources (in a manner analogous to how gold backs currency). Yet, excessive reliance on constraint generates high levels of alienation, making use of coercive assets counterproductive. Finally, power based on muscle alone is blind. The availability of units providing an informational capacity increases the prospect that resources will be used rationally, and, hence, it promotes greater effectiveness.

Centrality of Payoff

In contemporary societies, effectiveness is the most important ingredient of political viability. A modern polity can hobble along for a time without the efficient influence and even with low legitimacy but not without some payoff. Lipset notes that in certain settings, effectiveness is a substitute for legitimacy in the short run and can generate it in the long run. He suggests the republics set up in Germany and Austria in the wake of World War I survived as long as they did, although weakly legitimated, because they were perceived as effective through the late 1920s (1959, pp. 81–82). That is, strategic societal actors went along with the rules of the game as long as the new states, which many despised, provided basic political, social, and economic amenities. Similarly, Lipset argues that the United States, as the "first new nation," coped with the absence of pervasive national identity, loyalty, and legitimacy during its infancy partly becuse the Union demonstrated effectiveness; it was seen as providing a payoff in economic goods and a rising living standard. Tangible results allowed the new nation time to sink its moral roots and to build up a reservoir of legitimacy (Lipset 1963, pp. 45–60).

However, the need for payoff poses special problems for the viability of a polity. In advanced nation-states (as well as in those new ones that have adopted "modern" institutions and expectations) the ability to provide effective payoff is often outstripped by the expanding demand for economic growth and more social services. Democratic systems especially find it difficult to cope with

the spiralling political agenda, but other polities are hardly immune. Rather quickly, this may lead to a lowering in the efficiency
of political influence. Key groups may stop making regular contributions, either by reducing or withdrawing confidence or by
refusing to process their demands through institutionalized channels. (The nature of political influence and the social costs of
decining efficiency are discussed in a subsequent section of this
chapter.) Dissatisfaction with payoff is also an acute problem for
weakly legitimated polities (e.g., Weimar Germany). But it
presents difficulties in other systems, if the dissatisfaction persists
over a long period of time. The chronic ineffectiveness of the
Czarist regime, which World War I exacerbated, helped to erode
the legitimacy of Imperial Russia and thus contributed to the success of revolutionary forces.

Roots of Payoff's Primacy

What are the roots of today's open-ended push for more payoff? I
think it has three sources: first, it flows indirectly from themes in
modern political cultures; second, from the nature of the twentieth-
century state, and third, from the characteristics of contemporary
political influence.

Political culture In chapter 2, reference was made to how modern political cultures indirectly help weaken the viability of their
polities. Although few systems as yet have purely rational-legal
legitimations and thoroughly responsive institutional values, the
political cultures of advanced societies seem to be drifting in that
direction, however episodic the movement may be. Most political
cultures contain features of both already, including a stress on rationality in political life, a belief that societal problems require
state intervention, and a positive evaluation of some public mobilization for collective goals.

One focus of these themes is economic growth, which, according to Daniel Bell, "has become the secular religion of advancing industrial societies: the source of individual motivation,

the basis of political solidarity, the ground for the mobilization of society for a common purpose'' (1974, p. 42). The other focus of political themes is more equality. What equality means varies from society to society and even within them. But whether the systems are capitalist democracies or state socialist regimes, all are committed to the furtherance of some kind of equality. As I noted in the previous chapter, sometimes the impulse toward equality has been microsocial, sometimes macrosocial; at times opportunity is stressed; at others, the emphasis is on result. Yet, whatever its manifestations, equality, and not just economic growth, is at the center of our secular religion.

These twin ideals raise two dilemmas. First, the themes of economic growth and equality contain incompatible elements that foster contradictions in the culture and strains in the society and polity. Much of the literature on the conflict between the values of achievement and of equality is, in fact, about this topic. (See especially Lipset 1963; Milner 1972; Nisbet 1974.) In this regard, I concentrate on the quandaries faced by a twentieth-century state committed to pursuing both as operative collective goals (see below). The second dilemma is that neither ideal allows for closure. The theme of economic growth, by its nature, has no terminus; it is pure process, not a fixed point to be reached. Equality, as the last chapter detailed, is also open-ended; the conquest of one inequity only makes new ones and reemerging old ones more visible. Thus, both foci promote intense demand for payoff in political life. Needless to say, most states find it difficult to satisfy such demands completely or permanently.

The modern state The nature of the twentieth-century state also promotes the growing call for payoff. The crucial elements here are the state's activist character; its continuing relative ineffectiveness; and its difficulty in optimizing economic growth and equality simultaneously.

The state, as now constituted, is inherently activist. Its size, bureaucratic structure, and personnel make goal multiplication and goal succession inevitable. Goal multiplication occurs because of the resources, manpower, skills, and professional interests now concentrated inside the state (particularly in the national executive and administrative branches). Economic use of these dictates that more and more goals be adopted and pursued. (See, for example, Blau's study of the expansionist character of a federal regulatory agency in *Dynamics of Bureaucracy*, 1955, pp. 99–179.) Moreover, the attainment of any one goal leads to the development of additional ones in order to give renewed purpose to established bureaucratic commitments. (See Sills 1957, especially pp. 253–70.) The multiplication and succession of goals creates demand where there was none before, and it heightens expectations regarding the quality of payoff where some demand has previously existed.

However, the relative ineffectiveness of modern states makes discontent inevitable. Neither Marxian nor capitalist states are good at sustained goal attainment. The grounds for political ineffectiveness require more comparative research. As Brzezinski and Huntington's pioneering contrast of the United States and the Soviet Union (1964) makes clear, different kinds of political systems have different bases for faltering payoff. The former, for instance, is inclined to slow, fragmented, episodic policy formation, while the latter is vulnerable to the pitfalls of stifling centralization under a succession of master plans. Both provide less than satisfactory effectiveness. An irony of modern polities is that failure creates more demand for planning and goal formation—not less.

The greatest difficulty for twentieth-century states is balancing economic growth and more equality. The two goals, which are at the core of today's political agenda, are mutually supportive and antagonistic. The pursuit of each, coupled with their (at least partial) incompatibility, dampens the prospects for unmitigated success in either area. The tension between the two goals does not cool the ardor for state intervention; it stimulates the state's activist orientation and the public's demand for payoff. Marxians (such as O'Connor 1973) as well as neoconservatives (Bell 1974, pp. 33–44) recognize that states that advance both goals are in a bind. Economic growth requires the stimulation of capital accumulation, that is, the expansion of utilitarian resources as inputs for economic production. Special emphasis is put on such assets as factories, buildings, machinery, and transportation facilities, all of which generate revenue. While every segment of society benefits from economic expansion, the most privileged (the business elite) tend to be the chief beneficiaries of capital accumulation. Hence this goal is likely to exacerbate intermember disparities. At the very least, capital accumulation probably widens the relative gap between groups at the top and those near the bottom, even if the absolute wealth of each increases.

Programs for economic growth tend to conflict with the vested interests of those advocating more equality. Confrontation will be particularly intense when choices must be made concerning allocation of limited state resources. This conflict underlies the debates over ways to overcome recessions and unemployment, with some arguing for the stimulation of capital accumulation and others calling for improved benefits for the unemployed and the less privileged.

Economic growth, however, is essential for programs striving to dispense societal resources more equally. Capital formation fuels social services by providing the revenues (through surpluses and taxation) that pay for improved education, welfare, and health care. Moreover, an argument can be made for the long-range economic advantages of a better-educated, healthier, and happier public. But, in the short run, social-service activities show no tangible profit: hospitals do not pay for themselves the way a factory or a dam does. When inflation and recession slow capital accumulation, more than economic growth is impeded. The fiscal basis for more equality is weakened as well.

The dilemmas of balancing the two goals stand out starkly in democratic polities. The push for more equality sooner or later needs more than economic growth as fuel. Comprehensive income redistribution via radical tax reform appears to be the only feasible alternative *or* complement to economic growth in this regard. The United States still finds this approach to be politically unpalatable. Even nations that have had such programs (Sweden, Denmark) now encounter political resistance from middle- and higher-income

groups. Totalitarian regimes, on the surface, seem to be less susceptible to these strains. After all, they can resort to draconian
measures to compel workers, farmers, managers, and intellectuals
to be more productive, while also striking at the roots of macroinequality. Yet, they have not proven more effective overall. To a
large degree, alienation resulting from their reliance on coercion is
a major factor here. Attempts to counter these adverse effects with
normative (i.e., "ideological") appeals have not been uniformly
successful; heavy doses of ideology and propaganda seem to generate cynicism as often as enthusiasm.

The impact of political influence The political-influence process
is the final basis for the contemporary stress on payoff. The essence of democratic politics entails provoking demand for new
programs. "A good case can be made for occasional Government
inaction," Russell Baker observes, "but no party ever swept to
glory by promising, if elected, to do nothing" (1976, p. 39). Elections offering a choice among candidates and parties are organized
around issues. These issues are not always real or new, but competitors struggle to make them look that way. Elections create a
general expectation that the winners will do *something* that has not
been done before—if only to return the country to "normalcy."
Totalitiarian regimes are not faced by exactly the same problem,
although they too feel the need to appear receptive to public demands from time to time. Moreover, since modern totalitarian systems have been more activist than capitalist democracies, they
sometimes must take inchoate demand into account against their
will. Activist goals require mobilization of the public, and this is
difficult to accomplish without stimulating new political requests. I
find it hard to believe that a nagging disaffection with payoff
is merely a "democratic distemper" (as Samuel Huntington
suggests: 1975, pp. 9–38). Demand for payoff is now universal insofar as political influence is found in all systems; discontent with
payoff is probably universal too.

In sum, effective social control by no means coincides with
political viability. Unless influence is efficiently incorporated and

the institutions are legitimated, payoff alone will not carry a system over the long haul. Further, satisfying levels of payoff are unlikely to persist for generations if the other two exigencies are not dealt with. Nevertheless, the nature of modern political life makes effectiveness the *primus inter pares* of the ingredients of political viability.

Efficient
Political Influence

Confidence and Demand

Talking about the effectiveness of a polity centers our attention on downward processes in which the state emits commands. The topic of efficient influence deals with upward processes through which the public funnels contributions to the state. Talcott Parsons suggests that these contributions have two parts: generalized support and demand. Generalized support is "a broadly based confidence in those assuming responsibility for leadership in governmental affairs which is necessary to enable them . . . to make far-reaching decisions responsibly in the sense that the elements of the population that are affected will accept the consequences" (1959, p. 84). The main target of this confidence tends to be the governmental or national executive component of the state. When granted, confidence gives the state a "zone of indifference" so that it does not have to sell each directive or to expend inordinate amounts of resources to obtain acquiescence. Political commentators point to this phenomenon when they say newly elected governments have "mandates" or are on "honeymoon periods." The notion of a honeymoon period implies that confidence is greater early in the life of a regime; later, its credibility becomes tarnished by repeated political combat.

Generalized support should not be confused with legitimacy. Although the two are related, they are logically and even em-

pirically distinct. Generalized support means confidence in a particular set of officeholders, often clustered in and around the national executive. Legitimacy refers to the degree of moral approval
for the rules of the game, *apart* from the incumbents or contestants. For example, confidence in the Truman, Johnson, and Nixon
administrations in their last year or so (in 1952, 1968, and 1974)
was dipping sharply, but the moral acceptance of the American political system remained relatively high. Legitimacy provides a
foundation for generalized support but cannot guarantee it. Conversely, a series of governments whose credibility is weak is likely
to set off an erosion in legitimacy (albeit a gradual one). After
more than a decade of controversy over Vietnam, there were more
challenges to the morality of American political institutions than in
the early 1960s. The original band of antiwar protesters never
imagined how deeply some of our fundamental political arrangements would come to be questioned because of their lack of confidence in those waging the war.

Two good indicators of confidence or generalized support in
the United States are ratings for a president in Gallup or Harris
Polls and his party's fortunes in off-year elections. A valid indicator of low legitimacy, on the other hand, is the growth of parties
and movements rejecting the rules of the game and seeking to impose new ones. In democratic societies this means the transfer of
allegiance to "extremist" parties advocating one-party states.

"Advocacy of policy" is the second contribution examined
by Parsons. Others (including Parsons in later works) call it *demand*. (See, for example, Easton 1965, pp. 37–340; Parsons
1967a, pp. 355–82.) To focus on demand is to consider a polity's
responsiveness. A political system is responsive if members have
access to the state. The core issue is how adept groups are in
organizing to channel their wants upward and having them acted
upon by centers of political power.

Demand and confidence are, of course, linked. Groups with
less access to the state are likely also to have less confidence in it.
Still, in democratic systems, demand tends to be broad enough so
that confidence does not rest on the enactment of each petition.

Confidence only begins to slip when a group senses that many of its demands are being evaded—especially in comparison to those of other groups. A typical Pluralist view is that a loose association between demand and confidence is beneficial. When demand becomes too specific, the argument goes, it is disruptive, for it robs the state of its zone of indifference and weakens the prospect for bargaining and compromise.

There is nothing wrong with this formulation—as far as it goes. But potential negative consequences must not be neglected. The weaker the relationship between confidence and demand, the lower the responsiveness of the state tends to be; that is, the less the state will feel obliged to move decisively toward relieving society's problems. Most modern regimes suffer less from an intemperate harnessing of specific demands to confidence than from a smug sense that token initiatives will suffice to keep generalized support flowing upward.

An efficient eliciting of confidence and demands is a prerequisite for effective action in all political systems. Without contributions from the public, the state would seek to maximize domination. But state power that lacks public confidence and has no incentive to respond to demand (like control without legitimacy) tends to be alienating. Hence it will probably become overly dependent on coercive power. Conversely, overenthusiasm for mobilizing support and a willingness to respond to all (or most) demands weakens the state's capacity to lead effectively. In such situations, the state resembles a small ball buffeted by the waves of public sentiment and subject to the deep pulls by the currents of unequal intermember power. Totalitarian states have erred more in the former direction and liberal democracies in the latter.

The Influence Process

The channeling of demand and confidence is a little like the conversion of knowledge into information (see chapter 4). Influence too is "created" and put aboard a macrosocial conveyor belt before it can affect political decisions. Influence and information are both subject to blockages. But critical differences between the two remain.

When we talk about the informational capacity of a political power wielder, the focus is on knowledge-creating and knowledge-processing units that are directly (e.g., the Department of Health, Education and Welfare) or indirectly (e.g., universities receiving federal research grants) linked to the state. Influence-processing units are normally more independent. They are found on lower levels of the polity.

With a single critical exception, the macro actors who process influence were discussed in chapter 5. Those previously treated are macrosolidary groups and localities, associations, and organizations. As we move from the first to the last of these, cohesiveness, consciousness, and mobilization increase, while size decreases. Macrosolidary groups and localities are the public level of influence. They sometimes resemble quasi groups, but the more intense their associational webs, the greater their solidarity. Publics as quasi groups include more participants than when associational life is added; but they also are more dormant. Organizations represent a decisive step in the mobilization for political influence. As I noted in the previous chapter, organizations are instrumental agents that strive to act for macrosolidary groups, particular segments within them, or constituents which crosscut them. Organizational arms have the fewest, yet most active, participants.

The basic workings of the influence process are as follows: demands and varying degrees of confidence (or no-confidence) percolate on the public level; some of these are crystallized and conveyed upward via associational webs; organizations choose among these and mobilize to press them; finally, organizational arms compete in the most direct and immediate exercise of political influence. (This last step corresponds roughly to Joseph Schumpeter's classic model of elite pluralism. See 1950, especially ch. 22.)

Associations and particularly organizations "do something" to influence analogous to what knowledge-processing units do to information. In both instances, something is altered and reduced while value is added. Like knowledge processors, organizations act as gatekeepers. They restrict, remold, and edit confidence and demand, permitting some aspects to pass upward and holding others back. The dangers of distortion are very real, for organizational imperatives rather than public need often shape what is processed. But in advanced societies, the only practical alternative to distortion by organizations is the creation of less distorting ones, not the abolition of "organizational society." The public and its associations do not contain the skills and procedures for regular access to policy-forming bodies.

All three levels (the public, associational, and organizational) need to be taken into account for a full understanding of influence formation. The typical public-opinion survey focuses on inchoate influence within macrosolidary groups and localities. The more sophisticated of these avoid reductionism and tap macrosocial processes when they run their aggregated data by several respondent attributes simultaneously (for example, by ethnicity, occupation, and religion) rather than one at a time (since, as noted in chapter 5, macrosolidary groups are based on more than a single trait). Yet those relying on the survey tend to ignore the role of associations and organizations as well as interorganizational rivalry. In turn, researchers who concentrate on the latter factors (e.g., interest-group politics) frequently overlook political sentiments percolating in the less organized, public sectors of macrosocial life.[3]

Two modifications to the upward-flow imagery are necessary. First, the impetus for demand and confidence can originate at any level: in the "public opinions" within macrosolidary groups, in the associational webs that weave these groups together, or in the organizational arms acting in the name of vested interest. If they occur above the public tier, the initiators must convey the sentiments downward to optimize political efficiency. That is, if organizations originate the idea, they must convince the associational webs as well as their publics; if initiatives begin in associations, they must be sold on the public level before they are processed upward to the organizational tier. Nothing "turns off" political decision makers faster than the discovery that an "interest group" has no constituency and is speaking only for itself. Exceptions occur only when authorities believe compliance to the influence of such organizations is profitable. Bribery is perhaps the crudest instance of this. The shuttling of personnel between regulatory agencies and the industries they regulate is a less stigmatized manifestation.

The second modification to the upward-flow imagery is that not all publics have equal organizational capacities. Generally, less privileged groups have lower access to organizations. Theodore Lowi has warned that the success of existing organizations "is a mortgage against the future of new needs that are not yet organized or not readily accommodated by established groups" (1971, p. 5). (The implications of the persistence of unequal influence is discussed later.)

Organizations often impinge directly on political decision making. The role played by lobbyists vis-à-vis federal agencies is a clear-cut illustration of this pattern. The immediate impact of organizations on state activity is most evidence in nonelected arenas (e.g., in Miliband's administrative "element"). Yet, elected positions are also affected, as the access to Congress by pressure groups attests. Both Pluralists and Elitists tend to see organizations as the pinnacle of the influence process. Such views underestimate the importance of the one component I have not yet discussed, the political party. Its role is most visible in the electoral process, but the party channels other forms of influence as well.

The modern mass political party is at the interface of the state and the public-association-organization influence structure. Several kinds of political entities use the label of "party." Some groups calling themselves parties are merely organizational arms and do not engage directly in the electoral process (such as, the Black Panther Party). Some parties are the elite agencies of dictatorial states (the Communist Party in the Soviet Union, ruling cliques of one-party states in developing nations). Others are revolutionary groups aiming at the violent overthrow of a political order and not at garnering votes. Still other entities represent elite elements in societies where the franchise is circumscribed (the Whigs and

Tories in England before the Reform Acts of the nineteenth century). None of these, strictly speaking, is a party in the sense of
the mass political party that prevails under liberal democracy. Unquestionably, the advent of political parties in this last sense is due
primarily to the extension of the franchise in the nineteenth and
twentieth centuries. Today, the right to vote is virtually universal
in Western democracies. I will not dwell on the social forces that
led to this expansion of citizenship rights. Rather, my concern is
with the consequences of the expansion. (These are discussed in a
subsequent section on parties and the electoral process; see pp.
152–68.)

In sum, the party is the fourth and crowning tier of the influence process. Organizations frequently lack direct access to political power. It is at this point that political parties play the decisive
role in determining how efficiently demand and confidence help
mold effective actions.

Dilemmas of Influence

Political systems differ radically in how they deal with the mobilization of contributions. In the contemporary world, the issue boils
down to saying that totalitarian systems wrestle with the problem
differently than democratic (i.e., two- or multiparty) polities. Yet,
both must incorporate influence to be effective.

The major totalitarian leaders of the twentieth century (Stalin,
Hitler, Mao) all have been committed primarily to transformation
and not to the maintenance of the privileges of conservative elites
(as, for example, Franco was in Spain). Totalitarian rulers cannot
accept the inevitability of the constraint-alienation cycle. To transform a society means to mobilize its members. Satisfied citizens
work harder and better than alienated ones. A public that is alienated will either actively resist mobilization (e.g., the East Germans
in 1953, the Hungarians in 1956) or passively withhold contributions (e.g., the Czechs in 1968). Thus, the totalitarian state cannot
ignore the issue of efficient influence. In a sense, it deals with it by
standing the question on its head—by converting the influence

issue into a problem of social control. Totalitarian governments seize the agencies that stand between the state and the public. By capturing control of associations and organizations, the state tries to prevent them from articulating the sentiments and aspirations brewing on the public level. They become instead arms of the state and help impose acceptance of its edicts. Confidence is sought *after* decisions are made, not in conjunction with demands. For example, in Nazi Germany and the Soviet Union, labor unions were converted from potential voices of the workers to tools of the state to implement official policy and render it acceptable. The campaign to whip up public support for Chairman Hua's accession to power is a recent example from China. In the final analysis, the key question for the totalitarian state is how to build confidence in leadership without whetting the public appetite for demand.

The relationship between influence and policy is very different in democratic polities—and it raises different problems. In totalitarian systems, the regime (or the Party) first makes policy and strives to implement it; later it moves to churn up generalized support. In democratic polities, policy and implementation ordinarily occur after the activation of demand and confidence processes. True, influence is frequently slanted in favor of the most privileged groups in the society. Yet diverse voices are raised (although some much louder than others), and major initiatives rarely come unilaterally from above.

Democratic systems are plagued by substantial time lags between the advocacy of a program and its enactment. The state's ineffectiveness is one cause. But also important is the relative inefficiency of influence processes. Organizations, political parties, bureaucracies, legislatures, and executives do not seem to be adept at sifting, adjudicating, and compromising demands from below without delaying or watering down proposed policies. The history of federal aid to education, first proposed in 1937, is instructive. It took until 1965 for a bill to be passed with the approval of most strategic political and societal forces. (See Munger 1967, pp. 11–16.) Other examples come to mind readily—civil rights, Medicare, and legal rights for labor unions.

Analysts of democratic polities believe that such inefficiency derives from incompatible attributes in the citizen role. That is, viable democratic systems need members with conflicting characteristics. The reason that these incompatibilities can be reconciled at all, it is argued, is that not all actors embody all the contradictions. A democracy does not have to be a system of micro- or macro-schizophrenics. Rather, incompatible traits reside in separate parts of the same groups as well as differentially among several groups, in a hetergeneous public. (See Berelson, Lazarsfeld, and McPhee 1954, pp. 305–23.)

The final chapter of *Voting* (1954) provided the inspiration for a generation of political analysts cataloguing the dilemmas of democratic influence. The authors of this book located five sets of contradictory attributes a democracy's public must contain. These pairs occur on different social-system levels, on different levels of abstraction, and at different points of a causal chain. Over the years, two pairs assumed an especially important place in the literature, not only because of their pivotal roles but also because they seem to subsume the issues raised in the others. These two are cleavage versus consensus and involvement versus indifference.

Each of the four poles was felt to be vexing for democracies, but the strongest concern has been with the snares of cleavage and involvement. Classical democratic theory had seen intense competition by an informed and aroused public as the surest safeguard for democracy. Berelson, Lazarsfeld, and McPhee, and those following them, notably Lipset (1959), were no longer so sure. They saw these verities cast into doubt by the rise of fascism and Stalinism abroad and by McCarthyism at home. All three events occurred in the vortex of passionate political mobilization. They asked themselves: When does competition become polarizing cleavage? When does involvement produce uncompromising conflict?

True, they said, a degree of cleavage is indispensable if a polity is to remain flexible in coping with new problems developing in the society. Flexibility requires some competition among the groups in the influence process, since emerging strains and prob-

lems are experienced differently by various localities, macrosolidary groups, associations, and organizations. These actors are
bound to disagree over which strains are appropriate political
issues as well as over how they should be handled. If there were
no disagreement, problems could not be faced or solved.

However, the argument continued, a political system loses its
flexibility when conflict becomes so bitter that an issue divides society into antagonistic camps among whom there is little prospect
for contact and compromise. This phenomenon is called polarization; Karl Marx long ago saw it as a prerequisite for revolution.
The great danger of polarization is that it cannot be confined to one
issue: it tends to spill over to a spectrum of other issues, preclud-
ing compromise on them as well.

Balancing involvement and indifference is seen as an equally
vexing dilemma. In some respects this issue resembles the problem
of how to link demand with confidence. The language of involvement versus indifference, however, casts the question in more general terms. It visualizes an efficient democratic influence system as
one in which: (1) groups are sufficiently mobilized so that they
care whether the state behaves responsively; and (2) groups are
sufficiently passive and deferential to the state to provide leeway
for workable decisions. The underlying fear is of an aroused public
that is susceptible to "extremist" blandishments; that is, that an
ideological and politicized citizenry will hasten polarization and
conflict. Overinvolvement narrows the maneuverability of political
parties and the state and weakens the prospects for compromise.

Another sign of overinvolvement is when publics and their
agents react *de novo* to each new issue. This pattern is also a threat
to the flexibility of the polity, for it generates a situation marked
by erratic demand and unpredictable policy. The prospects for
forging alliances and negotiations are weakened and the specter of
polarization again looms large.

**Some Mechanisms
 of Amelioration**

The same analysts also recognized that democratic polities are not
completely at the mercy of excessive cleavage and overinvolvement. Two mechanisms for ameliorating disruptive effects
have received special attention: moderated traditionalism and
overlapping group attributes. Neither is a new force in advanced
democracies; both have been around for some time and they have
operated with little deliberate intervention (with one exception in
the case of overlapping affiliations).

Moderated traditionalism Moderated traditionalism focuses on
how confidence and demands flow from the public through associations and organizations. It reminds us that the flow is not totally
contingent on new issues, new events, and "objective" vested interests. The process is also shaped by remembrance of things past:
past conflicts, old issues, and traditional ties. In other words, the
public's response to new situations is refracted through a prism of
earlier issues (as the history of anti-Semitism promoted Jewish
commitment to civil rights and civil liberties) as well as older
loyalties (for example, the attachment of the Irish-Americans to
the Democratic Party). Influence does not fluctuate wildly, but
is modified gradually. Berelson, Lazarsfeld, and McPhee see contributions at any given time as a moving statistical average of reactions to past political events as well as to new ones. In their study,
conducted in Elmira, New York, of the 1948 presidential election,
they show how the voting patterns of middle-income Catholics are
explained by memories of issues of the Depression and old dis-
criminations, as well as by new economic and international issues
(especially communism and the Cold War). The tug of the old
issues and loyalties kept this constituency more Democratic than
their preferences on the new issues might have indicated. The authors of *Voting* suggest that, at any given time, macrosolidary
groups (and their representatives) embody remnants of issues from
the past so that there is always an overlap between old and new

political sentiments. They conclude: 'All the people vote *in* the same election, but not all of them vote *on* it'' (p. 316). The same can be said of all political influence, particularly demand, not just voting behavior.

Overlapping group attributes Overlapping group attributes stem from two features of modern stratification systems discussed in chapter 5. Their fluidity means that localities are more "real" than overarching macrosolidary groups. The internal heterogeneity of the latter creates a situation where social attributes crosscut group boundaries and promote the chances that diverse localities share some key characteristics and interests. As I indicated in the last chapter, a community composed of the families of Jewish businessmen now more closely resembles a community of white Protestant executives and their families than a low-income Hasidic neighborhood in Brooklyn.

How do overlapping affiliations help overcome political strains? There are two ways, the second being more deliberate and more explicitly macroscopic. The first arises directly from the heterogeneity in and among macrosolidary groups. It is not hard to get people worked up about a particular issue and to rouse hostility toward the opposition. But some members of our own group have traits different from ours and members of other groups have traits they share with us. This provides a brake on how intense political conflict will become. After all, the opposition may contain members of our macrosolidary group or locality; it may include actors with whom we share social characteristics or with whom we have common bonds, down to the kinship level. Elections, for instance, in modern democratic societies do not precipitate extreme emotions, physical assaults on the opposition, riot, looting, or burning (in short, the kinds of behavior elections kindle in many premodern societies). Awareness that the opposition is not a "stranger" is one reason for this. The opposition contains groups like us—people we may live and work with, go to church with, and relax with. Overlapping traits limit extreme cleavage or overinvolvement because they temper political passions with a sense that the opposition includes people who are like us in some ways.

The second (more macrosociological) way that overlapping affiliation regulates cleavage and involvement is by the organizations and political parties it spawns. Societies marked by extensive cross-cutting attributes often have organizations and parties that draw supporters from several constituencies (e.g., U.S. labor unions, the women's movement, environmentalists). In these societies, many new issues do not correspond with the prevailing macrosolidary groups but impinge on selected pockets within various groups. Efforts to articulate demand thus require mobilization across groups. Organizations struggle to forge a base, drawing on several sectors of society. Even more than the organization, the mass political party looks for diverse adherents if it truly aims at victory at the polls. (See the discussion of parties below.)

Organizations and parties with partisans in two or more groups help hold the polity together. Because they activate heterogeneous constituencies, these units are inclined to stress conciliation and compromise. They strive to curb "true believers" as a matter of rational political strategy, because zealots shrink the base of support. In a word, they develop styles that regulate the levels of cleavage and involvement. These administrative styles operate over and above the spontaneous mechanisms fostered by a sense that the opposition is like us.

The Persistence of Inefficiency:
The Role of Unequal Influence

However, moderated traditionalism and overlapping affiliation do not eliminate inefficiency in democratic influence. These mechanisms are safeguards against cleavages and involvements that encourage rigid fanaticism. But the truth of the matter is that the two excesses are only occasional threats to the viability of "mature" systems.

The inefficiency of democratic influence is also the result of deeper strains in the polity, particularly a weak capacity to respond to less privileged members. Unresponsiveness is not necessarily the product of malice or conspiracy by elites. It usually stems from the political impediments associated with being less privileged.

Macrosolidary groups and localities with low intermember power are not unaware of inequities, and they generally favor greater state intervention on bread-and-butter and welfare-state issues. (See, for example, Hamilton 1972.) They are less indifferent (in the *Voting* use of the term) than inarticulate. They face more blockages in the upward processing of demands. These publics have long-standing grievances, but these only reach the political arena in short, intense bursts rather than in sustained flows. When these demands do enter, they appear in "distorted" form—frantic activation, unruly behavior, nonnegotiable priorities. Weimar Germany exemplifies a society in which such outbursts on both flanks could not be contained (owing to the absence of ameliorative mechanisms just discussed), thus paving the way for an inhumane totalitarianism. But in "mature" democratic polities, these explosions are commonly short-lived. The deeper grievances they are intended to express are, at best, only partly resolved. The less privileged then sink back into a period of decreased activation—but not necessarily indifference.

This pattern of political influence by the less privileged is due to factors on the public, associational, and organizational levels. These macrosolidary groups and localities are poorer by definition, not only financially but in such matters as self-esteem, health, education, modernity, and administrative skills. They care deeply about inequalities, but they have fewer resources to spend on something as extraneous to everyday survival as politics. Fewer resources along with less experience in mobilizing them reverberates to the associational and organizational tiers. Less money, time, and ability is available to sustain and nurture such artificial constructs. The associational and organizational lives of the less privileged tend to be improverished. They have fewer agencies of their own, while those that exist are not geared to their interests. Statistically this means the ratio of potential to actual political participants decreases as one moves down the stratification hierarchy.

(See Milbrath 1965.) This is so because it costs them more to process political influence (at least relative to the resources they have
on hand). Lower or less regular mobilization, then, is far more rational for these groups, as Anthony Downs has noted, than it may
seem superficially (1957, especially pp. 236–73). Yet, while lower
mobilization has rational aspects, it is a narrow and costly rationality—for the less privileged and for the viability of the entire
polity.

Unequal influence can create intense cleavage and involvement. Black militancy of the 1960s is a recent example of this phenomenon. Ironically, unequal influence also ensures that these outbursts probably will be brief. Both mobilization and its sputtering
character stem from the underdeveloped or blocked influence-
channels available to the less privileged. Their demands will flow
upward in sporadic bursts that are less mindful of the niceties of
democratic give-and-take. The demanders are in a hurry, which is
understandable in light of what mobilization costs them. This also
explains their impatience with the slow pace of payoff endemic to
democratic polities. The most likely result, as I have said, is that
their activation will subside quickly, and, for a time at least, the
less privileged will wind down organizational and associational involvement.

Another possible response to political frustration is to take
demands outside of institutionalized channels. Pluralist theory has
regarded unruly conduct as a "politics of unreason" and has tried
to use psychoanalytic categories to explain away what are essentially macrosociological events. But there is more rationality to
some unruly strategies than meets the eye. In fact, as William
Gamson (1975) has shown in his study of American "challenging
groups," unruly protest organizations are more likely to gain acceptance and new advantages than well-behaved ones. Thus, resort
to influence via constraint by the less privileged is more rational
than was once suspected.

The polity's more highly organized levels (organizations, parties, the state) are tempted to meet the demands from below
through "symbolic politics"—reassurances and gestures that de-

mands are being heard—rather than by "real" political actions aimed at change. Groups with low potential for mobilization tend to have the cutting-edge of their protest defected—at least temporarily—by such a tactic. (See especially Edelman 1964, ch. 2.) This deflection takes the steam out of mobilizing efforts and promotes the winding down of political activity. Unanswered demand, however, only stores up resentments on the public level and paves the way for a future mobilizing burst.

Electoral Politics

Elections are the prime corrective for unequal influence in democratic polities. Certain stages of the electoral process redress imbalances for groups low in privilege and mobilization. Since elections are based on one person-one vote, these groups have a decided edge. "God must love the poor,' Lincoln said, "because He made so many of them." Their voting-turnout rates are lower, but those with less privilege still provide a plurality of the electorate. The larger a constituency is, the more it is the object of a party's blandishments. Thus, elections have a populist bias. Once suffrage is universal, politicians must complete, however unenthusiastically, for the confidence and demands of weaker societal actors.

Elections also benefit the less privileged since the act of voting is itself not terribly costly. Elections occur only periodically and casting a ballot takes little time. On the other hand, costs jump the further away from election day we are. As we move back from casting the ballot—to being active in the campaign, to raising funds, to shaping platforms and issues, to putting forward and selecting candidates, and to keeping party structures alive between elections—the cost for weaker groups skyrockets. Only at the very end of the electoral process does the leveling effect of one person-one vote prevail. The more remote the event, the greater differentials in influence.

Do elections make any difference? Or are they merely shams to mask the "real" influence exerted elsewhere in the system? No one questions the inauthenticity of elections in totalitarian polities. These are manipulated by the regime to create the impression of confidence and legitimacy. However, many see democratic elections as *the* central mode of political influence. Others, of course, retort that electoral politics here is also a travesty because, historically, key constituencies and crucial issues have been underrepresented or ignored. These charges have some merit. Nonetheless, it is also true that the past hundred years has seen the relentless expansion of citizenship rights in all Western democracies, that is, the inclusion in the political (viz., electoral) process of previously excluded groups. This process began with the elimination of property criteria for voting; its most recent manifestation is enfranchisement of the blacks in the American South as a result of the 1965 Voting Rights Act. Yet, while citizenship had become nearly universal in capitalist democracies, the impact of voting on influence and on the quality of political decisions still is a matter of considerable debate.

It is safe to say that most democratic elections entail some "real" influence; elections make some difference compared to the manipulative function they have in totalitarian systems. At the very least, elections expand the audience of decisions which limits the authorities' discretion in setting collective goals. However, the electoral process never coincides with all political influence. Elections are more important for some elements of the state than for others. National and subcentral executives and parliments are ordinarily more susceptible to electoral influence than are the administrative, military, and judiciary branches. Much of our recent domestic political struggle has focused on trying to introduce mechanisms of accountability to these latter elements analogous to the accountability generated by electoral review.[4] The ability of special interests to shape the policies of the federal regulatory agencies that are supposed to police them is only one rather blatant example of how influence without accountability is distorted outside of the electoral process. (See, for example, McConnell 1966.)

Those groups that are most influential in nonelectoral sectors also tend to be the ones which excess leverage in the prevoting stages of the electoral process. Groups with more resources and skills for mobilization play a decisive role in the influence process between elections. They contribute more to the selection of candidates, to the shaping of issues, to the financing of elections, and their members are more active in campaigns. The choices in a voting booth are as much the distillation of a long sequence of events as any other facet of political influence and show the same marks of unequal leverage. Yet, with all its inefficiencies, voting remains the only major mode of influence with a built-in democratic corrective—albeit only at the last stage.

In sum, how much elections matter varies among polities, from one branch of a state to the next, and from election to election. They are always more than a charade in modern democracies. But, even if the electoral process were thoroughly democratized, inefficiencies in influence would remain. Elections are only one way to funnel confidence and demands. Whether the electoral model can be expanded to other sectors of political influence is problematic. The call for elections to enhance accountability in the judiciary, in regulatory agencies, and in a national health system may seem a dubious proposal; but it deserves more attention than it has received so far.

The Uses of Voting Data

In chapter 1 I noted that voting data can tell us things about a polity which, strictly speaking, fall outside the electoral sphere. These data often illuminate a society's intermember and political-power struggles; voting data provide indicators of other macrosocial processes besides electoral alignments. The consumer of sociological research is warned that not every study using voting data is really about voting. (Ironically, many that are not have greater macrosociological significance than those that are.)

The analysis of data about elections (polls and voting results) yields information about: (1) which groups support what political forces; (2) what kinds of issues mobilize different groups; and (3) the extent of conflict and polarization in the polity and society. For example, electoral statistics are a good source of information about the social bases of "extremist" movements. Lipset studied the rise of the Nazis between 1928 and 1932 using such records. He showed that support for the middle-of-the-road bourgeois parties, drawn mainly from small business people and white-collar workers, collapsed almost totally, and economic and political turmoil pushed those groups toward a totalitarian solution; they turned to the Nazis in greater and greater numbers (1959, pp. 131–52). Indeed, Lipset's analysis of Weimer voting records portrays the tensions and conficts wracking German society during the rise of National Socialism. This glimpse is a useful supplement to the usual qualitative historical data. (Nonetheless, while voting records offer instructive indicators of polarization, we may not infer that electoral politics played *the* decisive role in the fall of the Weimar Republic and the rise of the Third Reich. Certainly, such factors as the position of the military and industrial elites were of vital importance but not integral to the elections and voting.)

Parties and Electoral Politics

Since plebiscites are rare, democracies must contain additional mechanisms if votes are to deliver policy. If elections are to make a difference, units must exist to organize the electoral process. These units mediate between the public, association, and organizational levels, on the one hand, and the state on the other. They are commonly called political parties—in the modern, mass sense of that concept. Their task in contemporary democracies, according to Dowse and Hughes, "involves the practice and justification of political authority, the recruitment and removal of leaders, the mobilization of opinion, the ordering of public policy and the balancing of group interest" (1972, p. 339).

Universal suffrage played a decisive role in growth of mass parties. Polities with universal suffrage and with mass parties, in turn, are allegedly marked by two foci of political identification: status politics and class politics. Finally, the alternation between these foci has given Western political life a distinctive character, one which Dennis Wrong (1974b) has called "the rhythm of democratic politics."

Parties are the key device in democratic polities for organizing and processing demand and confidence. These systems have parties that approximate one of two types: parties of integration or of representation. (See Neumann 1956, pp. 403–5; Lipset 1959, pp. 85–87.) They differ on (1) the heterogeneity of their constitutents; (2) scope and pervasiveness; and (3) political moralism. In other words, mass political parties are classified by whether they draw votes cross few or many macrosolidary groups (homogeneity versus heterogeneity); whether or not party affiliations spill over into nonpolitical sectors (low versus high scope and pervasiveness),[5] and whether or not goals flow from ideological orthodoxy (low versus high political moralism).

Parties of integration have homogeneous constituencies, aim at high scope and pervasiveness, and are predisposed toward political moralism. They seek to represent one or only a few groups. Because they are concerned with the "purity" of ideals, they see their responsibility as extending far beyond the electoral activities. They attempt to encapsulate and form the total lives of their adherents by creating associations that restrict contacts with outsiders and by imposing values that are, strictly speaking, beyond political life (regarding sex, family life, and aesthetics, for example). Totalitarian parties are always parties of integration; some democratic parties are, too. Catholic and socialist parties in Europe, especially before 1939, sought to construct networks of associations that bound members together and excluded nonblievers. There were Catholic and socialist trade unions, youth groups, and fraternal organizations. Needless to say, to succeed, a party of integration must build a base broad enough to prevent annihilation at the polls: a national political party for American Indians is doomed from the outset. Yet, in Europe, parties of integration flourished for decades while drawing the bulk of their support from a single religious, linguistic, regional, or economic group.

Parties of representation, on the other hand, pursue potential adherents in as many groups as possible. They are inclined to be more interested in the winning of votes and less in the saving of souls. They have little concern with the day-to-day lives of constituents and feel that success is more important than ideological purity. Rather than trying to preside over a circumscribed constituency, parties of representation are tempted to widen their base of support and to ingratiate themselves with new adherents. They try to "bargain policies for votes" (Lipset 1968, p. 397). Of course, the social base for such a party is not so will-o'-the-wisp that it fluctuates wildly or disappears overnight. In a given election, a party of representation, like any other, is best advised "not to try to convert a sizeable number of those disposed to vote for its opponent but to do everything possible to get out the vote among its own supporters" (Lipset 1968, p. 390). Still, compared to a party of integration, the party of representation is set off by its continuing, albeit gradual, effort to reach electoral victory through bridge building, even if this means the sacrifice of ideological purity.

Polities are charcterized by one type of party or the other as a result, to some degree, of unique ("historical") circumstances. Yet, from a cross-national perspective, three features of polities play a considerable role. The first factor deals with institutions surrounding the national executive; the other two have to do with the procedures for choosing the national legislature. Polities with presidential systems more readily develop parties of representation than those with parliamentary systems. The existence of a constitutionally separate executive, more or léss directly elected, forces factions to come together prior to the election. The American system is prototypical here. The Gaullist constitution, if it survives, seems to be pushing France along a similar path. In a parliamentary system, factions are likely to loôk more like parties of integration which come together and bargain only after the election to hammer out a government and a workable political agenda.

Polities whose legislatures are chosen by proportional representation are likely to have parties of integration, while those with single-member districts are more often marked by parties of representation. Parties of integration more often occur in polities receptive to minority parties. In systems with single-member districts, voting for a minority slate is perceived as a wasted vote. Under proportional representation, on the other hand, such a vote is a rational device to ensure having one's view represented. Legislatures that consist of two dominant parties more commonly contain parties of representation than do those with multiparty systems. Two-party systems involve struggles for the "middle-majority" vote. Both parties compete for a foothold in many of the same constituencies by trying to capture the middle ground and labeling the opposition as extremists. Such parties are coalitions of diverse factions, and electoral success depends on holding onto as many of them as possible. Where there are several parties, the tendency is to specialize in a narrower political base.

It goes without saying that these three factors are related. Two-party systems particularly are often seen as the outcome of the other two. Presidential politics do encourage the reduction in the number of competing parties. But causality is not one-way. For instance, multiparty systems foster parliamentary government. Duverger (1954, p. 217) has suggested that the association between systems with single-member districts and a two-party polities is "most nearly perhaps to a true sociological law" as there is. And, indeed, the correlation is unmistakable. Yet, as Grumm (1958, pp. 357–76) demonstrates, two-party-systems, once established, seem to be able to withstand the impact of a shift to proportional representation.

This suggests that the effects of the three factors are interactive. There is no theoretical reason for giving causal priority to one over the others. More historical research is needed for determining where and why one came first and how this shaped the development of the others. We can throw the integration-representation issue into such a matrix too. While type of party seems to be the outcome of these three factors, it may also feed back on them. Thus, in the American system, the character of our two giant parties of representation makes it likely that third (integration)-party movements will either be absorbed or ground under.

The party systems of mature democracies are not divided randomly between integration and representation. The trend over the

last generation has been toward parties that look more representational in character. Universal suffrage has been crucial here. The
pressure to win and hold large bodies of voters has made parties
more flexible, less dogmatic, and more tolerant of diversity. This
is true even of many of the so-called parties of democratic integration, such as European Catholic and social democratic parties. In
West Germany, the Christian Democrats and Social Democrats
have begun to resemble more the Conservative-Labour and Repub-
lican-Democratic splits in Britain and America than their sectarian predecessors in the Weimar Republic. All this has pushed political debate toward the center; to optimize their political
advantage, parties eschew sectarian appeals to the extreme right
and left out of fear of losing supporters in the middle.

This mode of political struggle first occurred in the United
States because the extension of suffrage began earlier here. Several
nineteenth- and early twentieth-century commentators noted the
fluid, pragmatic nature of American parties, as well as their single-
minded dedication to winning. Lipset has noted that Moisei Os-
tragorski and Max Weber predicted that the American pattern
would ultimately spread to Europe, but that both viewed this development with misgivings (1968, pp. 363–411). In essence, Os-
trogorski and Weber decried the penchant of American parties to
disassociate means from ends at the expense of the latter; that is,
to emphasize electoral success almost exclusively and to ignore the
"idealistic" purpose of winning.

But parties of representation provide the context for overlapping group affiliations that limit the excesses of cleavage and involvement. In contrast, the integrationist strategies of the Catholics
and socialists in pre-World War II Austria are blamed for polarizing that society and laying it open for the Nazi takeover. There,
each had a homogeneous constituency that was thoroughly antagonistic to the other. Although both were nominally committed to the
parliamentary system, each was incapable of the negotiations and
accommodation required to make such a system work. In short,
the modern mass party of representation has less character, since it
trades ideals for votes, but it is more attuned to the needs of the

diverse electorate typical of modern society and certainly more capable of mobilizing broad-based support.

The drift toward parties of representation is not uniform. The Republican Party in the United States has been sliding in the opposite direction for the past two decades. Compared to the last years of the Eisenhower administration, the GOP now has a narrower constituency and a more moralistic (i.e., conservative) stance—although it continues to be low in scope and pervasiveness. Of course, the Republicans are still nearer the representation end of a representation-integration continuum. But its drift in the other direction accounts for the party's declining success since 1958. Its presidential triumphs (in 1968 and 1972) and its close losses (in 1960 and 1976) obscure how badly the GOP is really doing. Better gauges of the situation come from the shrunken numbers of Republican governors, the failure to control state and federal legislatures, and the fact that only about one-fifth of the electorate currently identifies itself as Republican. The cry by the party's conservative-wing for even greater ideological purity will certainly further narrow the GOP's base and intensify its political moralism. It is a recipe for shrinkage—if not suicide—for it denies the representational character of the American party system. (See Nie, Verba, and Petrocik 1976.)

Parties of representation, on the other hand, are not without blemish. They homogenize demand, and this has political costs, particularly for the less privileged and less influential. Groups whose influence-channels are underdeveloped or blocked have less leverage in such parties, being swamped by better-organized factions. Of course, some redress is provided because they have more votes, especially in a.left-wing party. Yet, even here, as already suggested, maximum impact occurs with the casting of the ballot, and influence on party politics is weaker at other stages.

Thus, parties of representation can exacerbate the episodic and intense character of demand by the less privileged and less mobilized. This can take the form of ''extremist' ' takeovers of a party (Goldwaterites in 1964, McGovernites in 1972), which only precludes electoral victory. Or it can be expressed in third-party "revolts" which siphon off key votes (Wallacites in 1968). Both results leave the party structure at least temporarily shaken, but neither solves the problem of how to increase the political clout of less articulate groups.

Class and Status Politics

The conventional wisdom of political sociology is to view democratic political life as an arena for two great struggles: class politics and status politics. That is, two factors are reputed to provide the dynamics of party division: efforts to preserve or to alter the existing system of economic power and privilege (class politics), and efforts to protect or alter the prevailing distribution of normative resources, such as prestige, deference, civil liberties, and traditional styles of life (status politics). This formulation (derived from Weber's distinction between classes and status groups) has been used not only to understand electoral politics but, even more, to explain the nature of "extremist" movements challenging democratic systems.

Status politics and extremism Lipset's famous (and debated) thesis on "working-class authoritarianism" is built around these two categories (1959, pp. 97–130). He presents cross-national data suggesting that while working classes are liberal on economic issues, they tend to be illiberal on noneconomic ones, notably in opposing tolerance of dissent, civil liberties, and democratic procedures. As a result, he says, they are especially susceptible to extremist appeals of either the far right or the far left.[6] The link between status politics and extremism is most fully developed by Lipset in *The Politics of Unreason,* coauthored in 1970 with Earl Raab. I focus on this book because it is the exemplar of what is good and bad about equating status politics with extremism. The study purports to be a historical review of right-wing extremism in America from 1790 to 1970. The book runs into several problems that I have detailed elsewhere (Lehman 1972b). Here it is worth stressing that Lipset and Raab have difficulty conveying precisely what they mean by right-wing extremism and thus ultimately class versus status politics. Clearly, the authors intend to discriminate between conservatives and right-wing extremists. The former (e.g., William Buckley and his colleagues on the *National Review*) are committed to "preservation," to "maintaining or narrowing lines of power or privilege . . ." (p. 19), while still adhering to the pluralist rules. Right extremists, on the other hand, are "pre-servatist," advocating "the repression of difference and dissent, the closing down of the market place of ideas" (p. 6). Left-wing extremists also seek to close down the "market place of ideas" but in order to transform the system rather than to conserve it; they are "innovationist" rather than "preservatist." The capstone of all extremism is conspiracy theory, an extension of a moralistic version of history which sees political competition as the struggle of good versus evil.

Lipset and Raab's ultimate criterion of right extremism is whether or not a political phenomenon is based on "status deprivation." Their equating of status politics with rightist tendencies becomes explicit when they say:

. . . while the preservatism of the upper-class and often the middle-class may be both class-directed and status-directed, the preservatism of the lower economic class must be chiefly status-directed. Therefore, the common core of effective right-wing extremist movements is symbolic rather than instrumental in nature. This does not mean that such movements do not also have instrumental goals, but, it is the symbolic core which distinguishes them and gives them their particular aspect of similarity to religious movements. (p. 165)

Right-wing extremism thus comes to be defined as status politics of a particular variety (explicitly antipluralist). This raises two difficulties that haunt the literature on status politics and extremism. First, and perhaps more serious, is that the approach comes to rest on one grand tautology. Lipset and Raab's book is informed by one general proposition: Status deprivation is the single most important source of right-wing extremism throughout

American history. Whatever its merits, it receives no fair airing in *The Politics of Unreason* because right-wing extremism is implicitly defined as a form of status preservatism. Hence, 515 pages are anchored on the hypothesis that status deprivation tends to generate movements that aim at overcoming status deprivation—all other things, of course, being equal!

Apart from this logical difficulty, the definition of right-wing extremism in terms of status deprivation leads Lipset and Raab to employ a basic assumption about rightist movements in this country which derives from a psychoanalytic view of protest groups. The assumption is found in the very title of their book, which says that status-preservatist politics is the politics of *unreason*. (The politics of "reason," presumably, is class politics, particularly as it is institutionalized in interest-group articulation.) This perspective forces them to treat fundamentalist Protestantism and other traditionalist values as "cultural baggage" that express status anxieties but by no means cause them. They believe, for instance, that religious and racial prejudices do not foment right extremism. Rather, "status backlash has not so much emerged from the reservoirs of prejudice as the latter have emerged from, been activated by, been replenished by status backlash . . ." (p. 490).

Consequently, Lipset and Raab distinguish between status deprivation spawned by massive social change and the struggle to preserve traditional values, which they reduce to a response to status deprivation. Of course, once we empty the concept of status politics of its traditionalistic components, then class and status politics become nearly indistinguishable. All of the status-deprived groups that Lipset and Raab discuss are groups slipping in the capacity to affect the political and distributive processes of society (i.e., in power) or in their ability to command a given share of its valued resources, especially economic ones (i.e., in privilege). What difference remains then between class and status politics is not found in the sources or nature of the structural strain, but in the responses to it.

In other words, Lipset and Raab, when they are not talking about the structural bases of status politics, imply that the latter is simply class politics to which there is an "unreasoned" response and in which religious and other traditionalistic values are invoked largely as symbols of lost power and privilege. I think someone once called this phenomenon "false consciousness." Nowhere in their book is this interpretation put to the acid test. It seems equally plausible that some groups have real commitments to cherished beliefs, values, and styles of life, and that they sometimes enter the political arena to protect them, not just to use them as cultural or political baggage to safeguard slipping power and privilege. For example, perhaps those involved in the right-to-life movement really oppose abortion on moral grounds and are not acting out unconscious motives, as some of their opponents suggest.

In short, *The Politics of Unreason,* perhaps better than any other work, displays the difficulties in relying on the language of class and status politics to explain extremist political behavior. Status politics cannot simultaneously be an independent and a dependent variable. Clearly, as an independent variable, the notion of status deprivation is insufficient because (as I noted in the previous chapter) modern macrosolidary groups in general, and those in America in particular, are blendings of several elements—both class and status group in nature. The multiple strains these groups experience cannot be neatly packaged in an either/or classification. Lipset and Raab seem to be aware of this. (It probably accounts for their blurring of class versus status as a structural basis for politics.)

We are left, then, with class versus status politics as a dependent variable, as an outcome or an expression of structural strains. When the terminology is used in this way, we are speaking about the types of issues that can be invoked: economic ones versus those linked with basic values, styles of life, and traditional symbols. Once researchers have determined if one type of issue or the other is dominant at a given time, they still have not answered the question: Under what conditions is either type invoked and why? In other words, the structural (i.e., intra- and intergroup) sources for emphasizing one set of issues over another have yet to be explained. Furthermore, if the language of class versus status politics is restricted to political issues, we are not required to prejudge the false-consciousness question. This question may be rephrased to ask: Do a society's key groups conjure up religious creeds, traditional values, ethnocentric prejudice, and so on, merely as cultural baggage or because these themes are ends in themselves? The answer here must come via empirical research, not from the preferences of the social analyst.

Therefore, the highly touted language of class and status politics survives—but with considerably less explanatory power. It does provide a useful way to classify issues debated in the political arena. We can point out that certain groups at a given time are more susceptible to economic appeals, while others are open to more "moral" ones (and that this pattern may change later). Further, we can begin to study when status issues and when class issues are more likely to have an impact on the public. In this narrower usage, the terminology reverts to being more fruitful for analyzing electoral politics than for interpreting the origins and persistence of "extremist" movements.

Class and status politics in the electoral process Lipset himself is a major contributor in this regard, notably in an essay titled "Class, Politics, and Religion in Modern Society: The Dilemma of the Conservatives" (1968, pp. 159–76). Here he wonders: "If class remains one of the main sources of party division, and if the lower strata back parties that advocate greater equality—parties that oppose the privileged elites—how can conservative parties compete in democratic elections?" (1968, p. 159). Although some of the ambiguities of *The Politics of Unreason* are also found in this essay, Lipset alerts us to the political advantage sometimes held by parties of the Right. These parties are not only "preservatist" in the matter of economic power and privilege but also regarding the core values and beliefs of a society. Conservatives are typically seen as the guardians of religious principles and patriotic sentiment. Thus, while they are the protectors of the economic interests of an elite minority, on status issues they present them-

selves as the champions of the core values and traditions purport-
edly held by the majority. Indeed, they usually justify their economic views in the language of status politics ("free enterprise,"
"competition," the "work ethic," and so on). Conversely, parties
of the Left, who on economic grounds would control a majority,
are often thrown on the defensive by opponents who depict them
as subverters of moral standards, of public decency, of religious
devotion, and of love of country.

It is little wonder that parties of the Left and of the Right
employ different election strategies. Left-wing parties' best chance
for victory lies with bread-and-butter issues, whereas right-wing
parties prefer to stress moral, patriotic, or nationalistic (i.e., status) issues; these appeals cut across economic lines to some degree. The "silent majority" invoked by Richard Nixon in 1970 at
the crest of the Vietnam debate was (if it ever existed) a majority
grounded in status politics, not class issues.

The Rhythm of Democratic Politics

Dennis Wrong has analyzed the common practice of explaining
democratic (especially American) politics in terms of "swings of
the pendulum," "rising and ebbing tides," "cycles," and
"spirals." He prefers the phrase "the rhythm of democratic politics" because it is less deterministic in its implications (1974b,
pp. 46–55). Regardless of terminology, Wrong sees plausibility in
the assertion that there is periodicity to democratic politics—a
fluctuation between Right and Left, between more conservative
and more liberal times, between a focus on normative and utilitarian resources, between the ascendancy of status politics or class
politics; that in the process, the extremes of both sides tend to be
mitigated.[7]

Universal suffrage, plus the entrenched inequities in modern
societies, guarantee that parties advocating a more evenhanded
allocation of economic resources will triumph from time to time.
However, these class-oriented parties are likely to have moderate

programs. As noted above, the nature of mass party politics pushes
the contestants toward the center. Thus, the economic mandate of
parties of the Left in capitalist democracies is soon exhausted.
Reforms are instituted (e.g., social security and the Wagner Act
under the New Deal) and some acute economic distress is (at least
temporarily) ameliorated (e.g., policies are introduced to combat
unemployment, a recession, or a depression). The Left and its supporters become divided over whether to push on for more radical
changes or to consolidate their gains. Moreover, significant segments of the Left's constituency are appeased by incremental material gains, and they oppose further changes as potentially disruptive for, if not in direct conflict with, society's deeply held values.

All this allows the Right to regroup. Although based on a
narrower constituency, the Right, by virtue of its privileged base,
tends to have a special edge in the organizational skills necessary
for political mobilization. This provides it with an advantage in ex-
erting political influence—both inside and outside of the electoral
context. Stated simply, despite a smaller hard-core following, the
Right has a greater potential for political resilience than the Left.
Consequently, together with a promise not to undo past reforms,
the Right may call for national solidarity under the banner of patriotism, piety, or the preservation of hallowed values. In the absence of an economic crisis, these status-politics appeals may pre-
sage the electoral triumph of the Right. Yet, the Right is unlikely
to ensconce itself in power permanently. For one thing, insofar as
its mandate focuses on status themes, a conservative government is
inclined to be passive about endemic strains and inequities in the
economic realm. For another, if a conservative government does
intervene in the economic sector, it will probably do so with the
implicit suppositions of elite groups and often in explicit pursuit of
their vested interests; for example, with policies stressing capital
accumulation and economic growth over social services. Grievances will begin to accumulate in the middle and bottom of the society sufficient, *ceteris paribus,* to permit the class-oriented appeals of the Left to meet with success again. The process is often

accelerated by economic crises of differing kinds and magnitudes, such as depressions, recessions, inflations, periods of high unemployment, and scarcity of essential commodities.

A rhythmic interpretation of democratic processes, Wrong cautions, should not be used mechanically. All societies are subject to unique forces that prevent an unreflective application of the model. The history and present position of blacks in the United States makes the success of a simultaneous class-oriented appeal to black and white groups in similar economic situations more difficult than if there were no "race problem." Moreover, foreign relations and international politics have a way of intruding into national politics in a manner not accounted for by a rhythmic model. Foreign wars more commonly benefit the Right and short-circuit a phase of Left control. Yet, foreign-policy questions do not always redound to the benefit of the Right. While patriotism is a more traditional rallying cry of the Right, governments of the Left are not above jingoistic adventures or appeals.

In sum, a more modest use of the terminology of class and status politics—one that treats these categories as a way of talking about issues—is useful for interpreting the rhythmic character of democratic politics. But even here, exogenous factors preclude the unreflective application of the model.

Postscript: The Rhythm
of Democratic Politics
and Postindustrial Society

It may well be that in the future democratic politics will not fit this rhythmic model. Changes in economic life may have an impact. Many observers have noted a shift in the economies of advanced societies away from the industrial and manufacturing sectors. Whether or not this makes them truly postindustrial prompts heated debate among social analysts. Regardless of whether America and Europe are now in a new phase (with all the economic, social, political, and cultural implications of such a transition), it is safe to say that significant shifts have occurred since

World War II. All advanced societies have witnessed a more rapid growth in the production of services than of goods, a greater increase in service occupations relative to manufacturing ones, and growing reliance on informational capacities by public and private decision makers. These trends point to the growing importance of more abstract or intangible resources. Services, know-how, administrative skills, and theories are critical today, but they are more abstract than the utilitarian resources that marked nineteenth- and early twentieth-century industrial society.

This suggests that a blurring has occurred between some utilitarian and normative resources in the modern world. For example, the mass media are difficult to classify unambiguously as either utilitarian or normative resources. Indeed, to haggle over which theoretical pigeonhole they fit confounds the issue to some extent. The same may be said for other struggles and resources that are coming to center stage: the efforts by deprived elements to develop informational and organizational capacities; the fight for equal access to and accountability in education and health services; the call for more "meaning" in work. All of these demands might have been treated as a struggle over normative resources at other times, but one of the hallmarks of the contemporary order is that they have taken on a more utilitarian meaning. These resources are now more utilitarian because they represent something beyond differing styles of life; they are also looked upon as malleable assets that must be redistributed in order to promote material well-being and more equality.

In other words, the class politics of so-called postindustrial society frequently focuses on issues and resources that in earlier times would have been labeled unequivocally as normative. If the subject-matter of class politics is harder to disentangle from that of status politics, what does this portend for tomorrow's "rhythm of democratic politics"? At the very least, the beats and the tempo of the rhythm may change. In addition, the language we have been using to understand the rhythm (deriving as it does from Wilhelmian Germany) may have to undergo modification, if not replacement, in a postindustrial era.

Digression:
Political Influence
and Power Elites

Modern political sociology is obsessed with moldering, sterile controversies and is unwilling to drop them, to move beyond them, or to reformulate them. The so-called Power Elite debate is the perfect example. Students in political science and political sociology find the battlements of the Power Elite and Pluralist Schools looming before them. These approaches seem so irreconcilable and their judgments of each other so steeped in venom that a choice looks like the profession of one religious faith over another.

I do not intend to wander into this morass. In chapter 4 I scolded both traditions for minimizing the roles of political power and the state in the modern world while focusing excessively on the vagaries of intermember power. I wish only to add that both dally with straw men when they see the course of American society set totally by either the tuggings and haulings of roughly equal macrosolidary groups, associations, and organizations or a monolithic ruling elite. Each approach fails to confront the real world in all its complexities and ambiguities.

I do not degrade the contributions made by scholars who painstakingly map the contours of influence and political power in American society. (For a forceful review, see Prewitt and Stone 1973.) More detailed empirical work is needed. But the time has come to move beyond the old imagery and frameworks. Barrington Moore, Jr., provides the theoretical key for progress in his *Reflections on the Causes of Human Misery* (1972). He shifts the question from merely haggling over the description of American power structures to a concern with the prospects for *praxis*. Moore asserts that what radical critiques of liberal democracy "are ultimately trying to explain, and the point upon which they ultimately rest their case, is the *absence of change*—not the impossibility of change" (pp. 131–32). Moore says, in effect, that attention should turn to why there has been no significant opposition to what

he calls the "predatory" aspects of the American system and to an
exploration of the chances for transformation in the future.

He argues persuasively that the American polity and economy
is not wholly dependent on "predatory democracy."[8] Why, then,
he asks, have we failed to cut back our military establishment and
reorder our domestic priorities? His answer pinpoints the defects in
Pluralist theory (and *praxis!*) more sharply than a Marxian or
Power Elite perspective. The failure to develop countervailing
forces to the military-industrial complex stems from neither the internal contradictions of advanced capitalism nor the mystic permu-
tations of the Dialectic. Lack of any effective opposition is explained:

. . . if some segments of business make large gains at the expense
of the public welfare through military contracts, while other interest
groups take only minor losses or are able to make some gains of
their own, there will be no material incentive to alter the social
order. . . . Such a situation is not altogether unusual in human affairs. It is a far cry from predestined fate. . . . (pp. 143–44)

In this climate of political "indifference," some organizations exert inordinate influence on national policy, out of all pro-
portion to their numbers, "but . . . also far beyond what one
might anticipate on the more 'sophisticated' basis of knowing their
place in the social structure. . . ."

Moore's formulation allows us to reject a mindless determinism in political life without subscribing to the Pollyannaish
view that we reside in the best of all political worlds. It permits us
to ponder the potential for significant change with some hope of
success. But perhaps the major strength of Moore's approach is
that it avoids the sterile positions of Pluralism and Power
Elitism—and in a way that opens up the topics both sides raise to
falsification or verification as well as to change.

Legitimacy and Viability

The concepts of effective social control and efficient political influence focus on activities *within* political systems. The third ingredient of a viable polity, the legitimacy of its institutions, is an extrinsic element. Legitimacy points not to the properties of intrapolity relationships but of shared meanings associated with (but analytically distinct from) a political system. Legitimacy, as noted in chapter 2, is an aspect of political culture, not of a political system.

To put it differently: The viability of a polity is a direct outcome of how effective and efficient it is at any time; political culture is one of the conditions in the broader context which encourages or inhibits the structural forces that build viability. Hence, legitimacy's contribution to the success of a polity is more indirect. Its impact takes two general forms. First, legitimacy provides a frame of reference with which macro actors judge how the polity is doing. Second, legitimacy appears in "structural manifestations" which more immediately impinge on viability. The first impact deals with consequences of differing doctrines of legitimacy and how they influence subjective evaluations of effectiveness and efficiency. The second is concerned mainly with whether legitimacy is high or low (and less with whether it tends to be traditional or rational-legal). Certain structural problems in the polity are highly sensitive to levels of legitimacy. Indeed, these structural manifestations are a kind of litmus paper for legitimacy.

Legitimacy
and Subjective Evaluation

Social systems differ dramatically from systems in the physical and biological realms: a social system's parts have a reflective capacity not enjoyed by the members of the other two systems. Cells, clouds, and clams are not conscious of their roles or of their larger consequences. But in assessing political viability, a socio-

logical observer must consider subjective components, for, in the
final analysis, success in social enterprises is never based solely on
mechanical or objective factors. Political viability depends on both
objective, functional standards imposed by the observer, and subjective ones deriving from how members think the system is living
up to its highest ideals.

Doctrines of legitimacy (thoroughly rational-legal to purely
traditional) set the grounds for members' evaluations of a polity's
effectiveness and efficiency. The more political arrangements are
judged in rational, activist terms, the more grueling and volatile
the evaluation will probably be. Traditional judgments are likely to
be easier and less changeable. Yet whatever the impact of values,
beliefs, and sentiments, a clash between ''objective'' and ''subjective'' criteria always remains a real possibility in political analysis.
A complete scientific assessment of effectiveness and efficiency
must surmount this obstacle and somehow take subjective evaluations into account. Doctrines of legitimacy do not merely shape
what members feel about the system; they also have consequences
in political conduct. Criteria, judgments, and consequences must
be studied by the sociological observer opposed to an arid, mechanical interpretation of political events. This task is not easy.
Not all members share the same symbols. Moreover, as we saw in
chapter 2, not everyone has equal leverage in molding the operative standards. Thus, methodological questions persist for the social scientist who wishes to build legitimacy's ''subjective'' impact on effectiveness and efficiency into an assessment of viability.

Legitimacy and Its
Structural Manifestations

Legitimacy also has more immediate structural manifestations.
Strategic political activities often reflect the moral approval im-
puted to a polity. Here the question of degree of legitimacy (high
or low) is central, although the content of prevailing doctrines also
plays a part. Two structural problems in particular closely mirror a
polity's level of legitimacy. These manifestations are the availabil-

ity of third-party support and the smoothness of political succession. In turn, how both are dealt with has direct implications for a
polity's effectiveness and efficiency.

Third-party support At the heart of Weber's treatment of legitimacy is the idea of a morally inspired suspension of judgment by
those subject to commands. This approach roots legitimacy firmly
in the realm of meanings. Arthur Stinchcombe (1968, pp. 158–59)
sets out to rethink the issue of legitimacy by challenging both of
these elements.[9] He tells us: *"A power is legitimate to the degree
that . . . the power-holder can call upon sufficient other centers
of power, as reserves in a case of need, to make his power effective . . ."* [Italics in original] (p. 162).

Stinchcombe shifts the referent of legitimacy from the field of
meanings to the realm of social structure. He is less concerned
with legitimacy as an "estimation of the state of public opinion or
of . . . ideological enthusiasm" than with its manifestation in
social interactions. He also focuses concern away from the subject
of commands to the "contingency" of third-party support; from
"the acceptance of subordinates" to "the reactions of other
centers of power." In effect, Stinchcombe tells us that a key structural manifestation of legitimacy is the backing for commands by
other mobilized groups ("other centers of power"). He regards
this as more vital than compliance by those "who must take the
consequences."

He provides a graphic example of his support-of-third-party
approach to legitimacy:

A policeman . . . has power to jail a man who objects to the
degree that, when he has difficulty taking him to jail, other police-
men or the governor and the National Guard regard the arrest as legitimate. And the man stays arrested only if a grand jury and a petit
jury can be convinced of the legitimacy of the arrest. The reason a
policeman's authority comes to an end if the man is not indicted or
is not convicted, is that the policeman can no longer call on anyone
to back him up when the man wants to leave jail. In fact, the man
himself can call on the power of the state to force the policeman to

let him go. The "authority" of the policeman thus consists of the probability that his action will be backed up by other concentrations of power, and it is limited because the conditions under which others will back him up are limited. (p. 159)

Stinchcombe, like Weber, views legitimacy as linked mainly to downward processes. The main issue is how to make straight the path of political power. Yet, as we saw in chapter 2, legitimacy is also important for upward processes, that is, for the justification of political influence. Which groups are permitted to organize for political action and the types of confidence and demand they are allowed to generate requires legitimation too. In Stinchcombe's terms, this means that a group's attempt at political influence also depends on the legitimacy provided by "other centers of power," who are willing to back up its right to participate in political life.

What can we learn from considering Stinchcombe's reformulation? First, although there is no reason to turn legitimacy into a structural concept, Stinchcombe's work highlights backing by third parties as a key structural manifestation of legitimacy. Second, this manifestation applies less to support for a particular action (i.e., a specific command), but more to lining up behind classes of actions (i.e., the moral appropriateness of issuing sets of commands). Third, both influence and social control are facilitated by third-party support. When a national executive can count on the backing of the military, the parliament, and powerful groups outside of the state, it is endowed with a clear manifestation of legitimacy. Similarly, the ability of a macrosolidary group, an association, or an organization to call on backing for its right to exercise influence is also a manifestation of legitimacy.

The hardest legitimational problem for democratic polities is the right of defeated factions to try again. The language of third-party support is especially instructive here. Focusing on legitimacy solely in symbolic terms gives the impression that once a democratic creed is pervasive, the right of dissenters to dissent is never challenged. Nothing is further from the truth. Democracy is an "unnatural" state of affairs. Given the adversary nature of politics, we can never assume that one faction accepts the rights of its opponents with equanimity, regardless of lofty political themes. After all, the opposition is the "enemy" and they are advocating "error" (and perhaps they are after my job!). Therefore, a thoroughly legitimated democratic system needs periodic structural manifestations that third parties are willing to protect the advocates of "error." Ordinarily, the state itself plays a third-party role. (The courts in the American system are especially important.) Perhap the most perturbing aspect of the Watergate scandal is how far a national executive abdicated its responsibilities as a third-party guarantor of political rights and moved to deprive its "enemies" of the means to oppose.

To sum up: The ability to call upon third parties in the support of political actions is one structural manifestation of legitimacy. All else being equal, as the prospects for third-party backing become greater, social control increases in effectiveness and political influence becomes more efficient. The ability to count on allies reduces the probability that initiatives will be resisted. Thus, the state's ability to set, pursue, and implement goals expands. The American Civil War shows that a government cannot automatically count on crucial third-party support. Conversely, the presence of powerful forces who recognize a group's right to exert political influence inhibits those who might conspire to impede political participation. The growing backing for the right of black Americans to engage in the political process shows how a structural manifestation of legitimacy may make one group's political influence more efficient.

To keep this discussion within manageable boundaries, I have avoided introducing intermember power into the analysis. Let me note here that intermember power, like political power, is ordinarily less alienating if it is legitimated. Thus, third-party backing is probably a key structural manifestation of legitimacy in this domain of power too. Think, for instance, of the exploitative nature of management-worker relations during the early stages of capitalism and how this was backed by the coercive powers of the government and police, the strike-breaking injunctions of the courts, and antilabor pronouncements of moral and religious leaders. These manifestations suggest capitalist exploitation was probably widely legitimated during much of the nineteenth century.

Smoothness of political succession The smoothness of political succession is a second structural manifestation of legitimacy that may have a direct bearing on the viability of a polity. For Max Weber, the succession crisis is the principal event in the evolution of a revolutionary charismatic movement into a routine political order. In effect, Weber suggested that the viability of an established system depends (in part) on its ability to regularize the turnover in leadership, The problem is acute when the founder of the charismatic movement departs. Nevertheless, simply because successors are bureaucrats or traditionalistic leaders is no guarantee that routinized polities are more adept at handling political turnover. England's War of the Roses is an example of a succession crisis in a traditional order; the disruptions in the Communist Party of the Soviet Union after the death of Stalin is an example of a succession crisis in a bureaucratic one.

Legitimacy and succession are deeply intertwined. How the replacement for a charismatic leader is selected (by the drawing of lots, hereditary succession, or bureaucratization) helps shape whether a new system is legitimated in more traditional or in more rational-legal directions. Moreover, Weber implies that successful implementation of rules of succession is an important structural manifestation (indeed, a structural safeguard) of the new system. On the other hand, the unwillingness of key actors to accept rules regarding the circulation of political factions is a good indication of low regard for the entire system. Lyndon Johnson's smooth assumption of office following John F. Kennedy's assassination in November 1963 was considered normal by Americans, even in the emotional turmoil of the moment. Of course, there was nothing natural or normal about it. Johnson had been peripheral to the real power centers of the administration. Robert F. Kennedy, and not he, had been the second most powerful figure. Johnson's succession presaged the political decline of the Attorney General as well as of others in the Kennedy administration. Yet, Johnson's succession was never in doubt, nor was it challenged by either palace intrigue or the threat of a coup d'état. (It is illuminating to compare the unimpeded accession of Johnson in 1963 to Brzezinski and Huntington's account of Khrushchev's difficult struggle to the top after the death of Stalin in 1953 [1964, pp. 235–52]).

The smooth transition from Kennedy to Johnson is a structural manifestation of the moral approval of the system and its rules. Yet, smooth succession is more than a good indicator of legitimacy. The ability of a political system to avoid turmoil over the transfer of political power has important ramifications for its effectiveness and efficiency—and hence for its viability.

On the face of it, democratic polities seem to encounter the stresses of competition and succession most painfully. After all, they mandate periodic elections that raise the specter of a turnover in leadership. Indeed, for Lipset, "uninterrupted continuation of political democracy since World War I" is one of two key dimensions of "political stability" (1959, pp. 45–76). He believes that the inability to abide by the rules of succession demonstrates the existence of disruptive fissures within a polity that undermine its success. Although Lipset's indicator may be invalid for nondemocratic systems, his emphasis does alert us to how crucial smooth succession is for a democracy.

Nondemocratic sytems also face the problem of power struggle and succession. In fact, the absence of routines for succession is less a blessing than a burden. Brzezinski and Huntington regard the failure to provide a fixed term of office for the First Secretary of the Communist Party in the Soviet Union as a major source of instability (1964, pp. 182–90). They see the American system of regularized, prevacancy selection of leaders as more stable. In the Soviet system, opposition factions are deprived of institutionalized access to power (e.g., a mandated election for a First Secretary). Thus, they are compelled to resort to plotting and clandestine intrigues which may border on planning of coups d'état. Vacancies occur at the top only as the result of death (Lenin, Stalin) or because transient coalitions oust a leader (Khrushchev). Officially, the struggle for power never takes place. The informal struggle remains largely submerged until a leader shows weakness or a vacancy opens at the top. Brzezinski and Huntington report:

In the Soviet Union, the struggle for the top position automatically occurs when the position becomes vacant and involves the top Party leaders. Whatever his subjective, personal desires, a Soviet leader who is in the Party Presidium cannot escape the struggle for power. He must either compete for the position himself or identify himself with someone who is competing. Whatever his choice, his political and perhaps personal future is at stake. He cannot stand aside or retreat into neutrality. Having reached the top of the political ladder, he must engage in a Hobbesian war of all against all until a new Leviathan has emerged. (p. 237)

The inability of totalitarian polities to legitimate factional struggle weakens their effectiveness. During protracted struggle, the ship of state may founder, and payoff may become unpredictable. In the Soviet Union, for example, this has been so because the struggle takes place inside the government and in the absence of input from legitimated external constituencies. The competition is among leaders over who can shape policy rather than in appeals to the public. "Victories and defeats in the struggle for power," according to Brzezinski and Huntington, are ". . . directly reflected in the direction of government policy . . ." (p. 267). Key societal problems may be ignored in the fury of political infighting, strategic decisions may be delayed or not made at all; policies are advanced, espoused, or opposed simply to outmaneuver one's enemies in the government; foreign-policy initiatives may be erratic and hence diminish credibility with other states.

The failure to manifest legitimacy in turnover and succession impedes political efficiency too. Once again, strains occur more commonly in totalitarian systems. The effects of a succession crisis on efficient influence resemble our other structural manifestation, third-party backing.

Succession impinges on the efficiency of political influence through whether or not third-parties support the right of factions to enter a prevacancy competition. Insofar as the power struggle remains hidden, that is, without official sanctioning, as in the Soviet Union, such support cannot be counted upon. The advocates of opposition and "error" at best retain a dubious legitimacy; these factions must rely on guile and intrigue to marshall support. Their participation in the influence process is convoluted, costly, and highly unpredictable. Finally, defeat carries with it no promise of the right to try again. It usually guarantees just the opposite.

Summary:
Legitimacy and Viability

I have tried to show that legitimacy is an important ingredient of political viability, but in a quite different way than effectiveness and efficiency. The difference stems largely from the fact that legitimacy, as an aspect of political culture, is logically external to political structures. First of all, legitimacy is important because it forms the moral grounding upon which members evaluate their system. Subjective judgments mold action and hence feed back on objective functioning. Second, legitimacy implies a willingness to allow certain political processes to be carried out without interference. In the past few pages, I have examined two key structural manifestations of legitimacy: the availability of third-party backing and the smoothness of political succession. The presence of both indicates the existence of strategic reservoirs of moral approval in the polity; and both facilitate the effective exercise of social control and the efficient incorporation of political influence.[10]

Conclusions:
Political Viability
in The Modern World

This chapter has outlined the key ingredients of a viable polity. The categories of effectiveness, efficiency, and legitimacy provide a framework within which the success of different systems can be judged. Most of my examples have come from capitalist democracies (particularly the United States), but I have tried to move beyond the ethnocentric biases that haunted earlier studies of "political stability." I hope political viability can now be examined with less chance of ideological acrimony.

Underlying this discussion has been the assumption that modern society is preeminently political society. This chapter touched on the many reasons for this. Perhaps the most important one is the growing demand for payoff which typifies our times. Nowhere in the world are people content with the lot their parents or grandparents accepted. They expect the modern state to redistribute income, improve the delivery of health and educational services, preserve the environment from the excesses of industrialism and consumerism, while simultaneously curtailing the evils of state bureaucracy. Moreover, in democratic societies at least, the weaker competitors in the political struggle regard the state as the guarantor of their political rights. Paradoxically, this third-party role enhances state power, potentially the greatest threat to political rights, all the more.

The character of intermember power has also promoted political power. The absolutist monarchies of the seventeenth and eighteenth centuries were weakened by the evolution of intermember power. In contrast, today's intermember power has helped expand the role of the state. All competitors for intermember power want state intervention; they only disagree about the form that intervention should take.

"Postindustrial" theorists use such labels as postcapitalist, technochronic, postcivilized, postmodern, or postindustrial to explain the process. (For a review of these see Bell 1973, pp. 49–54.) Whatever their differences, they locate the source of growing state intervention in contemporary intermember processes. They focus particularly on the stresses created by economic changes—shifts in occupational structures, technologies, knowledge accumulation, and so on. But "postindustrial" factors are not the whole story. Our inability to surmount past intermember stresses also has an impact. We need only recall that racial justice has been a key source of state intervention in our own society. Race problems stem not from the postindustrial present but from the conflicts of a feudal (Southern agrarian) part. Consequently, the exigencies of late- or postindustrialism alone do not account for the growth of political power.

The indeterminacy of intermember power has also helped expand political power. Modern stratification systems are in flux. Neither Marxian nor Weberian categories can fully explain what is going on. A major realignment in the macrosolidary groupings of advanced societies is a possibility. As intermember power blurs, political power expands to fill the void. Today, the state offers many of the welfare services that in the past were the preserve of kinship groups, communities, or their organizational or associational arms.

To conclude, modern political power is anything but epiphenomenal. It grows in scope and pervasiveness. It is a source of hope and a presence to be feared. Hence, a fuller grasp of its morphology and dynamics, and of its limitations and potential, is essential for those who wish to harness its energies to alleviate human misery.

Part Four

Epilogue

chapter seven

The Limits to Transformation

Men make their own history, but they do not make it just as they please; they do not make it under circumstances chosen by themselves, but under circumstances directly encountered, given and transmitted from the past. The tradition of all dead generations weighs like a nightmare on the brain of the living.

—Karl Marx, *The 18th Brumaire of Louis Bonaparte*

IN the opening chapter I called for a tighter linking of theory and *praxis*. Yet, the failed hopes of the 1960s tempt one to belittle the prospect. After all, isn't the lesson of this shift in mood that deliberate change is not so easy as it seemed back then? Humane values and good ideas alone cannot melt ingrained inequities and discontent. Still, while good intentions do not magically overcome resistance, the probing for comprehensive change does not have to be mere wishful thinking. If the lesson of dashed hopes is that transformation is never easy, the message of the macrosociology of politics is that it is possible.

But what is the lesson of macrosociology? In fact, there is more than one. In this final chapter I want to focus on the bearing of sociological theory on successful policy. I shall suggest that macrosociological theory is most helpful in tracing the boundaries to transformation but less handy for finding specific policy levers. I shall describe three key elements of the macrosociological message: (1) change is possible; (2) macrosociology helps identify zones of malleability; and (3) macrosociology can zero in on the deep-seated barriers to successful change.

The Bearing
of Sociological Theory
on Policy Analysis

Sociological theory consists of a set of abstract concepts organized into statements called propositions. Ideally, propositions form a hierarchic system and are logically related to one another. The aim of concepts, propositions, and theory is to summarize and explain apparently disparate processes in the "real world." Policy analysis is far less abstract than theory. It is concerned more with particular problems and actions and less with classes of problems or actions. The aim of theory is to explain what is in the most general terms possible. The goal of policy analysis is to spell out what can be as concretely as possible. Policy analysis "is concerned with mapping alternative approaches and with specifying potential differences in the intention, effect, and cost of various programs" (Etzioni 1971, p. 8).

Abstract sociological theory is not an ideal guide to social-policy formation. "Grand" theory, whether Parsonian, Marxian, or somewhere in between, can gauge the theoretical possibilities for deliberate change. It can also be helpful for defining the constraints that limit the success of policies. But theory based on abstract terms does not lend itself directly to the solution of specific problems. Before such formulations can have any impact, they must be translated. Two steps are essential. First, the dimensions underlying each concept must be spelled out. Specification must be in the direction of lower levels of abstraction than the original category. Second, one or more valid empirical indicators for each dimension must be found. The effectiveness of social policy increases the more it is based on valid social measurements and the more it is evaluated in terms of such procedures. (See Lehman 1971.)

Theory need not be pessimistic or conservative, especially if we recognize its strengths and limitations. Yet, the fact that it can better pinpoint the constraints on deliberate change than locate the levers for particular changes might give such an impression.

Both Marxians and neoconservatives are pessimistic about the prospects for social policy that works. Their pessimism has different roots; but one feature they have in common is the quality of their theorizing. Neither approach is deeply interested in detailing the less abstract dimensions of concepts nor in their valid measurement. That is, Marxians as well as neoconservatives are partial to abstract theory and tend to be commentators on empirical research rather than practitioners. Marxians are less intrinsically pessimistic (and somewhat more research-oriented) but see effective change as possible only in the context of a transforming revolution. The alleviation of underlying miseries within capitalism is impossible, they feel, in light of the contradictions of the prevailing system.

Neoconservatives, such as Daniel Bell, Irving Kristol, Nathan Glazer, and Robert Nisbet, are more fundamentally pessimistic, for they are dubious about successful change before or after revolutions. It is no accident that these thinkers are conversant in classical "grand" theory and rarely carry out empirical work of their own. They are adept at invoking Tocqueville, Durkheim, Weber, Mannheim, and even Marx. But, as I have indicated, these formulations do not lend themselves to the immediate explication of policy. Rather, they are better suited for explaining why the "exteriority and constraint" of the larger system often washes out the efforts of social planners.

So long as we keep before us what theory can and cannot accomplish, it may be of significant value for those concerned with social policy. A recognition of the limits of what can be accomplished is itself a worthwhile contribution—at the very least, it reins an unbridled utopianism that leads to dashed hopes. A sociological theorist who tells you how to leap from abstract concepts to *praxis* in one giant stride must be viewed with caution, if not incredulity.

We tend to associate such leaps with Marxian analysis. Yet, the most flagrant instance in recent times has been a jump from "establishment" theory. A requirement for "maximum feasible participation of the poor" in community antipoverty programs was added at the last minute to the 1964 Economic Opportunity Act. This mandate represented an effort to spell out the policy implications of the Mertonian theory of "social structure and anomie" (see 1968, pp. 185–248). But the hasty addition produced chaotic results, for it contained no clear definition of participation, no specification as to how it was to be effected, and no mechanisms for assessing its consequences. (For a detailed description of the project, see Moynihan 1969.)

Amitai Etzioni (1971, p. 11) has recommended an "in-between discipline," called policy science, to bridge the gap between theory and policy recommendations. Policy science would be a less formal, less analytical discipline. Its link to the analytical behavioral sciences (sociology, psychology, economics, political science, and so on) would be analogous to the relationship of engineering to physics, medicine to physiology, and international relations to economics, sociology, anthropology and political science. The last example is instructive since it is drawn from the social realm. It suggests that policy science must seek practical knowledge across established disciplines and must not depend on only one. Certainly, anyone attempting to run a mental health organization on the basis of Weber's model of bureaucracy will soon learn that practical experience is more useful. Information of this kind will have to be gleaned from several specialities. In a sense, policy science entails acquiring practical "tidbits" from such analytical areas as psychology, organizational theory, and political science.

This book has tried to show that not every branch of sociological theory is equally important to policy science. Macrosociology holds a special position. In the sections that follow, the prin-

cipal contributions of a macroscopic perspective to policy analysis
are outlined.

Change
is Possible

Chapter 1 identified three features of the macrosocial domain that
give it a big edge for *praxis:* the longevity of macrosocial forces,
their control of strategic resources, and their malleability. Each
declares the possibility of decisive change.

An item probably falls within the realm of macrosociology if
its life span is longer than that of the people who are involved at
any time. History feels the pull of societal, political, and cultural
factors, but is less affected by the idiosyncratic behaviors of individuals. This is the theoretical basis for the old bromide; "We are
all born into a world we didn't make."

But this assertion is not grounds for gloom. True, most
macrosocial forces predate and outlive us, and they tend not to
bend to personal styles. All the same, they are not immutable—
they are not the reflections of God's essence, or a part of the
ontological order, or the emanations of chemical or biologic factors. Those who see them in this way have ideological axes to
grind. (It goes without saying that these, more often than not, are
tilted in a conservative direction.) Of course, pessimism is not restricted to those who reduce macrosociology to theology, metaphysics, biology, or chemistry. There is a slide toward gloom
among sociologists who view society as a totality with the relationships among its parts given (or predetermined) by the nature of
the overarching system they form. Theories of this kind are often
fond of biological analogies (e.g., comparing the body's capacity
to maintain steady temperature despite changes in the environment
to society's tendency to control deviant behaviors or social movements) even while proclaiming the distinctiveness of social facts.

Their needless pessimism becomes explicit when social change is treated. Social change is viewed as possible, and even likely, but it is "mindless." The members of society are held to have a low capacity for transformation because they are "not in command"; societal processes and changes are seen as unconscious unfoldings under the sweep of large-scale, impersonal, and unmanageable forces.

However, no sociological view of society is ever totally bleak about the prospects for reasoned change. Even those practicing the kind of "collectivistic" sociology just outlined are more optimistic than those who reduce macrosociology to theology, metaphysics, chemistry, or biology. All sociological perspectives assume that however much human actors are the creatures of society, they also serve as its creators, for the ultimate stuff of social life is human interaction (as it is manifested in the relations of individuals and groups). Thus, although we did not mold today's world, our actions, and the actions of the groups we belong to, sustain, modify, weaken, or overthrow the existing order. Paradoxically, even if we did not *make* the world we live in, we *are* the world we live in and hence the creators of tomorrow's world.

Unmediated individual initiatives may produce changes on the micro level, but are hardly the vehicles for overhauling society. Individualistic self-help philosophies that allege that by "lighting one little candle" you uplift yourself and redirect history are therefore wildly off the mark. You are more likely to burn your fingers than to ignite the fabric of society. The search for personal improvement and transcendence may make you a different, perhaps better, person; it may make your friendship groups, work cliques, and family life richer. But it cannot locate and defuse the major sources of misery and discontent.

If society is to be redirected, it will be because of the activities of those macroscopic actors capable of exercising and reorganizing political power, political influence, and intermember power and privilege. Only they have the longevity and tenacity to prevent efforts from being washed out by larger historic forces. For example, every attempt by individual physicians to provide better

quality care, to charge fairer fees, and to become more responsive
to the nonmedical needs of patients is laudable; but these private
efforts will not change the delivery of health services. The entire
American health system must be altered before it can provide better and more comprehensive care, become more economical, and
benefit from increased citizen input and professional sensitivity to
the psychosocial needs of patients. This can only be accomplished
by political activity that affects the system's macroscopic actors—
major medical centers, pharmaceutical companies, insurance companies, hospital associations, and key federal agencies.

Change is also possible because most of the resources necessary for transformation are found on the macro level. If we recall
the groups discussed in the last chapter (the national executive, the
military, organizations and associations, and political parties), we
realize that the principal assets they wield belong to them and are
not the property of micro actors. Regardless of whether we choose
coercive, utilitarian, or normative resources (or some combination)
for history making, the ones chosen, in all probability, will reside
in the macroscopic realm.

This is heartening. For the first time in history the instruments
for reshaping the societal landscape either exist or are feasible.
The disheartening fact is that to date these assets have been employed largely for destructive purposes. Insofar as they have begun
to make a difference in the political sector, it has been mainly for
subverting real change. After all, Watergate is, to some degree,
the outcome of both long-range trends in American politics and organizational and technological innovations focusing on "image
management" and surveillance. Such capabilities become potent
weapons in the arsenal of totalitarian states, or, in our own case,
of groups with a predilection for repressive tactics.

Moreover, the resources for making history abound in the intermember rather than in the political domain. Most important
technological and administrative innovations have been cultivated
and refined by industrial and business interests for the sake of narrow economic advantage. There are those who believe that the
modern corporation's dependence on informational capacities will

lead to its transfiguration; that reliance on practical knowledge will change it from an agency pursuing private interests to one concerned with the needs of society and increasingly committed to the public interest. It seems to me that no trait of technical knowledge or informational capabilities, nor of the personnel who wield them, indicates that they can break the cycle of intermember power and privilege. The macroresources for redirecting society are neutral. In isolation, they tell us little about courses for the future. We must focus on the groups who use them—and the power contexts in which these groups operate. Only then are we able to speculate about their chances for reducing misery and discontent.

Finally, the malleability of macrosocial factors also promotes the prospects for change. To inquiry about malleability is to ask, "Can it be fixed?" The assumption that macrofactors are more easily modified than individual or microfactors has been a keystone of this analysis. Malleability is perhaps the most important concept macrosocial theory has to offer policy science. "Can it be fixed?" is only one of several issues in macrosociology; in policy science it is *the* central one. Because policy science is less analytical and draws from several disciplines, it is better than macrosociology (or economics or political science) at ranking factors by how well they can be modified. Yet, policy research is indispensable for a precise delineation of the most malleable factors in any situation as well as the conditions under which less malleable ones become more open to modification.

Zones
of Malleability

Macrosocial theory points us toward "zones of malleability," that is, to the types of factors most and least susceptible to fixing. Part 2 of this book focused on the choice of an organizing concept for a macrosociology of politics. I argued that we should not search for the levers to transformation in the realm of culture. Such a decision does not require an outright rejection of diagnoses suggesting that there is something amiss in America's moral, aesthetic, or ideological life. But remedies for these problems can only be prescribed by treating the structures of society and polity to make them more responsive to public need and to enforce our basic values.

Culture's glacial movement yields weak explanatory variables and points to items with low malleability. A macroscopic perspective tells us that power-structure factors explain more of the world and are more readily modified. Thus, macrosociology treats America's malaise primarily in organizational terms—although it does not make the spiritual dimension irrelevant.

Macrosociology also reminds us that not all aspects of structure are equally important for policy. In the modern world, the system of political power is decisive, for it represents the networks built around the setting, pursuit, and implementation of collective goals. A hallmark of advanced societies is the structural separation of political power from intermember power. If political power is to guide society, it must develop specialized structures and acquire a capacity to penetrate intermember power in order to check the vicious cycle of power and privilege, misery and discontent.

Macrosociological analysts agree that success within political systems depends on two sets of process. One is downward and focuses on the ability to develop policy and overcome resistance: I have called this social control. A viable political system includes effective agents to impose control. But it must also possess efficient upward mechanisms called political influence. A state's ability to act is only partly determined by its control of the public; it also depends on how closely the goals and means it has chosen coincide with those preferred by others. The term "responsiveness" is often used in this regard.

Limits
to Transformation

"Futurology" is a tricky business. The superior works in this field remain closer to informed prophecy than to scientific prediction. Thus, I am not going to engage in what Dennis Wrong derides as "the melodramatic prophetic mode that pervades contemporary culture and has by no means left the social sciences untouched" (1974a, p. 26). Instead, in the concluding pages, I will sketch some of the entrenched impediments to viability which constrain successful policy. I do not offer spanking new recommendations. My final remarks focus on the outer limits on pursuing societal change.

Let us begin by acknowledging that constraints do not evaporate with introductions of democratic institutions. Those of us trained in the Western tradition tend to see a vague bond between political viability and democracy. Actually, the relationship is subtle and precarious. It is unfortunate that many of those who have studied the association have obscured the issues by speaking about "democratic political stability." In the process, the notions of democracy and viability (or stability) have been fused into a single theoretical construct. Hence, democracy and viability are joined as a matter of definition. Their interplay dissolves into a nonproblem via a semantic device.

Real problems in the real world cannot be wished away by word games. Engaging in the political processes under democratic rules has some advantages, but it also seems to impose limits on greater viability. For example, in a study of sixty Western and Third World countries, Robert W. Jackman (1974, pp. 29–45) finds that political democracy, as indicated by such processes as electoral participation, political competition, and access to an uncontrolled mass media, exerts no significant effects on levels of societal inequality. This finding is not surprising if we recognize that Pluralist theory treats democracy as an upward phenomenon. But I have previously suggested that the success of a political system flows from effective downward processes too. Jackman's analysis reminds us that the redistribution of intermember power and privilege needs more than smoothing out the influence process. The democratization of influence is indispensable for making it more efficient; but it is no substitute for the capacity to develop social policy, nor for the ability to make it stick.

Reaffirming our commitment to democracy, therefore, will not suffice. In the remaining pages I consider attributes of social control and political influence that foster deeper resistances to transformation—that is, the limits imposed by both downward and upward processes. I also touch on the limits to viability arising from the fact that modern polities are part of a larger ("global") network of intermember power.

Downward Processes

The preceding chapter argued that the principal downward problem of contemporary polities is the spiralling pressure for payoff. The state's need to demonstrate effectiveness is now the core feature of political life. How can it keep pace with demand? Even greater centralization looks like the most handy remedy. In America, for instance, this would lead to one national planning agency for each sector of society (e.g., a U.S. national health service). But while solving old problems, this approach is a source of new ones. In theory, greater centralization promotes more rational, comprehensive, and rapidly formed policy. Without question, our polity would benefit from better coordinated planning. Yet, in practice, centralized planning may stimulate unresponsiveness, insensitivity, and even ineffectiveness.

State bureaucracies tend to be external. They form control centers outside the "action-space" of the actors they coordinate. This externality fosters unresponsiveness. State bureaucracies are set apart from the others in a polity, and this makes it hard for them to incorporate what the public wants and feels. The rationality and professionalism that mark the modern bureaucracy only widen the gap. In all advanced societies, the feeling prevails that the government does not listen to local communities or even to local leaders. The extreme form of this unresponsiveness occurs in totalitarian systems, where the conventional mechanisms of political influence are turned upside down, into means of political control. But the American experience in the past decade suggests that unresponsiveness is neither transient nor trivial in democracies.

Externality also promotes insensitivity. An insensitive system is one that treats the targets of control mechanically, as objects of manipulation. A major feature of bureaucratic control is the production and processing of records. Now, in an industry that manufactures standardized items (such as cars), a product and the records about it are linked intrinsically. However, in social policy the raw materials being processed are often people and groups— hardly standardized items. The link between product and record thus becomes more problematic, and commonly the two become confused. The stated aim of health services, for example, is to make the sick well. Unfortunately, the bureaucratic imperative frequently succeeds in making the record, not health, the ultimate product. In some medical settings, social reality is constructed in terms of an arbitrary case record and not the real needs of patients.[1]

Insensitivity is, of course, linked to unresponsiveness. But the two are analytically, and at times empirically, distinct. The concept of insensitivity makes us ask whether a political system treats the public as subjects or objects and hence whether social policy is best processed via the strategy and tactics used in producing cars or toasters. The concept of responsiveness focuses on whether political power promotes or impedes influence. State bureaucracies that treat citizens with the same logic as inanimate objects probably also resist public demands. Still, the relationship between insensitivity and unresponsiveness is not one-to-one, and the nature of their association undoubtedly is modified by other political, societal, and cultural factors.[2]

Centralized coordination also threatens effectiveness. The most serious constraint is the phenomenon of goal displacement, a mirror image of goal multiplication and succession, discussed in chapter 6. (See Merton 1968, pp. 249–60.) Goal displacement involves a zeal for bureaucratic techniques that leads to slavish veneration for administrative rules and a neglect of official goals. Under such circumstances, concern is diverted from policy making to the refinement of organizational routines. Goal displacement in an organization interferes with its adjustment because it loses the "bounce" needed to cope with situations not envisaged by existing rules. The irrationality of our foster care bureaucracies, staffed by persons with impeccable humanitarian credentials, is a prime illustration of this organizational pathology. Organizational routines tend to keep children in foster care rather than return them to biological parents or place them in adoptive homes.

Goal displacement further increases ineffectiveness because it makes a bureaucracy more external. In fact, goal displacement and externality each reinforce the most negative features of the other. A bureaucracy's external position raises the chances that it will cope with new problems through ritualistic dependence on standard operating procedures. Attempts to explore the etiology of emerging problems will be discouraged. Conversely, when an agency stresses bureaucratic routines, it ignores the nonstandardized nature of citizens; thus the gulf between state and public widens, and the agency's external status hardens.

However, even if the state scotches goal displacement, its external character raises obstacles to effectiveness. Not all are impediments to the upward transmission of demands; some hinder the downward transmission of perspectives. A state benefits from downward transmission because this reduces differences in outlook among different parts of the public. The ability to bridge constituencies or to build consensus strengthens a bureaucracy's chances of bringing about significant change. If the state lacks this ability, and if it aims for substantial impact, it may be tempted to make policy that coincides with the prevailing structure of power. This neutralizes the strongest hotbeds of potential resistance. The temptation is most pronounced when a power center seeks immediate results, as new governments, administrations, or regimes are likely to do. The pursuit of immediate gains is enhanced when decisions favor the powerful. The New Deal succeeded in some measure because enlightened elements of American business went along, since they stood to gain from FDR's policies.

In short, centralized state bureaucracies, which at first glance seem to be a boon, actually are subject to pressures that make success questionable. On the one hand, to be truly transforming, a bureaucracy must have sufficient clout to reshape intermember power. On the other hand, an agency often needs tangible results. It can better obtain them when policies coincide with the existing contours of power. Paradoxically, then, centralized control tends to drift away from comprehensive planning toward piecemeal decisions that foster the prevailing distribution of power and privilege (however much the resources in society are expanded).

This implies that centralized coordination is hardly a complete answer to spiralling demand. Imagine, for example, what would happen if a national health service began to allocate resources in favor of the less privileged (the poor, the elderly, the medically indigent, and such providers as municipal hospitals and nonuniversity voluntary hospitals) at the expense of the more privileged (the affluent, elite providers such as university medical centers). The privileged would generate enough opposition to undermine the implementation of the policy. The opposition's rationale would be that elite providers have greater capabilities (human and material, professional and administrative) for effective and economic use of newly available resources (e.g., research grants, new programs or services). The less privileged, they would tell us, "waste" such resources. In other words, opposition, they would argue, is justified because elites offer a more rational use of assets.

Mixed planning is advocated by some to lessen the side-effects of bureaucratic power. Such recommendations try to keep the baby and throw out the bathwater by proposing centralized coordination which sets broad policy but assigns responsibility and resources for implementation as close to the local level as possible. On the face of it, this plan seems to retain the benefits of comprehensive planning while allowing specific decisions to be made closer to home. But there are limitations here too. To begin with, a bureaucracy is a bureaucracy regardless of geographic proximity. A local bureaucracy is liable to be as external to the action-space of citizens as a national one; externality speaks of sociological and not physical distance. Moreover, local control means more bureaucracy not less, because mixed planning elaborates bureaucratic layers rather than diminishes them. New local agencies are linked with the rise of central ones to coordinate their activities. Thus, the bureaucratic dilemmas outlined above may be sharpened rather than resolved. The fact that, in American history at least, local power has been more corrupt, less competent, and more particularistic further complicates matters.

Finally, political cohesion is also threatened by an unreflective enthusiasm for local control. Heterogeneous societies are marked by diversity among localities and regions. These differences in traits and interests are, by themselves, a potential source of political disintegration. Centralized state power is a check on dissolution in all modern polities. Local control entails some shift of responsibility and resources away from political cohesion and toward local diversity. If political power backs up local diversity too strongly, the chances for concerted political action decline. In the extreme, it may strengthen neofeudal (or neoanarchist) forces; here, central authority becomes a facade and a mere creature of local potentates.

Of course, the probability that Western democracies will disintegrate into feudal fiefdoms is more remote than are the dangers of totalitarianism. (The twentieth century, after all, has witnessed a surge in the latter direction more than in the former.) Yet, centrifugal forces exist in many modern societies, as witnessed by the cultural, ethnic, or linguistic tensions wracking Yugoslavia, Great Britain, Canada, Belgium, and even Switzerland. Backing diversity with state power is a risky business. Political disintegration or neofeudalism may not be just down the road, but regression to even the level of political activation of the pre-New Deal United States could be disastrous in light of current problems.

Upward Processes

Unequal influence In the previous chapter, I argued that the persistence of unequal influence is the greatest block to upward political processes.

The less privileged have fewer resources and skills; hence political mobilization is exceedingly costly for them. Their political participation is lower or more episodic. As long as vast differences in intermember power and privilege continue, striking variations in political involvement are inevitable. Some mechanisms for dampening the extreme manifestation of unequal influence are possible. Universal suffrage, for example, has played a significant role. Yet, in the final analysis, there are tendencies to inequality in all influence, even the electoral process.

A polity's existing mechanisms of influence often magnify unequal privilege. Historically, mechanisms have rarely been neutral. Most frequently, the rules governing political influence have been slanted in favor of elites in general, and older elites in particular. The pattern is found even in electoral politics. Restrictions on the franchise are the most blatant examples of how electoral rules enlarge the influence of the privileged. Voting barriers based on property, wealth, region, religion, race, sex, and age have been too common to require further elucidation. The composition of the Estates-General at the beginning of the French Revolution, the persistence of rotten boroughs in Britain into the nineteenth century, and the overrepresentation of whites and men in state and federal legislatures in the United States, all illustrate how electoral mechanisms can perpetuate the political influence of declining elites. (Some defenders of democratic politics see advantages to retaining certain areas of disproportional representation. Certainly, no serious opposition exists to the composition of the U.S. Senate, which gives all states, regardless of population, two seats. Moreover, prospects for the reform or abandonment of the Electoral College seem to be receding, as of this writing.)

Rules governing suffrage and representation do not exhaust

the ways existing mechanisms can distort influence. The nature of delegated authority makes all representation disproportional. Since procedures must be created to allow a few to act the many, not all the attributes and interests of the public can be reflected perfectly in its representatives. Even if all authorities were chosen by statisticians using random sampling techniques, we know that some variations on selected characteristics between sample and population would probably appear. All mechanisms of influence in the "real world" are infinitely more distorting.

Moreover, some disproportional representation is intrinsic to democratic processes. Democratic polities usually contain parties with multiple and skewed constituencies. When such systems work, political actors draw support from across camps, but the composition of any given party is not a replica of society as a whole or of other parties. The same groups may be represented in all or most parties, but rarely in the same ratios. Since there are winners and losers in each political contest, those on top after a particular competition speak for a distorted cross-section of society. The "rhythm of democratic politics" (see chapter 6) can contain the extreme effects of this form of disproportional representation. Yet, the rhythm is not automatic and neither are its beneficial effects. Hence it is improbable that representatives ever precisely mirror all the interests "below" at a given moment. Indeed, if they did, it would be a sign that something was amiss with the democratic process.[3]

Up to now, I have sketched a static picture of the problem. Although all stratification systems are in flux, those in Western societies have experienced more change than the average, and, hence, the fit between political and intermember power systems becomes more difficult. New groups or those experiencing rapid change in intermember power find access to political influence more difficult than established ones. Prevailing political structures, including the state, generally reflect accommodations to older patterns of intermember power and influence. Thus, not only does lower intermember power mean less influence, but in addition, the morphology of political power mirrors yesterday's intermember power configurations, not today's. In short, the organization of the polity tends to fall behind changes in the rest of society. Strains become acute when intermember power changes rapidly.

If systems of intermember power were macrosociological see-saws, this lag would be all to the good. Groups who were down today would still have influence reflecting a more privileged past and vice versa. Yet, modern systems of inequality are marked by the periodic emergence or expansion of new groups and the slippage or disappearance of others. This change has long-term, detrimental consquences. There are no "mindless' mechanisms for catching up or for smoothing out the lag. It is an abiding aspect of modern politics. No single reform can permanently overcome the strain. At best, reforms help the polity to catch up more quickly.

Of course, polities are not doomed to be exploded by new intermember power as the forces of production explode the relations of production in Marxian theory. To argue in this manner would mean surrender to the collectivism criticized earlier in the chapter. If political power is to be more viable, then authorities must increasingly anticipate and guide the contours of tomorrow's intermember power. Nevertheless, no system, not even the most ruthlessly totalitarian, has yet developed such a capability.

Direct action The persistence of unequal access makes it likely that all segments of a society are sometimes dissatisfied with the political order. At least a few disaffected groups will charge that injustices exist in political influence. When disaffections become intense, a temptation to resort to direct action develops. The array of potential noninstitutionalized outlets is broad. In our own country they range from such quasi-legal activities as demonstrations and sit-ins all the way to the pursuit of violent overthrow of existing systems (by, for example, the Weather Underground, the Black Liberation Army, and the Symbionese Liberation Army). In the discussion that follows, I focus on direct action which stays on this side of revolution.

While institutionalized mechanisms of influence constrain efficiency, so do the efforts to circumvent them. Both the "excesses'' of direct action and the efforts to avoid them hinder political viability. The sociological study of direct action has most commonly focused on social movements.[4] These treatments usually make a point of differentiating social movements from workaday organizations or interest groups. The former are seen as the expressions of discontent with routine political processes. Whether they are radical, liberal, conservative, or reactionary, social movements reject current policies as, at best, too incremental. (This is not to say that all social movements advocate the same levels of transformation. Smelser's [1963] distinction between value-oriented and norm-oriented movements has become a sociological shorthand for comparing more transforming and less transforming movements.)

Differences in structure also set off social movements from routine organizations or interest groups. Social movements are not strictly complex organizations. True, there is often a complex organization at the hub of a movement (e.g., the Southern Christian Leadership Conference in the Montgomery bus boycott). But the movement has access to other followers who, by most criteria, are not organizational members. The availability of this loosely attached mass is what gives a social movement its propensity for direct action. Compared to mere organizations, movements are better at churning up crowds, carrying on demonstrations, and conducting ''confrontation politics.'' Even the organization at the center of a movement displays less bureaucratization. At points of peak functioning, social movements are marked by intense activation by participants, both organizational members and followers. This activation is possible because most participants are true believers; they are the persuaded, not the induced or constrained.

As I noted in chapter 6, Gamson (1975) has found that movements that indulge in ''unruly'' behavior receive more acceptances and advantages than pacific challenging groups. Yet, the noninstitutional character of all social movements poses difficulties for efficient political influence. The very act of stepping outside of existing channels further distorts the upward flow of demands and confidence. This is the core dilemma of left-wing forces in liberal democracy: to engage in electoral politics is to relinquish hope in short-cut transformation in favor of civility, bargaining, and gradualism; to abandon the democratic route is to ensure the electoral triumph of law-and-order elements committed to the status quo or to tokenism. In this latter instance, the success of entrenched elites is advanced, not only because transforming forces have deserted the electoral arena but also because direct action appalls "respectable" people, who might otherwise be sympathetic. Efforts to straddle the fence can have more dire consequences than choosing one alternative or the other, as the history of the Allende regime in Chile demonstrates.

Social movements that opt for direct action to affect policy face additional quandaries. Their initial nonbureaucratic character is one. The intense enthusiasm associated with a social movement at its inception is useful for mobilizing dormant constituencies. But total reliance on enthusiasm dims the prospects for a lasting impact. Without institutionalization, the long-range commitments necessary for sustained policy input is hard to achieve. The student radicals of the 1960s failed to learn several lessons; but their organizational illiteracy was perhaps their greatest weakness.

On the other hand, institutionalization robs a social movement of its moral energy. Leaders become functionaries, activists paid staff, and followers disappear into the passive periphery. The social movement is now just an interest group. Many have written of this phenomenon, but none more lucidly than Max Weber, who spoke of the "routinization of charisma." Essentially, to routinize means to reenter the official political game through the back door while giving tepid lip-service to the rhetoric of direct action. In the end, social movements must choose between episodic activation with a faint hope of sporadic impact or sustained, albeit low-keyed, mobilization as one bureaucratic agent among many.

The choice of routinization not only has costs for the social movement but also for the larger network of political influence. While direct-action strategy disrupts the institutionalized channels of influence, the threat of collective protest sometimes generates greater responsiveness. The history of the U.S. labor movement, civil rights groups in the 1960s, and the women's suffrage movement in Great Britain in the early 1900s are examples of this. Direct action, judiciously employed, is an antidote for unequal influence. However, in striving for long-term impact, movements tend to bureaucratize. As just another organization with behavioral (if not symbolic) adherence to established procedures, champions of the weak lose the political edge they once enjoyed. Hence, their ability to check skewed influence gradually evaporates.

The proliferation of interest groups (through the routinization of political movements) also leads, some have suggested, to a "stalemate society." Daniel Bell argues that America is not a "mass society" because there is more participation today than ever before. Both on the local and national levels, the number of activist groups has multiplied in the past twenty years (Bell and Held 1969; Bell 1973, p. 160). This, Bell says, leads to a paradox: ". . . the greater the number of groups, each seeking diverse or competing ends, the more likelihood that these groups will veto one another's interests, with the consequent sense of frustration and powerlessness as such stalemates incur" (p. 160). In effect, Bell senses that we are reaching an organizational glut in the political marketplace. Stalemate erodes efficiency and effectiveness. But low success only spawns discontent, then more social movements, and ultimately more routinized organizations. Is Bell's pessimistic vision an abiding constraint in political life? Or is it only a backwash of the intense and unfulfilled activation of the 1960s? Only time will tell.

In short, some impediments to efficient political influence are endemic to the process itself. But others derive from attempts to correct institutionalized mechanisms that have become too rigid. Both the resort to direct action and its routinization can, under certain circumstances, hamper the development of more successful policy.

The global system In chapter 3 I said that proper use of the language of political and intermember powers requires the delineation of system-levels. What is political power on one level is intermember power on the next higher one. The power of a state within a society is political, but among societies it is intermember. This clarification is valuable when trying to grasp the contraints on transformation. Political power has become autonomous within modern societies—the most crucial element in them. But polities are nested in a global system where the exigencies of intermember power dominate and specialization in political power remains retarded.

The acclaim for Immanuel Wallerstein's *The Modern World-System* (1974) symbolizes the renewed interest in "global sociology" among macrosociologists. But, as Wallerstein demonstrates, the constraints from the world-system are hardly new, as any historian, economist, or student of international relations could have told us. American sociologists were lulled into overemphasizing the intrasocietal because of the bipolar world that emerged after World War II. Between 1945 and 1960, America and the Soviet Union did much as they pleased within their spheres of power. Global constraints were mainly those that one imposed on the other. No wonder American sociologists felt so comfortable with the terminology of social system and society and felt little need to look at the larger setting in which such actors were lodged.

The bipolar world is gone for good, having been the product of unique circumstances that arose after the collapse of the Axis powers. Formally, the international scene now looks more like Europe between the Congress of Vienna and World War I. The presence of the new, Third World nations, of course, makes the actual picture substantively more complex. Nevertheless, today's world system is one of multiple centers of power, shifting alliances, and local blocs of varying power and integration. No one nation or bloc can impose hegemony; but some nations, notably the United States and the Soviet Union, retain disproportionate political, military, and economic leverage.

The demise of bipolarism has been coupled with increased concern over availability of strategic resources, notably food and energy. No society is self-sufficient. There is a growing fear that there will not be enough to go around—or, at least, that the cost of resources will be so high so as to provoke a world depression or a world war. Some look for a "mindless" mechanism to save the day. For them "interdependence" has the same mystic resonances as "free enterprise" had at an earlier time. But Geoffrey Barrachlough notes that invoking interdependence in the face of international scarcity clouds the issue. He says: "No government, probably, rejects the concept of interdependence as such, provided it can secure it on its own terms. The question is how the terms are defined. We may all be in the same boat together; but the first question, notoriously, among shipwrecked mariners, is whom to throw to the sharks . . ." (1975, p. 24).

Today, the Hobbesian nightmare lurks closer to the surface on the international scene than in most intrasocietal settings. The record of international coordination—of enlivening the global capacity to pursue collective goals—has not been promising. The unchecked pains of the international cycle of intermember power-privilege pose a graver threat for the global system than the same cycles do in most modern nation-states.

Thus, the most massive constraints to transformation may come not from within nations but from the absence of a workable world-system. Unless international coordination expands in the coming decades, our struggles against misery and discontent may be futile. Yet, the struggle is not hopeless, for the relationship between the international system and individual states is not one-way. We know that subsystems can shape suprasystems on the societal level. Similarly, while the international order imposes constraints, a world made up of nations striving to be more effective, efficient, and legitimate may be a better one. Richard Rubinson (1976, pp. 638–59) has studied the effect of the world economy on inequality within societies. He found that "state strength" still affects levels of inequality. Thus, despite the impact of transnational forces, Rubinson's results indicate that the viability of polities continues to make a difference. Nation-states are not just pawns in the world-system.

The goals of a more viable polity and of a more viable world-system are not incompatible. Indeed, nation-states with enlarged confidence in their creative capacities are more capable of rising above the question of whom to throw to the sharks. More viable polities are probably the most reliable first step to a more viable world order.

Conclusions

Macrosociology's strength in locating the structural constraints to transformation should not fill us with dread, for it also tells us where the zones of malleability are. Moreover, when mixed with inputs from other analytical specialties, macrosociology helps policy science in its search for practical levers to change. Still, macrosociology cannot guarantee the success of policy. This may make us somber about history making, but, as Barrington Moore notes: "A somber view is not . . . a passive and fatalistic one. One task of human thought is to try to perceive what the range of possibilities may be in a future that always carries on its back the burden of the present" (1972, p. 193). Macrosociology can be a significant contributor to this task.

This chapter has been an argument for the sociological possibility of reasoned change. But it has also been a warning against the siren song of what Moore calls "static utopias." I discussed why the viability of polities tends to run down regardless of how initially effective and efficient they may be. In other words, no political arrangement is ideal for all time, although some are better than others. Since all contain the seeds of contradiction and potential destruction, the building of a more viable political system is not a temporary phase in human history. The effort is never complete, and failure becomes inevitable only if people view any project as a total success. In politics there is no beatific vision, only renewed stumbling and struggling for each generation. To treat political goals as a step to religious salvation is to freeze a transient accommodation into an eternal verity. Misery and discontent may be never-ending problems, but lightening the burden is a cause worth taking up and a torch worth passing on.

Notes

1. Why Macrosociology?

1. See Martin Jay's treatment of this issue in his study of the Frankfurt School (1973, especially pp. 83–84).

2. See Etzioni's treatment of longevity and concentration of resources (1968, pp. 52–53).

3. For a more recent sociological treatment of the Hobbesian problem, see Ellis (1971, pp. 692–703).

4. The phrase "who gets what, when, how" is from Lasswell (1936). For an overview of the two perspectives, see Gamson (1968, pp. 1–19).

5. A similar view of the two interpretations of America's "current crisis" is found in Steinfels (1976).

2. Political Culture

1. The basic statement of the Almond School may be found in Almond (1956, pp. 391–409). In addition, see Almond (1960, pp. 3–64), Almond (1963, pp. 3–10), Almond (1965, pp. 183–214), Almond and Powell (1966, especially pp. 21–25, 50–72), Almond and Verba (1963) and Pye and Verba (1965). However, the concept is by no means absent in other schools in political science. See, for example, Easton (1965, especially pp. 100–116).

For efforts at a general overview, see Kim (1964, pp. 313–36), Lehman

(1972a, pp. 361–70), and Pye (1973, pp. 65–76). Overviews on the general concept of culture are provided by Barber (1955), Kroeber and Kluckhohn (1952), and Kroeber and Parsons (1958).

2. See Lehman (1972a, pp. 361–70). This distinction between institutions and legitimations is taken from Berger and Luckmann (1966, pp. 47–123). I recognize the potential confusion in making the term "institution" an aspect of culture. Institutions ordinarily refer to structural properties or some mixing of structural and cultural properties. However, I feel it is more confusing to resort to additional neologisms and thereby obscure the Berger-Luckmann terminology on which the distinction is based. Political institutions include both rules about how the political system operates and values about how it ought to operate. This combination of cognitive and evaluative symbols brings us close to what many contemporary social scientists call "ideology." See Parsons (1951, pp. 348–59). For other discussions see Geertz (1964, pp. 47–76) and Sartori (1969b, pp. 398–411). I prefer to retain the label "political institutions" in this present context because the concept of ideology tends to blend institution and legitimation, which I see as worth keeping separate. My own recommendations on how to employ the concept of ideology are detailed later in this chapter.

3. The categories of responsive, dormant, totalitarian, and liberal institutions are derived under the influence of classifications offered by William Kornhauser and Amitai Etzioni. Kornhauser classifies societies as mass, communal, totalitarian, and pluralistic (1959, pp. 39–73), while Etzioni labels them as active, passive, totalitarian, or drifting (1968, especially pp. 466–68). The key difference between my approach and theirs is that they attempt to characterize societal structures, while I seek to portray political institutions as an aspect of political culture.

4. Weber's work, of course, remains fundamental (1960, pp. 4–13), but the concept pervades practically all of Parsons' work. (For an example of how it is used in his later work, see 1966.) For other recent sociological works that have relied heavily on the notion of legitimacy, see Blau (1964), Gamson (1968, pp. 127–35), Lipset (1960; 1963), Mitchell (1961), Stinchcombe (1968), and Wallerstein (1961). For general critiques of Weber's treatment of legitimacy and authority, see Parsons (1937, pp. 640–86), Bendix (1960, pp. 289–449), and Blau and Scott (1963, pp. 30–36) and Blau (1963, pp. 305–16). A recent effort to incorporate legitimacy into Marxian analysis is found in Habermas (1975).

5. On the nature of supramembership properties as distinct from membership properties, see Lehman (1971).

6. See, for example, Coser (1956), Dahrendorf (1959), and Ellis (1971, pp. 692–703). A detailed history of and apologia for the Normative School is to be found in Parsons (1937). Three works on modern sociological theory underscoring the ideological vortex within which it was forged are Bramson (1961), Nisbet (1966), and Gouldner (1970).

7. For a fuller treatment of specifications as one form of elaboration as well

as of other variants of the latter, see Kendall and Lazarsfeld (1950, pp. 148–58) and Hyman (1955, pp. 275–327). See also Stinchcombe's treatment of "environmental effects" (1968, pp. 201–32).

8. One theoretical tradition in the behavioral sciences has, however, consistently used general culture categories to account for variations in political behavior: the so-called Culture and Personality School. See, for example, Ruth Benedict's effort to explain Japanese political life largely in terms of general Japanese culture patterns in *The Chrysanthemum and the Sword* (1946). For an overview of this tradition, see Spiro (1968, pp. 558–63).

9. Sociological use of the notion of ideology does not come directly from Marxism, however. Mannheim (1936) is a more immediate influence.

3. Fundamentals of Social Power

1. Important recent works include: Alba (1972), Bachrach and Baratz (1962), Blau (1964), Cartwright (1959; 1965), Clark (1967; 1968), Coser (1976), Dahl (1957; 1968), Danzger (1964), Emerson (1962), Etzioni (1961; 1968), French and Raven (1960), Gamson (1968), Goode (1972), Hawley (1963), Kadushin (1968), Lehman (1969), Lenski (1966), March (1966), Olsen (1970), Parsons (1967a; 1967b; 1967c), Rogers (1974), Rose (1967), Schermerhorn (1951), Silvert (1970), Stinchcombe (1968), Westby (1966), and Wrong (1968). Slightly less recent but no less important are Barnard (1938), Bierstedt (1950; 1954), Goldhamer and Shils (1939), Lasswell and Kaplan (1950), and Neumann (1950). Of course, the works of Max Weber remain the classics of the field: Gerth and Mills (1946, pp. 180–264) and Weber (1947, pp. 324–406).

Unless a work is explicitly cited in the text, the reader may assume that the points made explicitly or implicitly pervade all or most of these works—notably the most recent ones. Especially important are the works of Blau (1964), Etzioni (1968), Gamson (1968), Parsons (1967b), and Wrong (1968).

2. To view power as an attribute of social structure does not preclude treating it as "social process." Marvin Olsen (1970, pp. 2–10) makes a skillful case for the latter approach. Yet, as Parsons (1961, pp. 219–39) notes, structure and process are analytical distinctions. What is structure on one level, is process on the next. I focus on power as a structural attribute mainly for heuristic purposes; because, in macrosociology, structure is the more fundamental of the two categories.

3. I here seek to reconcile the approaches of Etzioni (1961) and Gamson (1968). Etzioni generates a typology of resources (or "assets") in order to generate three analytically pure kinds of power. Gamson offers a classification of "influence" which in the last analysis heavily stresses the behavior outcomes (domi-

nation) desired by the power (i.e., influence) wielder. His classifications of inducement, constraint, and persuasion are close approximations of Etzioni's categories of utilitarian, coercive, and normative assets and power. I offer a series of classifications that tries to link resources with modes of acquiescence or domination. It is worth noting that the Gamson categories themselves represent an effort to clarify and to condense the Parsonian typology of social control (Parsons 1967b).

For similar classifications see Boulding (1953, p. xxxi), Commons (1957, pp. 47–64), Deutsch (1953, p. 218), Janowitz (1960, p. 258), Neumann (1950), Olsen (1970, pp. 5–7), and Westby (1966).

4. This topic on the macro level has been most extensively analyzed by Thomas Schelling (1963; 1966). Etzioni (1968, pp. 338–42) has dealt with the same phenomenon and called it the "poker face" of power.

5. For modern social scientists, the difficulties of conceptualizing and measuring costs and benefits for a group remain formidable, however. The issue is made more complicated when the question of costs and benefits for each member of the group is added. One strategy is to argue that nothing is a common good unless benefits outweigh costs for all or at least most of the members. (See Olson 1971.) At the opposite extreme is the argument that the common good may be judged by the net benefits ultimately accruing to the overall system, although, in the short run, the costs to the members may make their lives miserable. Such a view lies behind the call by revolutionary regimes for sacrifice by all segments of society to further the revolution.

6. Charges as varied as being too conservative, too radical, teleological, tautological, and overly abstract have been leveled at this school. Ironically, it is only after modern functionalism's unchallenged preeminence in sociology has faded that appreciation for its internal diversity has grown. N. J. Demerath III (1966) has noted two distinct strands: Mertonian structuralism, which focuses more on tracing the several consequences of specific social items (e.g., "functions" and "dysfunctions") and Parsonian functionalism, which is more concerned with elaborating the limits imposed by the social system's patterns of needs ("functional prerequisites").

4. Macropower

1. Albert Biderman suggests that research data have been used for at least five "nonscientific" purposes: (1) to promote the claims for resources whose allocation is dictated by law or custom; (2) to serve as ammunition for various parties in intra- or interorganizational politics; (3) to promote "the cohesion of organizational alliances"; (4) to serve as symbols to rally public support; and (5) to

provide the grounds for or to reinforce national or institutional creeds (1966, p. 102). Consequently, information is continually reshaped by the people who collect and handle it.

2. This is not meant as a definitive theoretical statement on power and decision making in complex organizations. Missing, for example, is the observation made by severàl authors that wielders of systemic power in organizations are too dependent on other members. This, in turn, opens the door for extensive bargaining processes and the formation of coalitions not only among the inter-member power units but also between some of the members and the systemic power center. See, for instance, Cyert and March (1963, especially pp. 27–34) and Thompson (1967, pp. 30–36, and especially 132–43). Thompson consciously builds his work on the formulation by Emerson (1962) that power and dependence are reciprocal and that power relations necessarily entail interdependence.

These insights of coalition theory may also be useful in the analysis of social units that are more macroscopic than complex organizations. They are reductionist *only* if systemic power is presumed a priori to be an empty shell, merely reflecting intermember power relations—a pitfall that Cyert, March, Thompson, and Emerson carefully seem to avoid.

3. Naturally, all Pluralist theories are not so inherently reductionist. Some are the societal counterparts of the organizational coalition theories (see note 2). For example, see Dahl (1961), Lindblom (1965), and Truman (1953).

4. My use of the concepts of influence and social control comes close to Gamson's (1968, pp. 2–19). However, Gamson apparently feels the phenomena I have called "intermember power" and "systemic power" are implied by these categories. Therefore, he does not make a separate set of distinctions. I think that keeping the influence-social control distinction apart from the intermember-systemic one has potential theoretical and research benefits. Dennis Wrong, in a personal communication, has suggested that the term "social control" is too broad and that "imperative control" might be more precise.

5. The Morphology
of Intermember Power

1. The same is true of our new political philosophers. While sociologists wrestle with the ghosts of Marx and Weber, Rawls (1971) and Nozick (1974) seem to be wrestling with the ghost of Locke without transcending his individualistic assumptions. The same is also true, to some degree, of Jencks et al. (1972).

2. This distinction between recipients and resources is implicit in both Marxism and Structural-Functional theories. The classical Marxian model sug-

gests that inequality rests ultimately upon the exploitative distribution of utilitarian (i.e., economic) resources among groups created by the ownership or non-ownership of the means of production. A common Structural-Functionalist approach views social stratification as the outcome of two processes: the division of labor (i.e., structural differentiation in which society divides into functionally specialized units) and differential evaluation (i.e., the unequal distribution of "prestige" among the specialized units). I indicate later in the chapter that both traditions give undue primacy to one kind of resource. Marxism tends to see recipients too narrowly in class terms, but it is more macrosociological than Structural-Functionalism, which often sees the recipient units as specific occupational statuses.

3. This view of the Hindu caste system is based on H. C. N. Stevenson (1968). For a recent interpretation of the American experience which stresses the importance of local solidary groups, see Wiebe (1975).

4. Family and kinship structures are frequently discussed as recipients in intermember power. Here, on the other hand, the primacy of macrosolidary groups is stressed. In the analysis of premodern societies, the two approaches are not necessarily contradictory because people generally inherit membership in macrosolidary groups via familial ties. The family "transmits" group membership from one generation to the next. Moreover, in some societies, families—or more accurately networks of families joined into kinship structures—actually constitute macrosolidary groups or subgroups (the clan in Imperial China, royal families, and so on). However, these patterns are uncommon in advanced societies.

In advanced societies, families still influence the access of their members to macrosolidary groups. The kinds and quantities of resources they can stockpile as well as the liquidity of these resources are especially important. But, generally speaking, the family cannot guarantee entrance or permanent membership in a group. For example, a *nouveau riche* father may provide his son with the specialized education and funds likely to get him into Harvard and from there entry into the upper class. However, although attendance at elite universities is helpful in gaining access to the American upper class, it is neither a necessary nor a sufficient determinant. The father in question may be sorely disappointed. Perhaps he might even be tempted to ask for his money back.

Therefore, the family has some effect on which individuals belong to what stratification groups in all societies. However, unless the family itself is a macrosolidary group, it is not a key recipient in the processing of society's resources. Macrosolidary groups, along with localities, organizations, and associations are the principal actors in systems of societal inequality, not families or individuals.

Nevertheless, family rank plays a role in the inequality *within* macrosolidary groups and especially localities. All those within localities rarely receive exactly the same amounts of different resources. For example, a member of the business elite from a "good family" frequently has far more control over normative resources (via prestige, education, etiquette, and so on) than a neighbor and business colleague whose family origins are more humble. In addition, family ties tend to incorporate individuals into groups to which they would seem formally not to belong (e.g., wives and children of the business elite). See, particularly, Barber (1961, pp. 3–10) on the problems of family rank, locality rank, and societal inequality and how these do and do not fit together.

5. The differences between macrosolidary groups, on the one hand, and organizations and associations, on the other, are clarified further using Westhues' (1976) distinction between the class paradigm and the organizational paradigm in sociological theory.

6. Wiley uses this model of economic imbalance to offer a purely "class" interpretation of (1) why American workers and farmers did not make common cause in a mass radical movement in the nineteenth century, (2) the origins of the contemporary radical right and (3) the sources of the recent black protest movement (1967, pp. 529–41).

7. This process has been described by Pareto in his theory of the circulation of elites from the idealistic, violence-prone "lions" to the opportunistic, acquisitive, cunning "foxes." Pareto saw this cycle as inevitable and the shift from rule by the "lions" to rule by the "foxes" as a major source of societal "decadence." See Pareto 1935, especially vol. 3, sections 2026–59, vol. 4, sections 2233–36.

8. Nevertheless, to agree that every society—and hence every stratification system—requires an economy to survive, does not entitle us to jump to a narrowly materialistic interpretation of history or of inequality. "In other words," Anthony Giddens has observed, "it is not legitimate to claim that, because men must eat to live, their mode of life is necessarily determined by the manner in which they produce what they eat" (1973, p. 87). In the present case, this means the relationship between any society's techniques of economic production and the character of its macrosolidary groups is always a matter for empirical research and not of a priori assertion. It goes without saying that the modes of production are probably very important; but how important and in which ways still must be determined.

9. The reader recognizes that my discussion has omitted Weber's final dimension of stratification, the party. A party is oriented toward the acquisition and maintenance of political power, but it is not a "natural" societal unit pursuing power for its own sake. Rather, the party is an expression of the interests of a class or status community. It represents an effort to project these interests into the political sector; that is, parties are arms of classes or status groups. Thus some approximate what here has been called organizations, which I said act as the instrumental agents of macrosolidary groups. Others are on a higher level of influence (see chapter 6). Yet, parties or organizations are not in themselves macrosolidary groups in the way classes or status groups are, and to treat them as

such is to misinterpret their significance in the political system (see chapter 6). As Weber makes clear, parties are particularly salient in modern political systems where they develop considerable structural autonomy from their constituencies. But, let me reiterate, they remain artificial structures and are not macrosolidary groups.

10. I think Prewitt and Stone (1973), who are generally sympathetic to the Power Elite perspective, are convincing in this regard and marshall and consider evidence to support their position. See also Sale 1973.

11. The running debate between Andrew Greeley and his critics is the best example here. See, for instance, Greeley (1972). Dennis Wrong (1972) provides an excellent overview and analysis of the debate among American sociologists.

12. Here I am, of course, talking about Gans's *The Urban Villagers* (1962). Wrong (1972) provides cogent observations about the problems of disentangling class and status elements on the community level, especially pp. 279–81.

13. See Lehman and Lehman (1975). A similar and more fully developed agreement is found in Glazer (1975).

14. Mills's treatment of this issue remains compelling (1956, especially pp. 110–15). Michael Young's fictional account, *The Rise of Meritocracy* (1958), is also first-rate.

15. *The Future of Inequality* is, of course, the title of an important work by Miller and Roby (1970).

6. The Morphology
of Political Power

1. For an excellent review of the literature on so-called stateless societies, see Dowse and Hughes (1972, pp. 89–99).

2. Runciman (1969, pp. 35–42) provides an incisive critique of the logical and empirical deficiencies of Weber's definition.

3. A noteworthy exception is Munger (1967, pp. 11–16).

4. However, only the incredibly naïve believe that the deliberations and decisions of elected bodies and officials are totally explained by electoral politics. Among the factors that impose themselves here are the internal politics of a particular agency (e.g., a president's kitchen cabinet, the seniority system in the U.S. Senate and House of Representatives) as well as the external pressure from organized outside interests. The most institutionalized expression of this latter factor is the practice of lobbying, in which registered pressure groups maintain formal offices to exert influence on legislators.

5. For a detailed discussion of scope and pervasiveness, see Etzioni and Taber (1963, pp. 220–38).

6. For a detailed critique of this thesis as it applies to the United States,

which includes references to the extensive literature, see Hamilton (1972, pp. 399–506). The most complete presentation of the class and status politics thesis is probably found in Bell, ed. (1963).

7. I think the reader will find it instructive to consider Wrong's thesis in the context of Walter Dean Burnham's approach of critical elections (1965, pp. 7–28; 1970).

8. Moore cites the work of Stanley Lieberson (1971), Robert W. Tucker (1971), and Murray Weidenbaum (1969) to show both the military and industry as far from monolithic. He states that transformation of American society which curtails military spending is possible because only a small segment profits excessively from swelling military appropriations, while the overall economy does not. Moreover, Moore rebuts the arguments that the "predatory" component of our foreign policy is a necessary exigency created by the American economy's need for raw materials (Kolko 1969), or that it stems from the need for an extra margin of profit from foreign markets to stave off depression (Magdoff 1969), or, finally, that our stress on armaments is the only way to siphon off profits that cannot be otherwise productively invested and thus would inevitably lead to the stagnation of American capitalism (Baran and Sweezy 1966). (For a detailed treatment of these issues, see 1972, pp. 118–37.) For similar findings by a neo-Marxian sociologist, see Szymanski (1973, pp. 1–14).

9. Blau's treatment of legitimacy (1964, pp. 199–223) makes some of the same points as Stinchcombe. Particularly crucial is that both see its explicit structural manifestation as at least as critical as its moral vibrations.

10. The notion of the structural manifestations of legitimacy helps clarify a relationship I noted earlier in the chapter. Recall that I said that effectiveness can serve as a short-term substitute for legitimacy. In effect, what such an argument implies is that effectiveness may stimulate the structural manifestations of legitimacy—notably third-party backing and smooth succession—in the absence of deep moral commitment. As a consequence, a political system that can yield a payoff may be endowed temporarily with some of the external trappings of legitimacy. In this way, it may have bought time to foster the deeper allegiances necessary for long-term survival and viability. Certainly, it has insured that key structural problems ordinarily linked to legitimacy are dealt with for a time in its absence.

7. The Limits
to Transformation

1. I am indebted to Eliot Freidson for this point. It is developed in Freidson (1975).

2. At the moment, we do not know how much one of these factors affects

the other, or whether one (insensitivity or unresponsiveness) has causal priority, and certainly not how much of their covariation is the product of third factors (political, societal, or cultural). All these questions require more comparative research.

3. Of course, not all political agents are always concerned with winning. This seems to be particularly the case with political parties.

"The big game is the party game," E. E. Schattschneider said almost two decades ago, "because in the last analysis there is no political substitute for winning" (1960, p. 58). While there is merit in this formulation, some qualification is needed before we can accept it. There are times, Richard F. Hamilton reminds us, when modern mass parties prefer to lose elections (see especially 1972, pp. 4–11). Certainly Michels' "iron law of oligarchy" (1949) suggests that the leadership of a party sometimes prefers to preserve its entrenched positions rather than to win elections. Hamilton notes that the Democrats after the Civil War could have improved their electoral prospects by taking up the widespread demand for "soft money." "The Democratic leaders, however, being conservative, on this and most other issues, chose to lose these elections" (p. 4). An example in our own time is when moderate Eastern Republican leaders virtually abandoned the Goldwater candidacy in 1964.

Thus those who run modern mass parties hardly have a total dedication to winning. The fact that they can always try again further weakens their zest. Generally, the lower this dedication is, the weaker the responsiveness of the party system. The result is likely to be a polity whose actual level of efficiency falls below the possible level.

4. For an overview, see especially Gusfield (1973 and 1968, pp. 445–52); Killian (1965, pp. 426–55); Oberschall (1973); Pinard (1968, pp. 682–90); Smelser (1973); and Zald and Ash (1966, pp. 327–41).

Bibliography

Alba, Richard D. 1972. "Who Governs—The Power Elite? It's All in How You Define It." *The Human Factor* 10:27–39.

Alland, Alexander. 1972. *The Human Imperative.* New York: Columbia University Press.

Almond, Gabriel A. 1956. "Comparative Political Systems." *Journal of Politics* 18:391–409.

—— 1960. Introduction. In Gabriel A. Almond and James S. Coleman, eds., *The Politics of Developing Areas,* pp. 3–64. Princeton, N.J.: Princeton University Press.

—— 1963. "Political Systems and Political Change." *American Behavioral Scientist* 6:3–10.

—— 1965. "A Developmental Approach to Political Systems." *World Politics* 7:183–214.

Almond, G. A. and C. Gingham Powell. 1966. *Comparative Politics: A Developmental Approach.* Boston: Little, Brown.

Almond, G. A. and Sidney Verba. 1963. *The Civic Culture: Political Attitudes and Democracy in Five Nations.* Princeton, N.J.: Princeton University Press.

Arendt, Hannah. 1966. *The Origins of Totalitarianism.* 3d ed. New York: Harcourt, Brace and World.

Bachrach, Peter and Morton S. Baratz. 1962. "Two Faces of Power." *American Political Science Review* 56:947–52.

Baker, Russell. 1976. "Between the Acts." *New York Times,* November 30.

Baltzell, E. Digby. 1964. *The Protestant Establishment: Aristocracy and Caste in America.* New York: Random House.

Baran, Paul A. and Paul M. Sweezy. 1966. *Monopoly Capital: An Essay on the American Economic and Social Order.* New York: Monthly Review Press.

Barber, Bernard. 1955. "On the relation between 'culture' and 'social structure.' " *Transactions of the New York Academy of Sciences* 17:613–20.
—— 1957. *Social Stratification: A Comparative Analysis of Structure and Pro-
cess*. New York: Harcourt, Brace.
—— 1961. "Family Status, Local-Community Status and Social Stratification:
Three Types of Rankings." *Pacific Sociological Review* 4:3–10.
Barber, Elinor. 1953. *The Bourgeoisie in 18th Century France*. Princeton, N.J.:
Princeton University Press.
Barnard, Chester I. 1938. *The Functions of the Executive*. Cambridge, Mass.:
Harvard University Press.
Barraclough, Geoffrey. 1975. "Wealth and Power: The Politics of Food and
Oil." *The New York Review of Books* 22:23–30.
Bell, Daniel. 1973. *The Coming of Post-Industrial Society: A Venture in Social
Forecasting*. New York: Basic Books.
—— 1974. "The Public Household." *The Public Interest* 37: 29–68.
Bell, Daniel and Virginia Held. 1969. "The Community Revolution." *The Pub-
lic Interest* 16:142–77.
Bell, Daniel, ed. 1963. *The Radical Right*. New York: Doubleday.
Bendix, Reinhard. 1960. *Max Weber: An Intellectual Portrait*. New York: Dou-
bleday.
Benedict, Ruth. 1946. *The Chrysanthemum and the Sword: Patterns of Japanese
Culture*. Boston: Houghton Mifflin.
Berelson, Bernard, Paul F. Lazarsfeld, and William N. McPhee. 1954. *Voting: A
Study of Opinion Formation in a Presidential Campaign*. Chicago: University
of Chicago Press.
Berger, Peter and Thomas Luckmann. 1966. *The Social Construction of Reality*.
New York: Doubleday.
Biderman, Albert D. 1966. "Social Indicators and Goals." In Raymond A.
Bauer, ed., *Social Indicators*, pp. 68–153. Cambridge, Mass.: MIT Press.
Bierstedt, Robert. 1950. "An Analysis of Social Power." *American Sociological
Review* 15:730–38.
—— 1954. "The Problem of Authority." In Morroe Berger, Theodore Abel, and
Charles Page, eds., *Freedom and Control in Modern Society*, pp. 67–81. New
York: Wiley.
Blau, Peter M. 1955. *The Dynamics of Bureaucracy*. Chicago: University of
Chicago Press.
—— 1963. "Critical Remarks on Weber's Theory of Authority." *American Po-
litical Science Review* 57:305–16.
—— 1964. *Exchange and Power in Social Life*. New York: Wiley.
Blau, Peter M. and W. Richard Scott. 1963. *Formal Organizations: A Compara-
tive Approach*. San Francisco: Chandler.

Boulding, Kenneth E. 1963. *The Organizational Revolution.* New York: Harper and Row.

Bramson, Leon. 1961. *The Political Context of Sociology.* Princeton, N.J.: Princeton University Press.

Breslin, Jimmy. 1975. *How the Good Guys Finally Won: Notes from an Impeachment Summer.* New York: Viking Press.

Brzezinski, Zbigniew and Samuel Huntington. 1964. *Political Power: USA/USSR.* New York: Viking Press.

Burnham, Walter D. 1965. "The Changing of the American Political Universe." *American Political Science Review* 59:7–28.

—— 1970. *Critical Elections and the Mainsprings of American Politics.* New York: Norton.

Calleo, David P. and Benjamin Rowland. 1973. *America and the World Political Economy.* Bloomington: Indiana University Press.

Cartwright, Dorwin, ed. 1959. *Studies in Power.* Ann Arbor: University of Michigan Press.

Cartwright, Dorwin. 1965. "Influence, Leadership and Control." in James G. March, ed. *Handbook of Organizations,* pp. 1–47. Chicago: Rand McNally.

Clark, Terry N. 1967. "The Concept of Power: Some Overemphasized and Underrecognized Dimensions." *Southwestern Social Science Quarterly* 48: 271–86.

—— 1968. "The Concept of Power." In Terry N. Clark, ed., *Community Structure and Decision Making,* pp. 45–56. San Francisco: Chandler.

Collins, Randall. 1971. "Functional and Conflict Theories of Educational Stratification." *American Sociological Review* 36:1002–19.

—— 1975. *Conflict Sociology: Toward an Explanatory Science.* New York: Academic Press.

Commons, John R. 1957. *Legal Foundations and Capitalism.* Madison: University of Wisconsin Press.

Coser, Lewis A. 1956. *The Functions of Social Conflict.* New York: Free Press.

—— 1976. "The Notion of Power." In Lewis A. Coser and Bernard Rosenberg, eds., *Sociological Theory: A Book of Readings,* pp. 150–61. 4th ed. New York: Macmillan.

Cyert, Richard M. and James G. March. 1963. *A Behavioral Theory of the Firm.* Englewood Cliffs, N.J.: Prentice-Hall.

Dahl, Robert A. 1957. "The Concept of Power." *Behavioral Science* 2:201–15.

—— 1961. *Who Governs?* New Haven: Yale University Press.

—— 1968. "Power." In *The International Encyclopedia of the Social Sciences,* 12:405–15. New York: Macmillan.

Dahrendorf, Ralf. 1959. *Class and Class Conflict in Industrial Society.* Stanford, Calif.: Stanford University Press.

Danzger, M. H. 1964. "Community Power Structure: Problems and Continuities." *American Sociological Review* 29:707–17.

Demerath, Nicholas J. III. 1966. "Synecdoche and Structural-Functionalism." *Social Forces* 44:390–401.

Deutsch, Karl W. 1953. *Nationalism and Social Communication*. New York: Wiley.

—— 1963. *The Nerves of Government*. New York: Free Press.

Devine, Donald J. 1972. *The Political Culture of the United States*. Boston, Little Brown.

Domhoff, G. William. 1967. *Who Rules America?* Englewood Cliffs, N.J.: Prentice-Hall.

—— 1970. *The Higher Circles: The Governing Class in America*. New York: Vintage.

Downs, Anthony. 1957. *An Economic Theory of Democracy*. New York: Harper.

Dowse, Robert E. and John A. Hughes. 1972. *Political Sociology*. New York: Wiley.

Duverger, Maurice. 1954. *Political Parties: Their Organization and Activity in the Modern State*. London: Methuen.

Easton, David. 1965. *A Systems Analysis of Political Life*. New York: Wiley.

Edelman, Murray. 1964. *The Symbolic Use of Politics*. Urbana: University of Illinois Press.

Eisenstadt, Shmuel N. 1968. *The Political Systems of Empires*. New York: Free Press.

Ellis, Desmond P. 1971. "The Hobbesian Problem of Order: A Critical Appraisal of the Normative Solution." *American Sociological Review* 36:692–703.

Emerson, Richard M. 1962. "Power-Dependence Relations." *American Sociological Review* 27:31–40.

Etzioni, Amitai. 1961. *A Comparative Analysis of Complex Organizations*. New York: Free Press.

—— 1968. *The Active Society: A Theory of Societal and Political Processes*. New York: Free Press.

—— 1971. "Policy Research." *American Sociologist* 6:8–12.

Etzioni, Amitai and William R. Taber. 1963. "Scope, Pervasiveness and Tension Management in Complex Organizations." *Social Relations* 30:220–38.

Freidson, Eliot. 1970. *Profession of Medicine: A Study in the Sociology of Applied Knowledge*. New York: Dodd, Mead.

—— 1975. *Doctoring Together: A Study in Professional Social Control*. New York: Elsevier.

French, John R. P. and Bertram Raven. 1960. "The Basis of Social Power." In Dorwin Cartwright and Alvin Zander, eds., *Group Dynamics: Research and Theory*, pp. 607–23. New York: Harper and Row.

Friedrich, Carl J. and Zbigniew K. Brzezinski. 1965. *Totalitarian Dictatorship and Autocracy.* 2d ed. Cambridge, Mass.: Harvard University Press.

Galtung, Johan. 1967. *Theory and Method in Social Research.* New York: Columbia University Press.

Gamson, William A. 1968. *Power and Discontent.* Homewood, Ill.: Dorsey.

—— 1975. *The Strategy of Social Protest.* Homewood, Ill.: Dorsey.

Gans, Herbert J. 1962. *The Urban Villagers: Group and Class in the Life of Italian-Americans.* New York: Free Press.

—— 1972. The Positive Functions of Poverty." *American Journal of Sociology* 78:275–84.

—— 1973. *More Equality.* New York: Pantheon.

Geertz, Clifford. 1964. "Ideology as a Cultural System." In David E. Apter, ed., *Ideology and Discontent,* pp. 47–76. New York: Free Press.

Gerth, Hans and C. Wright Mills. 1946. *From Max Weber: Essays in Sociology.* New York: Oxford University Press.

Giddens, Anthony. 1973. *The Class Structure of Advanced Societies.* London: Hutchinson.

Ginsberg, Morris. 1953. *Sociology.* New York: Oxford University Press.

Glazer, Nathan. 1975. *Affirmative Discrimination: Ethnic Inequality and Public Policy.* New York: Basic Books.

Glazer, Nathan and Daniel P. Moynihan. 1963. *Beyond the Melting Pot: The Negroes, Puerto Ricans, Jews, Italians and Irish of New York City.* Cambridge, Mass.: M.I.T. Press.

—— 1974. "Why Ethnicity?" *Commentary* 58:33–39.

Goldhamer, Herbert and Edward A. Shils. 1939. "Types of Power and Status." *American Journal of Sociology* 45:171–82.

Goode, William J. 1972. "The Place of Force in Human Society." *American Sociological Review* 37:507–19.

Gordon, Milton. 1964. *Assimilation in American Life: The Role of Race, Religion and National Origins.* New York: Oxford University Press.

Gouldner, Alvin W. 1970. *The Coming Crisis in Western Sociology.* New York: Basic Books.

Greeley, Andrew. 1972. "The New Ethnicity and Blue Collars." *Dissent* (Winter): 270–77.

Grumm, John G. 1958. "Theories of Electoral Systems." *Midwest Journal of Political Science* 2:357–76.

Gusfield, Joseph. 1963. *Symbolic Crusade: Status Politics and the American Temperance Movement.* Urbana: University of Illinois Press.

—— 1968. "The Study of Social Movements." In *The International Encyclopedia of the Social Sciences,* 14:445–52. New York: Macmillan.

Habermas, Jurgen. 1975. *Legitimation Crisis.* Boston: Beacon Press.

Hacker, Andrew. 1975. "What Rules America?" *The New York Review of Books* 22:9–13.

Hamilton, Richard F. 1972. *Class and Politics in the United States*. New York: Wiley.

Harrison, Paul M. 1959. *Authority and Power in the Free Church Tradition*. Princeton, N.J.: Princeton University Press.

Hawley, Amos H. 1963. "Community Power and Urban Renewal Success." *American Journal of Sociology* 68:422–31.

Hechter, Michael. 1974. "The Political Economy of Ethnic Change." *American Journal of Sociology* 79:1151–78.

—— 1975. *Internal Colonialism: The Celtic Fringe in British National Development*. Berkeley and Los Angeles: University of California Press.

Heller, Celia S., ed. 1969. *Structured Social Inequality: A Reader in Comparative Social Stratification*. New York: Macmillan.

Hobbes, Thomas. 1956. *Leviathan*. Part I. Chicago: Henry Regnery.

Huntington, Samuel. 1975. "The Democratic Distemper." *The Public Interest* 41:9–38.

Hyman, Herbert. 1955. *Survey Design and Analysis*. New York: Free Press.

Jackman, Robert W. 1974. "Political Democracy and Social Equality: A Comparative Analysis." *American Sociological Review* 39:29–45.

Janowitz, Morris. 1960. *The Professional Soldier*. New York: Free Press.

Jay, Martin. 1973. *The Dialectical Imagination: A History of the Frankfurt School and the Institute of Social Research, 1923–1950*. Boston: Little, Brown.

Jencks, Christopher et al. 1972. *Inequality: A Reassessment of the Effect of Family and Schooling in America*. New York: Basic Books.

Kadushin, Charles. 1968. "Power, Influence and Social Circles: A New Methodology for Studying Opinion Makers." *American Sociological Review* 33:685–99.

Kendall, Patricia and Paul F. Lazarsfeld. 1950. "Problems in Survey Analysis." In Robert K. Merton and Paul F. Lazarsfeld, eds., *Studies in the Scope and Method of "The American Soldier,"* pp. 148–58. New York: Free Press.

Killian, Lewis. 1965. "Social Movements." In Robert Faris, ed., *Handbook of Modern Sociology*, pp. 426–55. Chicago: Rand McNally.

Kim, Y. C. 1964. "The Concept of Political Culture." *Journal of Politics* 26:313–36.

Kolko, Gabriel. 1969. *The Roots of American Foreign Policy: An Analysis of Power and Purpose*. Boston: Beacon.

Kornhauser, William. 1959. *The Politics of Mass Society*. New York: Free Press.

Kroeber, Alfred L. and Clyde Kluckhohn. 1952. *Culture: A Critical Review of Concepts and Definitions*. Cambridge, Mass.: Harvard University, Peabody Museum of American Ethnology Papers.

Kroeber, Alfred L. and Talcott Parsons. 1958. "The Concepts of Culture and Social System." *American Sociological Review* 23:582–93.

Kuhn, Thomas S. 1970. *The Structure of Scientific Revolutions*. 2d ed. Chicago: University of Chicago Press.

Lasswell, Harold D. 1936. *Politics: Who Gets What, When, How.* New York: McGraw-Hill.

Lasswell, Harold and Abraham Kaplan. 1950. *Power and Society.* New Haven, Conn.: Yale University Press.

Lehman, Edward W. 1969. "Toward a Macrosociology of Power." *American Sociological Review* 34:453–65.

—— 1971. "Social Indicators and Social Problems." In Erwin O. Smigel, ed., *Handbook on the Study of Social Problems,* pp. 149–76. Chicago: Rand McNally.

—— 1972a. "On the Concept of Political Culture: A Theoretical Reassessment." *Social Forces* 50:361–70.

—— 1972b. "Review Symposium: The Politics of Unreason." *Contemporary Sociology* 1:291–305.

—— 1975. *Coordinating Health Care: Explorations in Interorganizational Relations.* Beverly Hills, Calif.: Sage Publications.

Lehman, Edward W. and Ethna Lehman. 1975. "Equality: Some Social Costs." Paper read at the annual meeting of the American Sociological Association, August 24, San Francisco.

Lenski, Gerhard E. 1966. *Power and Privilege: A Theory of Social Stratification.* New York: McGraw-Hill.

Levy, Mark R. and Michael S. Kramer. 1973. *The Ethnic Factor.* Rev. ed. New York: Simon and Schuster.

Lieberson, Stanley. 1971. "An Empirical Study of Military-Industrial Linkages." *American Journal of Sociology* 76:562–84.

Lindblom, Charles E. 1965. *The Intelligence of Democracy.* New York: Free Press.

Lipset, Seymour Martin. 1959. *Political Man: The Social Bases of Politics.* Garden City, N.Y.: Doubleday.

—— 1963. *The First New Nation: The United States in Historical and Comparative Perspective.* New York: Basic Books.

—— 1968. *Revolution and Counterrevolution: Change and Persistence in Social Structures.* New York: Basic Books.

Lipset, Seymour Martin and Earl Raab. 1970. *The Politics of Unreason: Right-Wing Extremism in America, 1790–1970.* New York: Harper and Row.

Lowi, Theodore, J. 1971. *The Politics of Disorder.* New York: Basic Books.

McCleery, Richard H. 1957. *Policy Change in Prison Management: A Test Case for Administrative Analyses.* East Lansing: Governmental Research Bureau, Michigan State University.

McConnell, Grant. 1966. *Private Power and American Democracy.* New York: Knopf.

Magdoff, Harry. 1969. *The Age of Imperialism.* New York: Monthly Review Press.

Maitland, Ian. 1976. "Only the Best and the Brightest?" *Asian Affairs* 3:263–72.

Mann, Michael. 1970. "The Social Cohesion of Liberal Democracy." *American Sociological Review* 35:423–39.

Mannheim, Karl. 1936. *Ideology and Utopia.* New York: Harcourt, Brace, and World.

March, James G. 1966. "The Power of Power." In David Easton, ed., *Varieties of Political Theory,* pp. 39–70. Englewood Cliffs, N.J.: Prentice-Hall.

Marshall, T. H. 1950. *Citizenship and Social Class.* London: Cambridge University Press.

Marx, Karl. 1963. *The 18th Brumaire of Louis Bonaparte.* New York: International Publishers.

Marx, Karl and Friedrich Engels. 1956. *The Holy Family.* Moscow: Foreign Language Publishing House.

Merton, Robert K. 1936. "The Unanticipated Consequences of Purposive Social Action." *American Sociological Review* 1:894–904.

—— 1968. *Social Theory and Social Structure.* 3d ed. New York: Free Press.

Michels, Robert. 1949. *Political Parties: A Sociological Study of Oligarchic Tendencies of Modern Democracy.* New York: Free Press.

Milbrath, Lester W. 1965. *Political Participation.* Chicago: Rand McNally.

Miliband, Ralph. 1969. *The State in Capitalist Society.* New York: Basic Books.

Miller, S. M. and Pamela Roby. 1970. *The Future of Inequality.* New York: Basic Books.

Mills, C. Wright. 1956. *The Power Elite.* New York: Oxford University Press.

Milner, Murray, Jr. 1972. *The Illusion of Equality: The Effects of Education on Opportunity, Inequality and Social Conflict.* San Francisco: Jossey-Bass.

Mitchell, William C. 1961. *The American Polity.* New York: Free Press.

Moore, Barrington, Jr. 1967. *Social Origins of Dictatorship and Democracy.* Boston: Beacon.

—— 1972. *Reflections on the Causes of Human Misery and Upon Certain Proposals to Eliminate Them.* Boston: Beacon.

Moynihan, Daniel P. 1969. *Maximum Feasible Misunderstanding.* New York: Free Press.

Munger, Frank J. 1967. "Changing Politics of Aid to Education." *Transaction* 4:11–16.

Neumann, Franz L. 1950. "Approaches to the Study of Political Power." *Political Science Quarterly* 65:161–80.

Neumann, Sigmund. 1956. "Toward a Comparative Study of Political Parties." In Sigmund Neumann, ed., *Modern Political Parties,* pp. 395–421. Chicago: University of Chicago Press.

Nicolaus, Martin. 1969a. "The Professional Organization of Sociology: A View from Below." *Antioch Review* 29:375–89.

—— 1969b. "The A.S.A. Convention." *Catalyst* 1:103–6.

Nie, Norman H., Sidney Verba, and John R. Petrocik. 1976. *The Changing American Voter*. Cambridge, Mass.: Harvard University Press.

Nisbet, Robert A. 1966. *The Sociological Tradition*. New York: Basic Books.

—— 1974. "The Pursuit of Equality." *The Public Interest* 34:103–20.

Nozick, Robert. 1974. *Anarchy, State and Utopia*. New York: Basic Books.

Oberschall, Anthony. 1973. *Social Conflict and Social Movements*. Englewood Cliffs, N.J.: Prentice-Hall.

O'Connor, James. 1973. *The Fiscal Crisis of the State*. New York: St. Martin's Press.

Offe, Claus. 1974. "Structural Problems of the Capitalist State: Class Rule and the Political System. On the Selectiveness of Political Institutions." In Klaus von Beyme, ed., *German Political Studies, vol. 1*. Beverly Hills, Calif.: Sage Publications.

Olsen, Marvin E. 1970. "Power as a Social Process." In Marvin E. Olsen, ed., *Power in Societies*, pp. 2–10. New York: Macmillan.

Olson, Mancur, Jr. 1971. *The Logic of Collective Action: Public Goods and the Theory of Groups*. Rev. ed. New York: Schocken Books.

Ossowski, Stanislaw. 1963. *Class Structure in the Social Consciousness*. New York: Free Press.

Pareto, Vilfredo. 1935. *The Mind and Society*. New York: Harcourt, Brace.

Parsons, Talcott. 1937. *The Structure of Social Action*. New York: McGraw-Hill.

—— 1951. *The Social System*. New York: Free Press.

—— 1954. *Essays in Sociological Theory: Pure and Applied*. Rev. ed. New York: Free Press.

—— 1959. " 'Voting' and the Equilibrium of the American Political System." In Eugene Burdick and Arthur J. Brodbeck, eds., *American Voting Behavior*, pp. 80–120. New York: Free Press.

—— 1961. "Some Considerations on the Theory of Social Change." *Rural Sociology* 25:219–39.

—— 1966. *Societies: Evolutionary and Comparative Perspectives*. Englewood, Cliffs, N.J.: Prentice-Hall.

Parsons, Talcott, ed. 1967. *Sociological Theory and Modern Society*. New York : Free Press.

—— 1967a. "On the Concept of Influence," pp. 355–82.

—— 1967b. "On the Concept of Political Power," pp. 297–354.

—— 1967c. "Some Reflections on the Place of Force in Social Process," pp. 264–96.

Parsons, Talcott and Neil J. Smelser. 1956. *Economy and Society: A Study of the Integration of Economic and Social Theory*. New York: Free Press.

Pinard, Maurice. 1968. "Mass Society and Political Movements: A New Formulation." *American Journal of Sociology* 73:682–90.

Piven, Frances F. and Richard A. Cloward. 1971. *Regulating the Poor: The Functions of Public Welfare*. New York: Vintage.

Poulantzas, Nicos. 1973. *Political Power and Social Classes*. London: Sheed & Ward.

Prewitt, Kenneth and Alan Stone. 1973. *The Ruling Elites: Elite Theory, Power and American Democracy*. New York: Harper and Row.

Pye, Lucian W. 1968. "Political Culture." In *The International Encyclopedia of the Social Sciences*, 12:218–25. New York: Macmillan.

—— 1973. "Culture and Political Science: Problems in the Evaluation of the Concept of Political Culture." In Louis Schneider and Charles Bonjean, eds., *The Idea of Culture in the Social Sciences*, pp. 65–76, London: Cambridge University Press.

Pye, Lucian W. and Sidney Verba, eds. 1965. *Political Culture and Political Development*. Princeton, N.J.: Princeton University Press.

Rawls, John. 1971. *A Theory of Justice*. Cambridge, Mass.: Harvard University Press.

Riesman, David. 1950. *The Lonely Crowd*. New Haven, Conn.: Yale University Press.

Rist, Ray C. 1970. "Student Social Class and Teacher Expectations: The Self-Fulfilling Prophecy in Ghetto Education." *Harvard Educational Review* 40:411–51.

Rogers, Mary F. 1974. "Instrumental and Infra-Resources: The Basis of Power." *American Journal of Sociology* 79:1418–33.

Rose, Arnold M. 1967. *The Power Structure: Political Process in American Society*. New York: Oxford University Press.

Rosenberg, Bernard and Irving Howe. 1974. "American Jews: Are They Turning Right?" *Dissent* (Winter): 30–45.

Rubinson, Richard. 1976. "The World-Economy and the Distribution of Income within States: A Cross-National Study." *American Sociological Review* 41:638–59.

Runciman, Walter G. 1969. *Social Science and Political Theory*. 2d ed. London: Cambridge University Press.

Sale, Kirkpatrick. 1973. "The World behind Watergate." *The New York Review of Books* 20:9–15.

Sartori, Giovanni. 1969a. "From the Sociology of Politics to Political Sociology." In Seymour Martin Lipset, ed., *Politics and the Social Sciences*, pp. 65–100. New York: Oxford University Press.

—— 1969b. "Politics, Ideology and Belief Systems." *American Political Science Review* 63:398–411.

Schattschneider, E. E. 1960. *The Semi-Sovereign People*. New York: Holt, Rinehart and Winston.

Schelling, Thomas C. 1963. *The Strategy of Conflict.* New York: Oxford University Press.

—— 1966. *Arms and Influence.* New Haven: Yale University Press.

Schermerhorn, Richard A. 1961. *Society and Power.* New York: Random House.

Schumpeter, Joseph. 1950. *Capitalism, Socialism and Democracy.* 3d ed. New York: Harper.

Sennett, Richard. 1976. *The Fall of Public Man.* New York: Knopf.

Sills, David. 1957. *The Volunteers.* New York: Free Press.

Silvert, Kalman H. 1970. *Man's Power: A Biased Guide to Political Thought and Action.* New York: Viking Press.

Simon, Herbert A. 1957. *Administrative Behavior.* 2d ed. New York: Macmillan.

—— 1964. "On the Concept of Organizational Goal." *Administrative Science Quarterly* 9:1–22.

Smelser, Neil J. 1963. *Theory of Collective Behavior.* New York: Free Press.

Spiro, Melford E. 1968. "Culture and Personality." In *The International Encyclopedia of the Social Sciences,* 3:558–63. New York: Macmillan.

Steinfels, Peter. 1976. "Do We Need a New Cold War?" *Commonweal* 103:393–98.

Stevenson, H. N. C. 1968. "Caste" (Indian). In *The Encyclopaedia Britannica,* 5:24–33. Chicago: William Benton.

Stinchcombe, Arthur L. 1968. *Constructing Social Theories.* New York: Harcourt, Brace and World.

Szymanski, Albert. 1973. "Military Spending and Economic Stagnation." *American Journal of Sociology* 79:1–14.

Thompson, James D. 1967. *Organizations in Action: Social Science Basis of Administrative Theory.* New York: McGraw-Hill.

Tocqueville, Alexis de. 1954. *Democracy in America.* 2 vols. New York: Vintage Books.

Touraine, Alain. 1971. *The Post-Industrial Society.* New York: Random House.

Truman, David B. 1953. *The Governmental Process.* New York: Knopf.

Tucker, Robert W. 1971. *The Radical Left and American Foreign Policy.* Baltimore, Md.: Johns Hopkins University Press.

Wallerstein, Immanuel. 1961. *Africa: The Politics of Independence.* New York: Vintage.

—— 1974. *The Modern World-System: Capitalist Agriculture and the Origins of the European World-Economy in the Sixteenth Century.* New York: Academic Press.

Weber, Max. 1947. *The Theory of Social and Economic Organization.* New York: Oxford University Press.

—— 1960. "The Three Types of Legitimate Rule." In Amitai Etzioni, ed.,

Complex Organizations: A Sociological Reader. New York: Holt, Rinehart and Winston.

Weidenbaum, Murray L. 1969. *The Modern Public Sector.* New York: Basic Books.

Westby, David L. 1966. "A Typology of Authority in Complex Organizations." *Social Forces* 44:484–91.

Westhues, Kenneth. 1976. "Class and Organizations as Paradigms in Social Science." *American Sociologist* 11:38–49.

Wiebe, Robert. 1975. *The Segmented Society.* New York: Oxford University Press.

Wilensky, Harold L. 1967. *Organizational Intelligence: Knowledge and Policy in Government and Industry.* New York: Basic Books.

Wiley, Norbert. 1967. "America's Unique Class Politics: The Interplay of the Labor, Credit, and Commodity Markets." *American Sociological Review* 32:529–41.

Wrong, Dennis H. 1964. "Social Inequality without Social Stratification." *Canadian Review of Sociology and Anthropology* 1:5–16.

—— 1968. "Some Problems in Defining Social Power." *American Journal of Sociology* 73:673–81.

—— 1972. "How Important Is Social Class?" *Dissent* (Winter): 278–85.

—— 1974a. "On Thinking About the Future." *American Sociologist* 9:26–31.

—— 1974b. "The Rhythm of Democratic Politics." *Dissent* (Winter): 46–55.

Young, Michael. 1958. *The Rise of Meritocracy.* New York: Random House.

Zald, Mayer N. and Roberta Ash. 1966. "Social Movement Organizations: Growth, Decay, and Change." *Social Forces* 44:327–34.

Zeitlin, Maurice. 1974. "Corporate Ownership and Control: The Large Corporation and the Capitalist Class." *American Journal of Sociology* 79:1073–1133.

Index of Names

Index of Subjects

DATE DUE

FEB 28 '88			
GAYLORD			PRINTED IN U.S.A.